THE
AMERICAN SECRETARIES OF STATE
AND THEIR DIPLOMACY

VOLUME XVII

THE AMERICAN SECRETARIES OF STATE AND THEIR DIPLOMACY

ROBERT H. FERRELL, *Editor*

SAMUEL FLAGG BEMIS, *Advisory Editor*

COOPER SQUARE

NEW YORK

VOLUME XVII

JOHN FOSTER DULLES

by

LOUIS L. GERSON

PUBLISHERS, INC.

1967

PUBLISHED BY COOPER SQUARE PUBLISHERS, INC.
59 FOURTH AVENUE, NEW YORK, NEW YORK 10003

LIBRARY OF CONGRESS CATALOG CARD NO. 67-24039

MANUFACTURED IN THE UNITED STATES OF AMERICA
NOBLE OFFSET PRINTERS, INC., 419 LAFAYETTE ST., NEW YORK, N. Y.

For Liz

VOLUME XVII

TABLE OF CONTENTS

PREFACE TO VOLUME XVII

JOHN FOSTER DULLES was the only religious leader, lay or clerical, ever to become Secretary of State (although Edward Everett was a pastor and pulpit orator for a couple of years in his early twenties). Throughout mature life, until he entered the Department of State, he held a succession of lay offices in the Presbyterian Church, most actively as representative to various interdenominational and international conferences and commissions and councils of Protestant churches seeking formulas of world peace. A notable expression of this activity was his statement on "The Christian Citizen in a Changing World," prepared for the First Assembly of the World Council of Churches in Amsterdam in 1948, at which he served as Speaker. "Nobody in the Department of State," he once said, "knows as much about the Bible as I do." He felt that it was the duty of a Christian to stand up for religion throughout the world.

As Secretary of State he undertook to translate his ideals into American foreign policy. Amidst the allied conference at London in 1956, over the fateful Suez question, he stepped aside and knelt in prayer at St. Paul's Cathedral. He has been praised and ridiculed for his stout piety. Perhaps it was this Presbyterian staunchness that brought him the sobriquet of the Iron Secretary. He assessed Soviet policy as a godless determination to control the world; this would mean the end of freedom everywhere, including freedom of religion. He stood firmly against such an evil consummation repeatedly to the brink of war, a phrase much abused by his detractors, who were to use the word "verge" instead of brink: but when death struck him down the free world mourned a champion. Some individuals in the United States and abroad may not agree with the opinion of Konrad Adenauer, who considered Dulles "the greatest man" he had ever known. Dulles, Adenauer remarked, "thought ahead, with visions of what was coming, and he kept his word."

Historians and students of international politics will debate his triumphs and his mistakes for years to come. None can afford to ignore this volume in the preparation of which Professor Gerson has had a wider access to principals and papers, including those of Mr. Dulles himself, than yet vouchsafed to any historian, as reference to his Bibliographical Essay will show.

SAMUEL FLAGG BEMIS
Advisory Editor

New Haven, Connecticut
May 1, 1967

ACKNOWLEDGMENTS

To many I owe my gratitude: to Samuel Flagg Bemis, Advisory Editor of this Series, friend and teacher; G. Lowell Field and colleagues in the department of political science at the University of Connecticut; Dean Acheson who read the chapter on the Japanese Peace Treaty; Philip A. Crowl, David Dulles, Eleanor Lansing Dulles, Admiral Arthur W. Radford, John G. Rohrbach, and Gaddis Smith who read chapters and gave suggestions and criticism; Betty Seaver for utterly indispensable assistance in research and preparation of the manuscript for publication; Florence Selleck likewise for helping with the manuscript. My thanks also go to the University of Connecticut Research Foundation and the Rockefeller Foundation. I am grateful to William S. Dix and Alexander P. Clark of Princeton University Library; to Philip C. Brooks, James R. Fuchs, and Philip D. Lagerquist of the Harry S. Truman Library; to Elizabeth Drewry of the Franklin D. Roosevelt Library; and to Howard Gotlieb of the Boston University Library, formerly of the Yale University Library. For helpful and unhurried interviews I am much beholden to former Presidents Dwight D. Eisenhower and Harry S. Truman, and former Prime Minister Sir Anthony Eden (Lord Avon). I should also like to record my debt to the following individuals for graciously granting interviews: Dean Acheson, Sherman Adams, Charles Bohlen, Philip A. Crowl, Arthur H. Dean, Thomas E. Dewey, Allen Dulles, Eleanor Lansing Dulles, Janet Avery Dulles, Abba Eban, John S. D. Eisenhower, Milton Eisenhower, Joseph N. Greene, Jr., Jacob Herzog, C. D. Jackson, Sir Gladwyn Jebb (Lord Gladwyn), George F. Kennan, Gaganvihari Lallubhai Mehta, Robert D. Murphy, Herman Phleger, Arthur W. Radford, Walter S. Robertson, Eustace Seligman, and Vijayalakshmi Pandit.

With pleasure I express my parental pride in my children—Elliot, Bill, and Ann—for their cooperation which added much enjoyment to the writing.

Louis L. Gerson

Bombay, India
December 1, 1966

JOHN FOSTER DULLES

FROM THE PAINTING BY

ROBERT BRACKMAN, N.A.

in the Collection of the
Department of State

John Foster Dulles

JOHN FOSTER DULLES

1953-59

CHAPTER ONE

EDUCATION OF A STATESMAN

WHAT a bitter cold day in the nation's capital, that Wednesday, January 28, 1953! At noon, several thousand employees of the Department of State, chilled by a wintry wind, crowded the parking lot at the west entrance of the State Department building to hear the "inauguration address" of their recently appointed Secretary, John Foster Dulles. The weather bureau had been most unkind to the incoming Secretary. It had postponed the earlier scheduled meeting from an anticipated rainy Monday to a promised sunny Wednesday. Now the reverse was true. Dulles took comfort in the fact that President Dwight D. Eisenhower during his inaugural "had good luck on his weather," and concluded that as long as the President "can have good luck we can take tough luck now and then."

"To you people," Dulles told his audience, ". . . there is nothing very novel about seeing a new Secretary of State." He reminded those persons who had been with the Department for more than eight years that they had served under at least six Secretaries, and that while for them the novelty of seeing a new Secretary might have lost its excitement, for him it had not worn off.[1]

To them John Foster Dulles was a novelty. They had of course seen him before. They had seen the tall figure with graying hair, the solemn-looking and clear bespectacled Anglo-Saxon face, an individual whom people in Woodrow Wilson's day might have described as an "old Presbyterian." But they wondered about his thoughts and views on public matters, for he was the first Republican Secretary of State since Henry L. Stimson.

The Secretary's voice, terribly difficult to hear against the gusty wind, moved on through the speech. Dulles said he had awaited his tenure with confidence, for he came from a family with a long history of diplomatic service. "I could tell you that it is a wonderful thrill to me to feel that I can be here with you as your chief and Secretary of State. I don't suppose that there is any family in the United States which has been for so long identified with the Foreign Service and the State Department as my own family. [He forgot the Adamses—father, son and grandson.] I go back a long ways—I'd have to stop and think of the date—when a great-great uncle of mine, Mr. Welsh, was one of our early ministers to the Court of St. James. In those days, you know, they were ministers and not ambassadors." He recalled that his grandfather, John W. Foster, was Secretary of State under President Benjamin Harrison, and his uncle, Robert Lansing, served as Secretary under Wilson. Proudly he brought attention to the long diplomatic careers of his brother Allen, his sister Eleanor, as well as his own "sporadic association" with the Department of State and Foreign Service. "So you can see, from the standpoint of background and tradition, it is to me a very exciting and thrilling thing to be one with you here today, as Secretary of State."

1

John Foster Dulles was born on February 25, 1888, the year of the Great Blizzard, into a family that had stressed public service. Foster, for so he was called and known by his family and friends, was the first of five children—two sons, three daughters—of Edith Foster and Allen Macy Dulles. Ancestors on both sides of the family had come from Great Britain. Joseph Dulles (originally Douglas, or perhaps du Lisse [Fr.]), arrived in Charleston, South Carolina, in 1776; Matthew Foster (a name originally spelled Forster), an Englishman, settled in New York in 1815. Each side soon left a legacy of church and diplomatic service, and interest in world travel. The paternal grandfather was a missionary to Madras. The maternal grandfather—Civil War general, lawyer, journalist—was in the diplomatic service with assignments to Mexico, Russia, Spain, Japan, and China. At Watertown, New York, where the Reverend Allen M. Dulles was pastor of the First Presbyterian Church, young Foster grew up with a religious background and in Washington where John Watson Foster lived he acquired interest in law and early exposure to the fascination of international politics. From both branches he secured pride in family, moral purpose, love of country, a sense of mission. These influences and predilections were to remain with him as he moved through a succession of Americas, from the simple, safe, provincial America of his youth to the America of the 1950's, mighty but insecure.

Foster Dulles spent the first sixteen years of his life in Watertown and on the neighboring shore and islands of Lake Ontario. Here he enjoyed summer and winter sports; spent hours bird-watching, and collected birds' eggs (being "always careful to take only one egg from a nest"); and began a stamp collection which later became a prized possession of one of his sons.[2] He relished memories of summers at Henderson Harbor on Lake Ontario, twenty-five miles from Watertown, where Grandfather Foster had a cottage. Years later, Dulles was to build a cabin on Duck Island, the "goal of adventurous sailing . . . when he was a boy," about forty "crow's miles" from Watertown. At Henderson Harbor, young Foster, his brother, and three sisters spent summers and vacations until college days. Here Aunt Eleanor Foster had her vacations and met and married Robert Lansing, a young Watertown attorney and leading Democrat in northern New York.

During fishing and sailing excursions Grandfather Foster recounted experiences as soldier, lawyer, Republican politician, journalist, and diplomat. The grandsons were respectfully attentive. One time the younger Allen found his grandfather's conversation so enthralling that he wrote an essay, full of boyish misspellings, attacking British policy toward the Boers in South Africa. Grandfather was so delighted that he printed it privately, without correction, and circulated it among the family.[3]

John W. Foster's long and varied diplomatic service was truly a school for young Foster Dulles. And what exciting stories he must have told! Judging from his *Diplomatic Memoirs,* Grandfather Foster was a keen traveler, observer, writer.[4] One comment on John W. Foster may not be misplaced here. After his tenure as Secretary of State, he advised the Imperial Chinese Government at a conference ending the Sino-Japanese War in 1895. The famous Li Hung-chang then invited him to remain as permanent adviser to the Chinese Government "with a fabulous salary, a palace, and a staff of servants." Foster declined. Assuming a "serious tone" he told the Viceroy: "I had made an engagement with and a promise to my seven-year-old grandson, that I would come home in time to go a-fishing with him that summer, and that it would destroy all his esteem and confidence in me, if I failed in my promise!" Soon after return home he sent the Viceroy a photograph of his seven-year-old grandson Foster Dulles with a "fish on a gaff-hook hanging from his shoulder."[5]

In such a family the young Foster Dulles grew to manhood. His mother, Edith Dulles, a woman of social accomplishment, strong personality, and much energy, was proud of her first-born and early recognized his capacities. Especially did she watch his religious growth. On Foster's fifth birthday, February 25, 1893, she recorded in her "line-a-day" diary that her son "has developed fully during the past year—while he is not ready to receive instruction, yet he has fine acquisitive powers, and such things as interest him he very promptly takes hold of and retains. His lovely devotional spirit remains. He is reverential to a striking degree. His thought of God is of his Heavenly Father. Whenever he sees . . . his father or mother in the attitude of prayer, he will instantly assume the same attitude and so remain until his mother rises." She also was pleased that Foster was "growing toward self-control" and had fewer attacks of "naughty spirit," and that interest in mechanical things and natural objects continued. "Mentally," she noted in her neat handwriting, "he is really remarkable for his intellectual acuteness. His logical acumen betokens a career as a thinker . . . he reasons with a clearness far beyond his age." Her entry concluded that Foster's "sense of humor is as keen as ever. His 'funny' book is his great delight. He loves a joke intensely and sees one without any explanation."[6]

As for the Reverend Allen M. Dulles—his rule over the family was affectionate if firm. He was a liberal minister who contended that Christian religion did not depend on belief in the Virgin Birth, and was one of the early ministers to officiate at marriages of divorced couples. He was a kind and gentle man who had a "firm sense of duty and of the obligation to serve his fellow men."[7] The Reverend Mr. Dulles often used the word "righteousness." He expected the children to attend three Sunday services in addition to Sunday School, and prayer meetings each

Wednesday evening. Every week young Foster had to memorize a passage from the family Bible and a verse of hymn, not without occasional protest. His mother taught him, and his father listened to his recitations and applied discipline when needed. The regular schedule of worship which averaged over ten services a week made "an impression that was not always enjoyable," but the older that Foster grew and the wider his experience, the more he appreciated the early religious upbringing, seeing "how relevant" it was "in the far-flung and changing scenes of life." The Dulles children "never felt a conflict between the things they believed and the way they lived."

At Watertown, Foster Dulles attended kindergarten, grammar school, and high school from which he graduated at the age of fifteen. His experiences in public school were pleasant and instructive. More than a half century after graduation he recounted for his townsmen his school experiences, the lessons he had learned.[8] "My family could not afford to send me to private school," he said in 1952,

> and I am glad that they could not. I learned here solidly the fundamentals of reading, writing, and arithmetic, plus American history. I particularly remember the history. History was then taught me, as I believe it should be taught to the youth, so as to emphasize the best in our great American tradition. Today American history is often taught as a doctor would report his post-mortem examination of a diseased corpse. Historians today seem

to take pride in trying to find defects in our great national figures, and to show hypocrisy in our national conduct. Of course, our nation has not been perfect, and its leaders have not been perfect. No human beings ever are. But our national history is a great record, and the acts and utterances of the Americans who made it can be an inspiration and help to each new generation. I am glad that I was taught that way.

2

Upon graduation from high school, Foster Dulles accompanied by his mother and eldest sister Margaret went to Lausanne to study French; six months later he returned to Washington where after some tutoring he entered Princeton in the autumn of 1904. Dulles often thought he would have gained more had he gone to college at an older age. He remembered mainly "lying under the trees in the sun and playing mumblety-peg," debating, or playing chess. But he was a serious student. He "came to Princeton for an education and got one." A friend of that time described him as a "poler"—one of the "quiet harmless folk who concentrated on studies." At Princeton, Dulles expected to enter the ministry and studied philosophy under Professor, later President, John Grier Hibben, a specialist in pragmatism. His senior thesis on "The Theory of Judgment" helped election to Phi Beta Kappa, made him valedictorian of his class, and earned the Chancellor Green Fellowship, a year studying philosophy at the Sorbonne under Henri Bergson. As Secretary of State, Dulles in a letter to the *Daily Princetonian* recommended study of the classics of ancient times. "I was interested," he told the young Princeton men, "in the knowledge the authors of *The Federalist Papers* showed in Greece and Rome and how much Hamilton, Jay and Madison had benefited from a knowledge of the classics as the young men who founded this nation. Their knowledge of Greek and Latin was very important to them and the kind of education I got was along the same line."[9]

Foster Dulles had a first taste of diplomacy during his junior year at Princeton, when his grandfather took him to the Second Hague Peace Conference of 1907 where Mr. Foster represented the Chinese Government. The nineteen-year-old became secretary to the Chinese delegation, "and because of his knowledge of the French language was enabled to render useful service."[10]

As mentioned, Dulles received a Princeton fellowship to study abroad. Upon return home in the autumn of 1909 he entered George Washington University Law School where he crammed a three-year course into two years. He did not fulfill the three-year residence requirement, and was not awarded a degree until decades later. The degree then was dated 1912. What wonders a willing university administration can perform!

During law school he lived with his grandparents in their large four-story brick house at 1323 Eighteenth Street, Northwest. Robert Lansing and wife also lived with the Fosters. The house was a place of frequent resort for official Washington. Mrs. Foster's Monday afternoon teas were a Washington tradition. His grandmother "presided like a duchess."[11] While in Washington, Foster Dulles met the sons of President William Howard Taft, and the Taft boys and Foster visited each other's houses.

After passing the bar Dulles went to New York City, but found that in Wall Street there was little interest in a product of the George Washington University Law School. On hearing about his grandson's plight, John W. Foster wrote a letter of introduction to William Nelson Cromwell, senior partner of the firm of Sullivan and Cromwell. He recalled friendship with the late Algernon Sydney Sullivan, mentioned Dulles' excellent record at George Washington, and inquired whether "the memory of an old association" was not "enough to give this young man a chance?"[12] Foster Dulles at age twenty-three entered Sullivan and Cromwell in 1911 as a clerk at fifty dollars a month. At the end of the year his salary rose to one hundred dollars a month. Whereupon he married Janet Avery of Auburn, New York. Eight years later he became a partner in the firm, and in 1927 at the age of thirty-nine he became its active head.

During his initial years at Sullivan and Cromwell, Dulles went on assignments to Latin America. On one trip he came down with malaria, and while quinine effected a cure it left a permanently damaged optic nerve, a noticeable tic in his left eye, and a need for glasses. Early in 1917, possibly on recommendation of

Robert Lansing, President Wilson sent Dulles on a diplomatic mission to Panama to bring about the alignment of Panama, Costa Rica, and Nicaragua for defense of the Panama Canal (Sullivan and Cromwell represented the Panama Government, perhaps the reason for choosing Dulles for this secret and successful mission).

When the United States entered the World War, Dulles received a commission as an Army captain and later a major, assigned to the General Staff in Washington. In 1918 he became assistant to the chairman of the War Trade Board, Vance McCormick, and served as liaison between the Board and the General Staff. The Board sought to deny Germany trade from five neutral nations: Switzerland, the Netherlands, Sweden, Norway, Denmark. Major Dulles negotiated agreements with those countries which tightened the blockade and made neutral shipping available to the allies.

Association with the War Trade Board led to participation in the Paris Peace Conference, where Dulles circulated among the other young men President Wilson brought to Paris—his brother Allen, aged 26; Walter Lippmann, aged 30; Joseph C. Grew, aged 39; Adolf A. Berle, Jr., aged 24; William C. Bullitt, aged 28. Foster Dulles was chief American counsel on reparations and other financial matters. He drafted the clauses of the Treaty of Versailles dealing with reparations and related problems. The Peace Conference was exciting for a young man, to come in contact with world figures—Wilson, Lloyd George,

Clemenceau, Maynard Keynes, Herbert Hoover, Thomas W. Lamont. The latter, an associate of J. P. Morgan, was so impressed with the young lawyer that he offered a senior position in the Morgan firm, which post Dulles did not accept.

Within a year after return from Paris, Dulles as a member of Sullivan and Cromwell was advising industrial, commercial, and investment bankers. Because of acquaintance with private and government leaders of Europe, Latin America, and the Far East, he represented foreign financial and industrial interests in a variety of cases. He was special counsel to the American underwriters of the Dawes loan to Germany in 1924. He helped reestablish stable finances in many countries. As counsel to the Polish Government and banks of England and the United States, he helped with Polish monetary stabilization in 1927. On the Polish case he worked with Jean Monnet whom he had met at the Peace Conference.

In the early 1930s, as the world took a turn toward chaos, Dulles doughtily continued his legal work. He had become fairly well-to-do, and managed to preserve his funds despite the Great Depression. Now senior partner of Sullivan and Cromwell, he was chief counsel for American bondholders following the bankruptcy of Kreuger and Toll. At three successive conferences in Berlin he represented American creditors who had underwritten German securities or lent money to German companies. Dulles' colleague in those active years, Arthur H. Dean, remembers a man of great energy and vigor, "indefatigable, thorough and persevering." During discussions Dulles invariably had a lined, legal-size yellow pad on which he took notes or doodled. He was "fair, even tempered, with no pride of opinion, considerate and open-minded." He said little during a conference, occasionally interjected pointed queries, but mostly waited until its end when he would summarize and express his views clearly and precisely. He was always eager to do his best for his clients. Dulles was not, nor did he profess to be, a brilliant dialectician. While arguing a case he often had a preacher's fervor. He was warmhearted and sensitive, intense, at times austere. But he impressed colleagues with great powers of relaxation, particularly after a period of hard work.[13]

Dulles' career in law was successful, usually so. It brought financial security, reputation, and also (one must add) the designation of "Wall Street lawyer," a pithy phrase to those individuals who later would question his background for diplomacy.

CHAPTER TWO

RELIGION AND POLITICS

1

FOSTER DULLES was well into his forties when his mind began to drift away from the law, back to the idealism of Woodrow Wilson, back to the Christian ministry of his father, and the diplomatic service of his grandfather. His own years were passing rapidly. He had been forty-one when the Great Depression came; forty-two when his father died; forty-five when the fragile world structure he had helped build at Paris began to collapse; forty-eight when Adolf Hitler gave that structure a hammer blow in 1936 with German reoccupation of the Rhineland. In the early 1930's Dulles with his own life in order, wealthy and professionally secure, contemplated the economic despair of many of his countrymen; in the latter part of the decade his pride in America faced the uncertainty of American hopes for the world. Beginning in 1936 he addressed himself seriously to problems of war and peace, in speeches, articles, and a book published in 1939, *War, Peace and Change.*[1]

The future statesman at first sought to define his political philosophy. He viewed the international events of the mid-thirties as another page in the historic record of struggle "between the dynamic and the static—the urge to acquire and the desire to retain." Failure of the three dominant democracies, Great Britain, France, the United States, to hold back the aggressive tide of the three despotisms, Italy, Germany, Japan, convinced him that a peaceful world order could never prevail as long as victorious nations identified peace with *status quo*, stability with rigidity. He accepted the inevitable and universal nature of change, but advocated an order of life which would permit peaceful change. In an address at Princeton in March, 1936, "Peaceful Change within the Society of Nations," he urged acceptance of change even though one could not, he said, understand or accept the forces that compelled it. Opposition encouraged violence, often resulting in destruction of nations. "Change," he remarked with perhaps an overdose of philosophy, "is the ultimate fact to which we must accommodate ourselves." He noted that change had a variety of ways, some "gentle and benign." "Violent and destructive" changes occurred when a "rigid envelope" restrains a dynamic people, the former when restraints were flexible, allowing diffusion and expansion in a gradual, peaceful manner. In both cases the conspicuous instrument of change was force, implied or actual.

The ideas of sovereignty, "the right to be free from change by outside forces," and of national boundaries, the "restraining envelopes," Dulles believed, were the main obstructions which dammed forces until they irresistibly burst. These obstacles accounted for the constant coupling of change with violence. He recalled the statesmanship of President Wilson who had labored to eliminate force as an instrument of change. Wilson attempted to mitigate the obstructive character of national boundaries by creating "an elastic world" which would allow peaceful change. Wilson during the Peace Conference proposed to open the seas to all, "alike in peace as in war"; advocated a mandate system in colonial areas where territories would be in trust, excluded from ambitions of any single nation; urged removal of economic barriers between sovereign nations; recommended that national boundaries be subject to change by international action "whenever their rigidity threatened the peace."

The ideas of Wilson haunted Dulles. He believed that Wilson's program did not fail, because nations never had tried it. Postwar efforts disregarded Wilsonian premises. Neither the realists who thought that force could disappear only through superior force, nor the intellectuals who based their hopes on reason, nor sentimentalists who looked to emotion, had the right solution. Dulles continually urged a return to Wilsonian premises.[2]

The Dulles system for a new world order, one might add, appeared in extremely turgid prose, perhaps indicating that the future world statesman was unsure of his position, uncertain how to express it. But the speech showed his developing thoughts on foreign policy, moving out of the legal world in which he had lived for fifteen years.

Then, at last, in the terrible autumn of 1939, Hitler readied German troops to march into Poland. Dulles abandoned his earlier belief that a peaceful world order was a legal or even a political possibility. Although he recognized the propriety and indispensability of political devices, some of which he had urged for years, he now doubted their usefulness as long as "millions of people look upon the State, rather than God, as their supreme ideal." Christian leaders of various nations had deeply impressed him by calmly agreeing on general principles, but when the same Christian leaders sought to identify "righteousness with one or another national cause" he found himself greatly discouraged. As the world moved closer to war he began to doubt whether the church could repair the failure of political leaders. Many churches took the "easy way" by replacing Christian symbols with national flags and anthems, thereby allowing an "anemic" church to draw "vitality from the coursing blood of nationalism." Despairing over the inability of some religious leaders, Dulles urged evangelism to "vitalize belief in a God who is the Father of us all, a God so universal that belief in Him cannot be reconciled with the deification of Nation." This, he could say on the eve of the Second World War, was "a hard, slow way," but it was the way of Christ, a way which did not involve political controversy "and had little to say about the functioning of the state or even of war and peace," and only had "one solemn guide and warning, namely, that we should not render unto Caesar that which is God's."[3]

It was in the summer of 1939 that Dulles attended at Geneva a conference of the World Council of Churches, where he helped arrive at three principles, a Christian formula for world peace. The first demanded that "political power and responsibility should be coextensive," the second that "power should be exercised in accordance with the principle that all human beings are of equal worth in the eyes of God and should be so treated in the political sphere," and the last, which clearly reflected Dulles' thinking, that it was as "necessary to effect changes in the interest of justice as to secure the protection of the *status quo.*" Dulles was certain these principles could extend through the world: if nations would only agree to some dilution of their sovereignty. He saw no evidence of readiness to limit sovereignty either in the United States or the other democracies. The church alone, he contended, could dispel the worship of sovereignty.[4]

Despite increasing interest in religion Dulles did not disdain politics, and perhaps it was the newly discovered religious zeal with all its righteousness and repentance whch led him to attack the dominant world powers, his own country, Britain, and France, for "blunders so colossal that they must be paid for." Their responsibility, he said in 1939, cannot "be discharged merely by assuming a 'holier than thou' attitude and denouncing the evil creatures which their policies have spawned forth." He disapproved of President Franklin D. Roosevelt. He charged Roosevelt with weakening democratic process in the United

States by regimenting business; making Congress a rubber stamp; upbraiding and nearly destroying the Supreme Court; above all, by introducing the "leader" principle of government which equated criticism of the executive with disloyalty to the nation. "If war were to occur," he had said with some exaggeration in March, 1939, "our democracy would vanish." "It seems to many," he told the Foreign Policy Association, "that, with the world so divided, we need an *affirmative* policy in support of our ideals and cannot trust their survival to the chance of our being let alone." Roosevelt's foreign policies, he contended, had three major characteristics, all basically negative and futile: denunciation, armament, and a disposition to give economic and perhaps military aid to Britain and France "to repress the dynamic forces which are at work." Denunciation created in those who used it "a sense of moral superiority whereas the proper approach is one of humility and repentance." It strengthened the power of the persons they denounced. He had observed this phenomenon, so he said, firsthand in Japan, also in Germany.[5]

Such were the ideas on which he set his mind. In October, 1939, he spoke to a meeting of the YMCA in Detroit. "So I see," he said in his peroration, "neither in the underlying causes of the war, nor in its long range objectives, any reason for the United States becoming a participant in the war. Were we now to act, it would be to reaffirm an international order which by its very nature is self-destructive and a breeder of violent revolt."[6]

2

As the United States moved toward war, Dulles turned his restless energy to postwar planning. The church which he had criticized in previous months became the forum for his ideas, the sounding board for his politics. When in 1940 the Federal Council of Churches, representing more than twenty-five million Protestants and 120,000 churches, created a Commission on a Just and Durable Peace, Dulles became its chairman. His religious work soon identified him not only as an outstanding lay church leader but as a Republican Party spokesman on foreign affairs. His name became known throughout the country.

The speechmaking was tireless, indefatigable. "There is, in government," Dulles told the YMCA in January, 1941, "no effort to educate the people in terms of specific long range objectives." A full year before the Japanese attack on Pearl Harbor he had convinced himself that neither the government of the United States nor that of Great Britain was willing or able to assume responsibility to free public opinion by standing against hysteria and leading toward "the course of wisdom." The object of the two governments, he said, was "to mobilize the full, undivided strength of their people for a supreme national effort." They appealed to emotion and encouraged hatred of Germany. They were building an "ephemeral and dangerous" unity on these techniques. Dulles agreed that irrational appeals served "necessities of the moment." He feared the effect on postwar planning. He noted that Winston Churchill repeatedly declined to state the postwar aims of Great Britain, and that Roosevelt also "abstained." Public statements of the two leaders convinced him that they sought "little more than to recreate the very conditions which have bred the present war." Only rarely did a nation produce leadership "which dares to meet national emergencies other than with the dynamics of cheap emotion." Abraham Lincoln and Wilson were such rare leaders. Both sought understanding, not hate; both wanted to build, not destroy. Both failed. People did not support them. There needed to be, Dulles concluded, both enlightened leadership, such as that of Lincoln and Wilson, and support from "a steady weight of public opinion" which only churches could create.[7]

Postwar planning came to preoccupy him. The Atlantic Charter of August, 1941, gave the first major opportunity to project Christian ideas into this wider political arena. Dulles welcomed the declaration but felt it "tentative and incomplete." In the statement of criticism which he prepared and which the Commission on a Just and Durable Peace adopted, he cautioned that the end of the war would bring overwhelming power to one or two nations. This power should "create, support and eventually give way to international institutions drawing their vitality from the whole family of nations." He urged both governments to prepare for the relief of war-torn populations, seek ways to reorganize the political structure of Europe into a commonwealth, assure Japan access to materials and markets, develop plans to preserve China from domination by Japan or any other power, and bring all nonself-governing colonies under an international mandate system. After the United States entered the war, Dulles increasingly stressed postwar planning. At a conference at Ohio Wesleyan University, March, 1942, sponsored by the Federal Council, he urged a world organization dedicated to the welfare of mankind with allegiance "superior to that of any national allegiance," with powers "not subject to the ordering of any national sovereign." By these steps "we will have begun that dilution of sovereignty which all enlightened thinkers agree to be indispensable."[8]

Dulles, of course, took pleasure in his growing prestige among church leaders in the United States. Braving wartime conditions he went to England in 1942, fully expecting an enthusiastic reception from British churchmen. He found no particular interest in seeing him. No effort even to house him. No meetings arranged. "There was nobody to see, nothing to do." Ironically the people who did want to meet him were political leaders. In London he talked with some members of Parliament, particularly Vernon Bartlett who wrote for the *News Chronicle*. Dulles suggested that Great Britain "ought to take more interest in postwar planning," including a New Deal policy for the colonies "which could no longer be on an imperial or exploitation basis." He noted that the British Government did not persecute big business as much as did the United States and business therefore had more "inside position in the English government." He met the American Ambassador, John G. Winant, "quite an interesting person," and Winant's predecessor, Joseph P. Kennedy. From them he learned that the British Government had been ready to agree to the territorial demands of Russia in Europe, to make a treaty which would give the Russians a slice of Poland and all of Bessarabia and the Baltic states. Strong objection from the United States had forced the British to abandon these plans. Instead they made a twenty-year alliance with Russia, for which Anthony Eden received much praise. "Anybody who does anything for Russia gets a great hand." This British reaction, Dulles reported, had "buffaloed" Kennedy.

During his London visit Dulles met Foreign Secretary Eden who invited him to lunch. The only other person present was Eden's undersecretary. "He did not do a great deal of talking himself, but mostly listened to me," Dulles recalled. "I talked to him merely of the importance of taking greater interest in post-war conditions." Dulles found Eden "quite handsome," but the Britisher's eyes were "quite shifty." Eden did not indicate any estimate of Dulles during this first encounter. When in 1964 he recalled the occasion to the present writer he remembered only a pleasant visitor and luncheon. As for other members of the government, neither Clement Attlee nor Ernest Bevin impressed the visiting American; both lacked strength. Bevin especially disappointed him, boring him with his "theory of postage stamps and raw materials." Bevin, Dulles wrote in some contemporary notes of the trip, was "exceedingly barren of any ideas," for which his own countrymen criticized him.[9]

On return Dulles continued the campaign to educate American opinion to the need of world organization. He put great effort into his speeches (which practice he continued to an amazing extent as Secretary in the 1950s, despite competing demands on his time). Seldom did he repeat the same address, believing that each speech should represent an advance in his ideas. Audiences found him reserved, a lawyer concerned with logical order. He was not an impassioned speaker, had no oratorical tricks. Often his hands were at his sides, at times he would insert them in his trousers or vest pockets. He did not gesture to make a point. Together with leading ministers and other laymen he set up study groups on postwar planning and traveled about the country conducting so-called national missions on world order. These sessions produced many proposals which the Commission on a Just and Durable Peace fashioned into a pamphlet, *Six Pillars of Peace*, published in 1943.

Dulles was sure that this pamphlet warranted attention of President Roosevelt. As chairman of the commission comprising more than a hundred distinguished Protestants, he asked for and received an appointment with the President. In the company of the Presiding Bishop of the Protestant Episcopal Church, the Reverend H. St. George Tucker, and Dr. Roswell P. Barnes, he told Roosevelt on March 26, 1943, that

Six Pillars of Peace proposed that the American people commit themselves to international collaboration in six major areas. The first pillar required the victorious nations to provide a flexible peace, curative and creative, not repressive. The remainder urged international agreement on economic and financial matters; treaty revision to meet changing conditions; autonomy for subject peoples; control of armaments; the right of people everywhere to intellectual and religious liberty. Dulles called Roosevelt's attention to the statement's simplicity, lack of controversial detail, its main purpose being to evoke from the American people a mandate to their government. Both victory and peace required that "the unity of the United Nations be cemented, and the only cement that may work is the willingness of the American people this time to go the way of organized international collaboration," thus avoiding Wilson's defeat. Dulles thought it realistic to emphasize continuing collaboration among the allies "because the spirit that makes it possible to have lasting collaboration is a spirit that precludes any nation from imposing its will."

The President listened carefully, so his auditors believed. Roosevelt had heard many delegations before, and was clever at seeming to give attention and agreement. But this time he may have listened more carefully than usual, for he was hearing ideas which coincided with his own. He asked Dulles to leave a copy of *Six Pillars*, as well as other materials, with promise that he, Roosevelt, would find a way to make public use of them.[10]

Events then played into Dulles' hands, so well that he began to believe he had helped order them. By the end of 1943 he believed his campaign to influence public opinion had paid off. It "bore early fruit in Congress" when in the latter part of that year both Houses passed resolutions favoring world organization. His confidence increased when Roosevelt, "convinced that American public opinion would support another try," sent Secretary of State Cordell Hull to Moscow where in October, 1943, the allies (including China) issued the Four Nations Declaration which led to the Dumbarton Oaks Conference and eventually the United Nations. "Public opinion," Dulles later wrote, "had taken the lead, and in two years had transformed the attitude of the government."[11]

During the final apocalyptic months of the war Dulles began to look for ways to link Christian principles with political expediency to insure a peaceful world. There would be no wars if people only would change their desire for material possessions to a desire to share ideals. "If we all concerned ourselves with idealism, of which there is no limit," he reflected in a private memorandum of November, 1944, "there would be no competition for possessions. We would wish to share our spiritual values with all."[12] He recognized that the world was not about to turn to God. If some of the postwar plans included "*heavy* emphasis on a religious philosophy" they might nudge man in His direction. Training in the ways of God took a long time, hence political means had to accompany it.

The reasoning of this personal memorandum deserves attention. Nations like men, Dulles contended, shared a common failing in that they continuously wanted things and were impatient in acquiring them, although some nations were more patient than others. From this he deduced that in planning the future of Germany and Japan it was necessary to recognize the "characteristics" of the Anglo-Saxons, British and Americans, particularly since the two nations were likely to carry the burden of postwar responsibility. Both peoples did not hold hate, did not insist indefinitely on repressive measures. In impatience to "get back to normal" their "war psychosis" would evaporate. In thinking of what to do with the defeated nations, the allies should not take such concern with the immediate future as to ignore the world of thirty or fifty years later. A devastated and defeated Germany would be no threat during the first five or ten years. As for "characteristics" of the Germans, history convinced him that when Germans assimilated with other societies they made good citizens, and only when they were en masse did they rise to "white heat over the idea of racial superiority and all that heinous philosophy means." To prevent so horrendous a repetition Dulles suggested that the victorious allies should incorporate "German life" into the surrouding countries, "leaving only a nucleus of Prussia": the Rhineland should go to France, south Germany to Austria, eastern Germany to Poland. And to prevent resurgence of the war spirit a European federation of states should stand guard. Meanwhile plans should get underway to reeducate the

Germans, rewrite their history, and reintroduce religious teaching for the youth. The Germans needed rule by an iron hand, or they would have nothing but scorn for the rulers. "Let us make it impossible for them to murder the world. Let *us* make sure that civilization conquers and is not conquered."

A religious theme ran through all Dulles' wartime thoughts on international affairs, a theme he would repeat to the end of his days, something like the theme in Johann Sebastian Bach's great Passacaglia in c minor. When Dulles received opportunity to practice diplomacy he would remark that mankind could never enjoy peace unless moral and spiritual power supported it. He would get annoyed with people who talked about peace as something that could come with a simple stroke or some agreement, rather than by a way of living with one's neighbors. His first confrontation with Soviet ambition at the San Francisco Conference in 1945 confirmed that latter idea, and thereafter he became increasingly certain that only efforts derived from deep spiritual conviction could ward off the peril of world communism. The enlarging involvement of the American Government in projects of material welfare, so Dulles believed, tended to put individuals into spiritual, intellectual, and economic straitjackets. "I am convinced," he wrote privately early in 1950, "that we here need to make our political thoughts and practices reflect more faithfully a religious faith that man has his origin and destiny in God."[13] American and world society should organize around that central truth.

While he would at times lose confidence, he seldom despaired of the future. Despite lapses, he repeatedly pointed out that the people of the Western world believed in equal rights and dignity of all men, in the sacredness of individual personalities. This faith, begun in the hills of Judea where East and West met, held that all men regardless of race and color were the creation and concern of a universal God.[14]

CHAPTER THREE

POLITICS AND DIPLOMACY

1

THE YEAR of planning for the United Nations, 1944, was a presidential election year in the United States; according to the Constitution there had to be an election, war or no war. Secretary of State Hull, long an advocate of nonpartisan foreign policies, was anxious to keep the organization of peace out of domestic politics. "If that organization became a political issue," he wrote later, "it might well suffer the fate of the League of Nations in the Senate in 1919."[1] And so Hull in the spring of 1944 began a series of discussions with ranking Congressional leaders of both parties which culminated in an agreement that the UNO would not become "a puck of politics." Then something went awry. Confident of Republican Party support, Hull had organized a conference at the Washington estate of Dumbarton Oaks, beginning August 1. Unfortunately his "reasonable assurance" of a nonpartisan meeting came to grief on August 16 when the Republican candidate for the presidency, Governor Thomas E. Dewey, issued a statement criticizing proposals emanating from the Dumbarton Oaks Conference. "These indicate," Dewey claimed, "that it is planned to subject the nations of the world, great and small, permanently to the coercive power of the four nations holding this conference."[2]

Dewey's statement had an interesting background: John Foster Dulles, apparently, had proposed and written it. The press release revealed Dulles' long-expressed view that a world organization should have representation for small nations. Republican leaders by 1944 were recognizing Dulles as one of the party's leading spokesmen on foreign affairs, the undisputed choice for Secretary of State if Dewey won the election in November. A close friendship between Dulles and Dewey had begun in 1937 when Dulles, impressed with Dewey's record as special prosecutor in an investigation of New York racketeering, offered to make him a partner in Sullivan and Cromwell. Dewey accepted, but shortly thereafter when Republican leaders invited him to run for District Attorney he asked to be relieved of this commitment. Dewey won handily and launched a political career which led to the governorship of New York and nomination by the Republican Party for the presidency in 1944 (and again in 1948).

As Dewey's foreign policy adviser, Dulles took part in the Republican National Convention at Chicago during the last two weeks of June, 1944. He worked closely with Senator Arthur H. Vandenberg, the isolationist-turned-internationalist, who persuaded the platform committee to adopt the Republican advisory committee's "Mackinac declaration"—arranged at Mackinac Island, Michigan—which urged the party to support a future international organization. Vandenberg recorded in his diary that he was "greatly impressed by Dulles, we found ourselves in complete harmony." Dulles felt the same way. "I want to say," he wrote Vandenberg on June 20, "how much I feel the Party is indebted to you for the fine preliminary work you did as Chairman of the Mackinac Committee in getting up a foreign affairs plank upon which the Resolutions Committee and the delegates as a whole could substantially unite. Without that assiduous and painstaking advance work by you . . . there might have been serious disruption." Vandenberg commented carefully on the margin of this letter: "Dulles speaks for Dewey in respect to foreign relations—and will probably be his Secretary of State."[3]

It was shortly after the convention that Dulles got into a mediation over his own handiwork. Dewey's unexpected criticism of the Dumbarton Oaks Conference, arousing excitement in the newspapers, worried Secretary Hull, who called a press conference to assure Dewey that the party fears were "utterly and completely unfounded." He indicated willingness to confer with the Governor. The Republican presidential candidate accepted Hull's offer, and designated Dulles as his representative. Dewey's response delighted Hull, although President Roosevelt had been skeptical of any "nonpartisan agreement with the Republicans."[4]

Hull was careful with Dewey's emissary, Dulles. "I have seldom worked harder on any project," Hull recorded in his memoirs, "than on the preparation for and conduct of the conversations with John Foster Dulles. I was convinced that, if I did not reach a satisfactory agreement with him, successful American participation in an international security organization might be seriously jeopardized." Dulles, too, was aware of the importance of his mission. So was the American press; leading newspapers mentioned his name, heralding the appearance of a Republican statesman and future Secretary of State.[5]

Dulles' arrival in Washington on August 23, 1944, brought national and even world publicity and, one must add, a first exposure to public criticism. The new Republican spokesman had been suffering from a severe attack of thromboid phlebitis, making it difficult to get about without crutches. Aware of this incapacity, Governor Dewey had arranged for a New York State car to drive him down to the capital. The Washington columnist Drew Pearson censured Dulles for using scarce gasoline. The unjust comment at this historic moment in his life upset Dulles, but he was to learn that criticism, just or not, is part of the price of being a public figure.

The Hull-Dulles talks lasted three days, and were in Dulles' opinion a landmark of bipartisanship in foreign policy. Vandenberg accepted this view, although he thought bipartisanship antedated these conversations. "In practical operation the Dewey-Dulles-Hull arrangement in the campaign of 1944," he would recall, "was undoubtedly the first formal and formidable exercise of this policy. But of course it was preceded . . . by many expressions of purpose on my own part." Hull dispelled Dulles' fear that the future world organization would discriminate against small nations, and both men agreed that all Americans, regardless of party, should support a United Nations Organization. They were not able easily to secure a wording of the final agreement. Dulles insisted on the word "bipartisan," which he said connoted collaboration by both parties; Hull preferred "nonpartisan," arguing that two political parties could not share responsibility for foreign policy. He called attention to *Webster's New International Dictionary*, Second Edition, then an epitome of English usage, which defined "nonpartisan" as viewing foreign policies without party bias. Dulles reluctantly accepted "nonpartisan," a term incidentally that Vandenberg preferred. In Vandenberg's view bipartisan collaboration was a means to achieve a nonpartisan foreign policy.[6] Later the Senator would complicate the political lexicon by using an awful word: unpartisan.

Dulles' active and well-advertised role as champion of bipartisanship in creating the United Nations led to continuation of that policy in subsequent years. He felt disappointment when the American people reelected President Roosevelt for the fourth time, although Vandenberg's letter of November 11 consoled him; the Senator facilely informed Dulles that their friendship was a "most important" compensation for Dewey's defeat: "I feel that we are already 'old friends.' I looked forward to working intimately with you in the great 'peace adventure.' Indeed, I confess to a feeling of 'loneliness' as I look ahead to the responsibilities which I still confront. I beg of you always to feel free to send me your advice and suggestions. . . . I suspect you will find me knocking at your door more than once. I really think it is little short of amazing that our views on foreign policy should have proved to be so emphatically harmonious."[7] After Dewey's failure, and failure thereby of Dulles' hopes, nearly a decade passed before the New York lawyer reached the pinnacle. But it was a busy time, with service at the United Nations Conference, at ten subsequent diplomatic assemblages averaging two months each (all important, involving either the United Nations or meetings of the allies or sessions with the Russians), and lastly the Japanese Peace Treaty which Dulles undertook to negotiate for President Harry S. Truman, to which we shall give special attention later.

2

Before his bipartisan activity in American foreign relations moved into high gear, Dulles had a period of contemplation. "The American nation," he announced in January, 1945, "has not yet adjusted itself to the working conditions of collaboration. . . . We like collaboration as an idea. We fear it as a reality." In this opening address to the National Study Conference on The Churches and a Just and Durable Peace, held at Cleveland, Dulles alerted his audience to the corrosion of diplomatic collaboration agreed upon at the Moscow Conference of 1943. The

United States Government, he charged, did not wish to share responsibility in decisions on liberated areas of Eastern and Southeastern Europe. Responsibility had gone in large part to the Soviet Union and in smaller part to Great Britain. Who, he asked, was responsible for the "retrogression from the practice of cooperation?" (Here, truly, was a prescient query on the origins of the cold war, two years and more before the phrase—not to mention the idea—became current.) Dulles criticized Roosevelt for a temperament which made it "difficult to organize and delegate," preference for "lofty generalities, such as the Four Freedoms, upon which all can agree." Such behavior by political leaders was not unique, and hence the need for organized collaboration was imperative. He credited the American people for accepting "the proposition that international trouble anywhere is of potential concern." Theoretically this gave the American Government a mandate to take part in world affairs. In fact it was not so. The people, he said, "inspire our government with fears that it cannot collaborate and still retain the confidence of the people." He told his auditors that this was not without warrant: European problems aroused violent emotions in those Americans of foreign origin who remained ideologically and culturally tied to the ambitions and fortunes of native lands. These blocks of citizens were vocal, and from a standpoint of voting had strategic power. Other Americans "who judge their government as Americans" preferred their President to proclaim lofty pronouncements gratifying their sense of moral superiority, instead of leading the United States into world affairs. "Under such conditions, government is not disposed to work in such mire as much of the world is today. It is afraid of the criticism which will be heaped upon it when it comes back with some of the mire adhering to its hands and feet."

Dulles called attention to Poland, Greece, and other Balkan states. Any settlement of boundaries of Poland in which the United States participated was bound to attract criticism from Polish-Americans as well as Christians, particularly Roman Catholics, who would oppose cessions of Catholic areas to the atheistic Soviet Union. It was not surprising that the American Government had escaped responsibility in Poland and elsewhere and took refuge in generalities about noninterference in the internal affairs of another state. During civil war days in Spain, Dulles said, democracies used this principle of nonintervention as an excuse "for abandoning a people to armed cliques or to the intervention of others." They prevented the Spanish people from having a moderate democratic form of government. "The democracies kept their hands and feet clean, but did so at heavy cost to the Spanish people and in the long run to themselves."[8] It was not too late, he claimed, for the United States to return to active international collaboration and participate in decisions on the future of Europe. He urged the government to call on experienced Americans to render their services for world cooperation. "Collaboration, to be acceptable, must be skilled," sustained, so as to prevent crises and not merely solve them. American cooperation must be conciliatory and respectful of ideals and needs of others. For a principle Dulles recommended a phrase from the Lansing-Ishii Agreement of 1917—"territorial propinquity creates special relations between countries."[9]

Dulles early in February, 1945, made another speech and appraised American foreign policy against the world emerging from the war. "During the 19th century," he told the Economic Club of Detroit, "we had a simple, yet profound, conception of our role in the world."[10] The founders of America had dedicated the nation to aid mankind by showing how to build a beautiful spiritual society. For a hundred years after establishment of the great American experiment the United States by conduct and example "led other peoples to seek for themselves that which we demonstrated to be possible." Through the nineteenth century the peoples of the world admired and respected Americans, "not out of fear, not in the hope of largess," but because of desire to emulate the American way of life. This, and no accident of history or geographical detachment, he maintained, produced "a spiritual alliance" with the people of the world which gave America influence, opportunity, and safety.

Dulles warned of a widespread conviction that the American experiment had failed: the humiliating day had come—peoples of Europe, Asia, and South America were turning elsewhere. It was naive, he said, to debate the merits of isolationism against internationalism. Americans could no longer make this decision, it was being made for them. "We are being isolated, not because we want that, but because our example no longer attracts a following in the world." Foreign and domestic policies were intertwined; no foreign policy of the United States could be successful unless domestic policies created a society which recognized dignity and worth of the individual, promoted his spiritual and intellectual development, and gave economic independence; only then could the United States become an inspiring example. "This war will be won by that nation which provides the ideals which inspire the peoples of the world."

The major long-range objective of American foreign policy must be to regain prestige. Dulles did not expect this to happen quickly. For many years, he said, "we cannot count upon our example as sufficient to assure us safety at home and opportunity abroad." As the first and most necessary step toward a favorable environment the government of the United States would have to involve itself in international politics "as never before." He welcomed a world organization which would promote consultation among nations, but cautioned against optimism that the United Nations Organization would assure opportunity abroad and safety at home. World organization would not reverse dangerous trends. "We shall have to do that ourselves."

This second important speech given early in 1945 set out a considered point of view. As Dulles looked toward Europe in the winter of 1944-45, the eve of victory, he claimed the right for America to take part in rebuilding. "With our blood and with our treasure we have earned the right to have a voice in how the oft-charred structure of Europe is, this time, to be rebuilt." To evade this responsibility would be folly. He also saw need for more friendly relations with the Soviet Union, a difficult task. Soviet leaders were atheists and materialists and could not be trusted. Then, too, the Soviets, "on their side, have little reason to trust us." He recalled that America had opposed the Bolshevik Revolution of 1917 and given aid to counter-revolutionists, and for many years failed to recognize the Soviet Union.[11] To revert to prewar relations would be disastrous for the United States, the Soviet Union, and the rest of the world. "But it is a disaster that stares us in the face."

Dulles then listed four principles which he recently had recommended and which were adopted by the National Study Conference on The Churches and a Just and Durable Peace: the first called on the government of the United States to "adopt and publicly proclaim long-range goals which reflect our high ideals"; the second demanded that the government get into international politics and "battle" for those ideals; the third asked the government to give assurance that "no particular defeat is final" ("We may, at times, have to accept solutions which do violence to our ideals. But we cannot do that if thereby we become morally bound to their perpetuation."); the fourth, addressed to the American people, asked them to judge their government not by immediate results, often imperfect, but by "whether it works competently and skillfully to achieve the best practical results." These four principles of conduct, he felt, were necessary "to bring collaboration out of the realm of theory."

Shortly after this speech Dulles learned of the Yalta Conference, which he greeted as a clear mandate to make cooperation a reality, a mandate which he believed he had in some measure helped bring about. Yalta, he told the Foreign Policy Association of New York in March, 1945, opened a new era, the end of American aloofness and beginning of Soviet acceptance of "joint action on matters that it had the physical power to settle for itself."[12] Many people might not like some of the decisions, but collaboration could not bring perfection. One had to take chances. "Peace, like war," Dulles concluded, "requires that peoples go on taking risks." Only those who dared could bring peace to the world. "Let us hope that at San Francisco, the great powers will dare to give posterity a good chance."

3

Having arranged his ideas on foreign policy, somewhat theoretically, Dulles moved off into the world of diplomatic practice. At the San Francisco Conference in the spring of 1945 his real diplomatic experience began again, long years after the Paris Peace Conference of 1919. San Francisco and subsequent conferences in which he was to participate as unofficial Republican Party representative and official adviser to four Democratic Secretaries of State—Edward R. Stettinius, Jr., James F. Byrnes, George C. Marshall, Dean G. Acheson—gave opportunity to test his theories. He began his diplomatic odyssey with a conviction that peace like war had to be waged, and like war required idealism, sacrifice, courage, a "righteous and dynamic faith"; that the United States had responsibility to participate in world affairs; that cooperation with the Soviet Union was necessary; that peace treaties must allow for change; and that the policies of the United States needed bipartisan support. Through this period, 1945-51, he was grateful to the Democratic Administration for opportunity to serve his country in the cause of peace.

The United Nations Conference on International Organization, called to order by Roosevelt's successor Harry S. Truman at San Francisco on April 25, 1945, lasted until June 26. From all over the United States the new Truman Administration invited civic, religious, and political leaders as secretaries, advisers, observers. Among them was Dulles, whom Roosevelt originally had appointed to the official American delegation headed by Secretary of State Stettinius. Dulles worked hard and effectively at San Francisco. More or less by default he became the *de facto* leader of the United States delegation and was personally responsible for many of the clauses of the United Nations Charter. Most of the San Francisco delegates would return home full of evangelical fervor. Dulles' first encounter with the Soviet representatives Vyacheslav M. Molotov and Andrei A. Gromyko sobered his expectations. He was to leave the conference with a belief that the great powers did "dare" to give mankind a chance, but only a chance. The new world organization could not do everything, it was no substitute for foreign policy, it did not relieve the United States of major responsibilities, but in its operation it had possibilities which could make it a "cornerstone" of American policy. "The present Charter," he wrote in *Foreign Affairs* for October, 1945, "represents a conscientious and successful effort to create the best world organization which the realities permit. . . . The task of statesmanship, however, is to relate theory to reality."[13]

The London Council of Foreign Ministers in the autumn of 1945, to which Secretary Byrnes invited Dulles, gave another opportunity to relate theory to reality. If Dulles had thought Yalta had opened a new cooperation with the Soviet Union, the first major postwar conference of foreign ministers marked the beginning of the postwar American policy of "no appeasement." So he would write in 1950 as he recalled the diplomatic adroitness of Foreign Minister Molotov who tried to divide the allies and maneuver the United States to sacrifice the interests of weaker nations to preserve cooperation between the two superpowers. "Was *war* appeasement to be continued in the form of *peace* appeasement?" There was truth in the Soviet contention that if the United States and the Soviet Union could not agree it would threaten peace. Nevertheless he approved Byrnes's decision of September 30 to reject Soviet demands, which brought to an end the policy of appeasement.[14]

On return home Dulles in a radio report to the nation on October 6 said the London Conference "has not *created* difficulties. It has merely *revealed* difficulties of long standing which war has obscured. It is healthier that we now know the facts."[15]

To the student of recent American diplomacy it is interesting that not until some months later, in the spring of 1946, did Dulles become sure of his conclusions about the aims of Soviet foreign policy. Like many Americans, despite some mistrust he had expected the Soviet Union to welcome American cooperation and aid at the end of war. Soviet diplomats showed neither friendship nor gratitude. What was their motive? Nationalism, which drove them to seek control of nearby nations? Communist ideology, which propelled them to extend their social system throughout a world already shaken by collapse of old empires, a collapse that left vacuums everywhere? Was Soviet behavior a combination of both communism and nationalism? Perhaps it came from a fear of capitalist encirclement, or was it fear of the presence of American power in Europe? Internal tension within the Soviet Union? Whatever the reasoning, the actions of Soviet leaders were incompatible with the American hope to restore normal relations with the Soviet Union and establish a peaceful, secure world.

To find the right answers Dulles, by this time in his late fifties, turned to the study of communism. He added a new book—Stalin's *Problems of Leninism*

—to the volumes he most often consulted: his grandfather's *Diplomatic Memoirs,* the *Federalist Papers,* and the Bible.

"I have for some time felt," he wrote on May 8, 1946, to all members of the Commission on a Just and Durable Peace, "that our Commission has been derelict in not facing up to the Russian problem." The time had come. The Commission could no longer delay giving Protestant churches guidance on the most serious postwar problem. Dulles accepted responsibility for this delay in leadership, because he had not been sure about Soviet policy. Diplomatic experiences of a year and more had given him "clear understanding of the fundamentals, at least, of Soviet foreign policy." For the Commission he had prepared a paper expressing his thoughts on Soviet policy, and he requested a full meeting to study it.[16]

The Soviet challenge, he now believed, was double-barreled: one barrel aimed at social revolution throughout the world; the other at national expansion. The objects of Soviet foreign policy derived from the communist creed in Stalin's *Problems of Leninism,* and not from words of Soviet leaders often uttered to confuse. What should count were Soviet deeds—a contention he would repeat during his tenure as Secretary of State. He compared Stalin's work to *Mein Kampf*—statesmen had ignored the latter book at their peril and later regret. Soviet foreign policy was world-wide and sought a *Pax Sovietica.* Soviet rulers therefore had developed a program which divided the world into three areas: the

Soviet Inner Zone, Middle Zone, and Outer Zone. The Inner Zone comprised the Soviet Union, already much expanded. It had begun with Hitler's concessions during the Nazi-Soviet honeymoon which gave the USSR part of Finland, all of Estonia, Latvia, Lithuania, and large portions of Poland and Rumania. All this as a price for neutrality during Hitler's march upon the West. After Germany attacked Russia, the Western powers, anxious to preserve unity, made concessions to their new ally at Teheran and Yalta which extended Soviet land power in Europe and the Far East. The Soviet Middle Zone comprised the twenty-odd states on the Russian periphery, all under Soviet power, some within its orbit and the rest gravitating toward it. The Outer Zone was the rest of the world. Here the Soviet Communist Party through propaganda, infiltration, and fifth-column activity took advantage of mass discontent. In Latin America, the Middle East, Africa, Asia, and Western Europe, communist agents with help of local communists promoted a Soviet system of proletarian dictatorship. Dulles warned that all these policies were against the free world and threatened the traditions of Western civilization.

Americans must inform the Soviet Union by words and deeds that a *Pax Sovietica* could not succeed. "Twice within 25 years the U.S. has been drawn into a world war because the American people finally came to feel that aggressive policies in Europe and Asia threatened our conception of democracy and our ideals of personal freedom. In each case the foreign leaders would probably have followed a different course had they, at an early stage, realized that the American people would react as they did. In not making apparent, in time, our devotion to our ideals, we were guilty of contributory negligence. We must not make the same mistake three times in a generation."

Dulles was not certain that the United States could change the Soviet Union, but felt that Americans must act on the assumption they could do something. "If we do not go ahead on that basis, we shall almost surely fail," and war follow. He accepted change as a working hypothesis, and recommended courses for the American Government. He cautioned his fellow citizens not to react violently to the Soviet threat he had outlined; he was anxious to prevent the American people from following the advice of those persons who would rely on economic and military coercion. Such a program might not work because the men in the Kremlin are not "the kind of men who are easily coerced," and moreover such policy would divide the American electorate. No program could succeed, he wrote, if it was against someone or something. The United States must have constructive policies. He suggested two approaches. The first called for American military power to deter the Soviet Union. The Soviets, he said, respected force. The second recommended open competition with the Soviet Union for the minds of men everywhere, an American world policy which would recognize demands for political freedom and economic advance. Such a contest called for exposition of American ideals to peoples new to freedom in Asia, Africa, the Middle East, and elsewhere, in such a way that America's principles could compete with the simple Marxist ideology.

Dulles evidently did not believe American values were too difficult for non-Western peoples. By demonstrations America would indicate that its free society could fit modern times. The most important demonstration could be religious. "The overriding and ever-present reason for giving freedom to the individual is that men are created as the children of God, in His image. The human personality is thus sacred and the State must not trample upon it." This, Dulles contended, was the foundation of the American state. All the country needed was rededication to the faith of its forefathers, which would make apparent the futility of any world program based on suppression of liberty. America should demonstrate a willingness to help others toward economic, personal, and religious freedom. At the same time the nation must show its power. Both policies were essential to any plan for frustrating the Soviet design. Soviet leaders must realize that Americans are a people of "righteous convictions," and this only could come by adhering "steadfastly to principle not merely in word but above all in deed."

Dulles had returned to his prewar theme of peaceful change. Peace, he wrote, could not prevail easily through the *status quo*. Nor would it prevail after dynamic groups imposed on others a system which violated political and religious faiths. As long as the Soviet Union continued its expansion the United

States must resist. The many problems of the impoverished, emerging states were not economic but political, relating to the *Pax Sovietica.* Accommodation would come when the Soviet Union abandoned its grandiose plan and accepted a world in which it was only one of many nations, "each one representing a distinctive way of life."

4

Dulles sent copies of his evangelical remarks to President Truman, Senator Vandenberg, to his brother Allen, Dean Acheson, and Walter Lippmann, as well as to Gromyko among others. He felt pleased by the reaction (not, incidentally, from Gromyko, who did not answer directly; the Russians soon began to call Dulles a warmonger), and after minor revisions *Life* published his comments in June, 1946, in two installments.[17] *Reader's Digest* reprinted them. Before publication Dulles pondered for weeks whether the American people would see Soviet aims and not react foolishly; he concluded that it would be wise to trust the people. "If, as a people," he wrote Lippmann, "they do not have self-restraint, then we are not entitled to freedom, and, in fact, cannot keep it long."[18]

Here was quite a prescription. The ideas were vintage Dulles. If to a later generation they show much assurance, they must have made an impression on many millions of readers: the magisterial analysis and solutions, the stress on religion and on national if not personal self-righteousness.

Congratulations poured in. Senator Vandenberg believed Dulles' "Russian poem" magnificent, his definition of Soviet policy masterful. He was critical of Dulles' failure to mention the communists and fellow travelers within the United States, the direct instruments of the Soviet Union. It was an interesting letter from Vandenberg, all in the Senator's typical gee-whiz style, replete with mixed metaphors and double nouns, verbs, and adjectives. Still, under the fervor was approval. Dulles, one should add, did not accept the Senator's ideas on emphasizing the communist menace within the United States.[19]

The reaction of Allen Dulles to his brother's memorandum is of importance, for the future head of the Central Intelligence Agency did not think American foreign policy could assume that "dangerous aspects of Soviet policy may be altered." He agreed that it was a possibility, but did not accept it as a "certainty." Allen Dulles recalled that some statesmen had made the same assumption about Hitler in 1938. Allen felt that as long as the Soviet Union continued to suppress liberty within its "inner zone," it would consider liberty outside a menace. "There may be a method of insulating the two systems; I doubt whether there is a method of reconciling the two systems." The firmness and "demonstration" which Foster suggested could achieve sufficient insulation to keep the peace for a time. It was possible that during this period the Soviet Union might undergo some fundamental change which would allow personal liberty. He favored sitting down with the Russians to settle territorial issues which would give them better access to the seas and even military protection, but not on the basis of "another Munich appeasement." If the United States could have several years of peace, Russia "whether it likes it or not, will be brought so closely in touch with the rest of the world that a modification of the Communist system will result, which will mean that the liberties existing in the rest of the world will also be introduced into Russia." Then permanent accommodation would become possible, and the United States and the Soviet Union would adjust difficulties the same way the United States had done with France and Great Britain. The difference between the Dulles brothers was, as Allen saw it, that Foster hoped for some arrangement between the Soviet system and the American, and the younger brother doubted it. Allen agreed with the lines of policy directed toward that hope, because such tactics "may gain time within which a gradual change may produce a different kind of Russian government and social structure."[20]

Such were Foster Dulles' thoughts about Soviet foreign policy. He was to hold these views while he was Republican adviser to a Democratic Administration, and he would bring many of them to the Department in 1953. From 1944 until the campaign of 1952 he faithfully, and at times enthusiastically, supported these policies while working with the Truman Administration.

Dulles' public duties changed bewilderingly during the early postwar era. In early 1947 he attended the futile Moscow Conference of Foreign Ministers as an adviser to Secretary of State George C. Marshall.

President Truman on November 18, 1948, appointed him to the American delegation to the United Nations as acting chairman, which restored his waning political prestige after the Republican defeat in the presidential election. Early in May, 1949, he accepted Truman's invitation to join the American delegation to the foreign ministers meeting in Paris under leadership of Secretary of State Dean Acheson. Governor Dewey then appointed him on July 7, 1949, to fill the unexpired term of Senator Robert F. Wagner, Sr., who had retired because of physical disability. After defeat in the ensuing senatorial election he returned to the Department in 1950.

Dulles would look back with great satisfaction to his role during these years as champion and originator of bipartisanship. He continuously fought off prominent Republican spokesmen who thought bipartisanship a political mistake. In the campaigns of 1944 and 1948 he prevented conservative Republicans from dominating the party in its foreign policy pronouncements, but would not be successful in 1952. Privately and publicly he countered the attacks on bipartisanship by pointing out that American foreign policies could not be successful unless they were national rather than party policies. Foreign policies which change with shifts of domestic politics are not worth much, he said in 1945, because nations would not "adjust their conduct to meet our policies unless they feel that those policies are sufficiently stable so that long-term plans can be made in reliance on them."[21] When in the wake of Dewey's unexpected second defeat in 1948 prominent Republicans again attacked bipartisanship as one of the reasons for failure to win the presidency, Dulles although personally disappointed and even worried by the outcome of the election which denied him the office of Secretary of State, continued to defend it.[22]

Throughout the year 1949, and into 1950, an era of intense partisanship among political leaders throughout the nation, he warned fellow Republicans that the United States would never be able to lead the world if its foreign policies lasted only until another Congressional or presidential election. "Other governments will not risk their countries' future in reliance on United States policies that are partisan and subject to change without notice."[23] He recalled the "near-panic" that had gripped friendly governments in 1948 lest foreign policies of the United States, "into which they had geared their own, might be suddenly shifted," and how bipartisanship practiced by President Truman and the Republican presidential candidate Governor Dewey allayed their fear. In his book *War or Peace*, published in 1950, he defended his stand on the ground that "if, at a time of national peril, two Presidential candidates should compete in making novel and unseasoned proposals, designed primarily to win votes, the end of that campaign would leave our foreign relations in a shambles."[24] Within weeks after these views appeared in *War or Peace*, President Truman was asking Dulles to negotiate the Japanese Peace Treaty.

CHAPTER FOUR

THE JAPANESE PEACE TREATY: SHOWPIECE OF BIPARTISANSHIP

SOMETIME in the winter of 1949-50, Secretary of State Acheson decided to expedite a peace treaty with Japan, and for this task turned to his Republican bipartisan collaborator, John Foster Dulles. Preparation for a peace treaty with the former enemy had begun in the Department soon after the war. Secretary Byrnes had initiated the first plans in 1945-46, but nothing came of them. General Douglas MacArthur in 1947 began to press for an early, nonpunitive treaty. Not until late 1949 did the Department, hitherto unsure of the situation in Japan because of the informational screen surrounding MacArthur's headquarters, take a serious view of the General's warning that the occupation of Japan was encountering diminishing returns.[1]

Beginning in January, 1950, Secretary Acheson received ideas and drafts of treaties reflecting divergent opinions of the Department of Defense, MacArthur's headquarters, and groups within the Department of State. By the spring of that year a voluminous draft proposal of hundreds of pages with meticulous detailed answers to questions raised and anticipated was on Acheson's desk. The experts produced more questions than solutions. Could the United States afford a peace treaty which would free Japan? would a post-treaty Japan allow military bases which the Pentagon considered necessary? would Japan remain friendly? was the economy of Japan viable? should the United States support demands, from nations previously occupied by or at war with Japan, for heavy reparations or trade restrictions? how about the communist success in China, its effect on Japan's economic and political future and also national security? how about protection against possible resurgence of aggression, of particular concern to the Philippines and Australia? or defense in case of Soviet-Chinese aggression against a disarmed Japan? A treaty with Japan, with or without Soviet participation, was bound to produce difficulties.

The Secretary knew it would be difficult to negotiate a nonpunitive treaty with the principal former allies, who were not in a forgiving mood, and carry it through a hostile Congress. He needed support for a treaty which would ignore the Bataan march and the many subsequent Japanese barbarities, and which would call for closer relations including continuation of American economic aid. There was the possibility that the bitter domestic political argument about the Far East which had not yet involved Japan might well extend there. "Can you imagine my asking Congress for this kind of treaty? They would say, 'Here comes this communist, Acheson. Now he wants us to help the Japs!' " Acheson decided to enlist Dulles.[2]

Such a move would signal a return to the bipartisanship suspended in the aftermath of the presidential election of 1948, and in the Far East where American foreign policies continued to be scathingly criticized by Republicans who claimed they had not been consulted as they had been on European problems.[3]

There was some momentary difficulty about appointing Dulles. Acheson had to overcome a delicate political obstacle before asking Dulles to return to the Department. At that time Dulles was *persona non grata* to many leaders of the Democratic Party, including President Truman. In the autumn of 1949 Dulles, whose brief appointive term as United States Senator from New York was coming to an end, was persuaded, much against his inclination, to run against Herbert H. Lehman in a special election. At one point during this campaign Dulles, while upstate, referred to the Democratic strength in New York City by saying: "If you could see the kind of people in New York City making up this bloc that is voting for my opponent, if you could see them with your own eyes, I know you would be out, every last man and woman of you, on election day."[4] Lehman, his campaign managers, and the New York *Post* which supported him, immediately charged Dulles with bigotry and branded him anti-Jewish. Dulles' statement, which did not make any reference to American Jews, was of course maladroit. But political remarks during campaigns seldom are models of felicity. Lehman's accusation did not correspond to Dulles' views publicly expressed or privately held. It was a slender branch on which to hang such a heavy charge. Still, once on the record it proved difficult to explain. For years afterward many people would go on believing that Dulles was anti-Semitic and that he based his policies toward the Middle East on that feeling. The immediate controversy emanating from Lehman's campaign headquarters created a bad impression, spreading resentment in the Democratic Party, its national committee, and even the White House.[5]

The Department, sizing up Dulles, at first thought it must allow some time for the episode to be forgotten. Could another prominent Republican take Dulles' place? Late in March, 1950, Acheson asked Vandenberg for a recommendation. Vandenberg concluded that Dulles should carry the assignment. It was advisable to restore "unpartisan unity." Dulles, he informed Acheson, had his total confidence, and he would unhesitatingly give him his own proxy during his illness (Vandenberg was gravely ill). The Senator recognized that political considerations resulting from the senatorial campaign in 1949 had intervened and that they again might intervene in the autumn elections of 1950, should Dulles want to run, but should not be considered an insurmountable obstacle if Acheson and the President thought Dulles uniquely qualified to carry out this important work.[6]

Acheson decided to follow Vandenberg's suggestion. The next thing was to convince Truman. He called Truman, vacationing at Key West, on April 4, 1950, to tell him he was in accord with Vandenberg's strong endorsement and wished to recommend Dulles as consultant to the Secretary of State on bipartisan foreign policy. The President's first reaction was negative. Truman was irate, in no forgiving mood. Confronted with a presidential red light, Acheson did not press the matter, trusting that after some reflection Truman would put on the green light. This Truman did. The President, however, did not want Dulles made ambassador-at-large. While he would like the appointment to be one which would not harm Dulles' dignity, at the same time he felt that because of the ideas Dulles had expressed in the campaign of the previous autumn, particularly those relating to domestic affairs, he could not make him part of the Administration. He further suggested that Acheson clear the matter with Lehman. "If Lehman says it is all right, it will be all right with me." The same day Acheson cheered the ill Vandenberg with news of Truman's decision. The Senator immediately volunteered to urge Dulles to accept the invitation to serve and not be too concerned about his title. Next day Acheson offered the post to Dulles who promptly accepted even though he did not like the title "consultant." During their conversation Dulles told the Secretary he had no love for politics and disliked the thought of being in the Senate for six years where he would have to spend most of his time on matters of little interest. Sometime that day Acheson also called Lehman and told him that Dulles felt himself best qualified in foreign affairs and that his work with the Department probably would mean he would not run for the Senate. Acheson added that the President endorsed the Dulles appointment as advantageous, both for bipartisan foreign policy and for the Senator in the coming campaign. Lehman, who did not relish the idea of another contest with Dulles, agreed.[7]

Dulles, then, would come to work for the Department. It is interesting how Acheson, in light of his political problems before the country and especially the Senate, now moved carefully into his specific proposal to Dulles that the latter take on the Japanese Peace Treaty. Acheson suggested that Dulles come to Washington for the necessary briefings, to familiarize himself with major problems of foreign policy, and to help with consultation with members of Congress. He mentioned the problem of the Far East, and work toward the Japanese Peace Treaty. Dulles indicated that while he had great interest in the Far East he did not have the knowledge of that area that he had of Europe. Acheson replied that work in that area was not so much a matter of knowledge as of judgment.[8]

The Dulles appointment as consultant to the Secretary of State on broad problems in the field of foreign affairs was officially announced on April 19, 1950, and the New Yorker was sworn in on April 26. No mention that Dulles' duties would be exclusively the Japanese Treaty. Two days later Dulles had a long conversation with President Truman. He told the President he was glad to be working again on a bipartisan basis in foreign policy. He felt that his ability to serve depended on the President's confidence. Truman told him he should not concern himself on that point, because he, Truman, would not have invited him back unless he had great confidence in him. Dulles was aware of Truman's earlier adverse attitude, emanating from the New York campaign. He thought it useful to review these past events. He had accepted Governor Dewey's appointment as interim Senator, he told Truman, because he felt his influence on the Republican Party in the area of foreign affairs needed domestic political activity. His strength in the party had come from Dewey and Vandenberg. With Dewey's second defeat and Vandenberg's illness, it had seemed desirable that he gain some stature. He had not wanted to run for the Senate. Indeed he had informed Secretary Acheson before the recent campaign that if appointed to the United Nations prior to the New York State Convention he would accept the appointment rather than the nomination. Acheson had tried to do this, but circumstances had prevented. Under pressure from Vandenberg he had accepted the nomination and done his best in the campaign. He had not attacked the Administration's foreign policy, which had been a handicap. He had fought on domestic issues, expressing himself vigorously. He told the President he was deeply concerned and personally hurt by "vicious things" said of him.

Having "cleared himself," Dulles attempted to set out his position on bipartisanship. He reported that he had told the Republican leaders in the Senate—Taft, Eugene Millikin, Styles Bridges—that his present and future work in the Department did not assure bipartisanship in foreign policy or protect the Department from criticism. Should he find he could support foreign policies wholeheartedly, he was confident Republican leaders on the Hill and elsewhere would react sympathetically to his recommendations. Much would depend on whether he would work on policies he could endorse. The President assured Dulles that he understood his position.

At conclusion of the conversation Dulles recommended action in foreign affairs as quickly as possible, to strengthen trust of the American people in the government's ability to deal with the communist threat. It was this lack of confidence, Dulles was sure, that allowed men like Senator McCarthy to achieve prominence. Once the United States started on a course, the people would stand behind their government. Dulles was pleased that Truman agreed, delighted when Truman diplomatically said he had read and liked his "very good book," *War or Peace*, published that year.

Immediately after the appointment the Department began a series of conferences with Republican leaders, particularly Senator H. Alexander Smith, ranking Republican member of the Far East subcommittee of the Foreign Relations Committee. It became evident that Republicans were not willing to identify themselves with the Administration's policies in the Far East. The pleas of the stricken Vandenberg, urging "maximum cooperation at both ends of the Avenue in searching a final, *unified* foreign policy," did not make much impression. The Far East was a "soft area." Foreign policies there were risky, did not promise easy success. The Republican Policy Committee, believing failure in that area would be politically advantageous in future campaign strategy, would not give unqualified support. Only in one part of the Far East were they willing to offer bipartisan support: Japan.[9]

Before Dulles got down to work on the treaty he went on a fact-finding tour, and while he was in the Far East the Korean War broke out, which gave new urgency to the negotiation. On return he applied his fullest energies to the task. He relished the assignment, particularly since it met with his conviction, long expressed, that harsh and retaliatory peace treaties were self-destroying, and with his belief, recently acquired, that Japan must have a full opportunity to become an equal partner within the community of free nations and thus be a bulwark against communist expansion in the Far East. There was another incentive: his new work brought to mind his grandfather's part in negotiation of the Treaty of Shimonoseki.

Dulles would look back to this diplomatic assignment as one of the most important achievements of his life.[10] He was right. His work on the treaty was a magnificent piece of bipartisan statesmanship. Dean Rusk would later remark:

> From early in June, 1950, to after signing the peace treaty it would be hard to imagine any closer team-

> work with people of such diverse political origins as Mr. Dulles and the administration. It was reflected in many different ways, but in the first place, Mr. Dulles had been in Korea just before the Korean War broke out. He was on Wake Island when the President's first announcement on the use of forces in Korea was announced. He was wholeheartedly and completely in support of that policy. His telegram from Japan was one of the first telegrams we had urging actual intervention in this Korean affair, and that of itself helped to precipitate this period of the closest possible collaboration that was tested pretty severely at the time of the firing of General MacArthur.[11]

Dulles' tactics with the Peace Treaty are of interest to the student of his later diplomatic career. When Dulles saw the draft treaty prepared by the Department, a complicated and prolix document, he decided to simplify it. He wrote two documents on August 7: a letter of instruction for the President's signature outlining the main bases on which to proceed with the Japanese settlement, and a substitute draft of about eight pages of the treaty itself. President Truman, with approval of the Secretaries of State and Defense, signed the letter on September 8. This presidential directive gave Dulles a free hand to carry on his work, unmolested by the lower echelons. From then until the Peace Treaty was signed a year later on September 8, 1951, Truman, Acheson, and Rusk, the latter then in charge of Far Eastern matters in the Department, blocked all sorts of harassment and interference from the Pentagon and from allies, giving Dulles a clear field to carry the ball. Dulles was aware of this support, which he greatly appreciated.

The decision authorizing him to negotiate bilaterally with all nations concerned enhanced the assignment. Accompanied by a capable aide assigned by the Department, John M. Allison, he traveled to all the appropriate capitals (125,000 miles)—London, Manila, Tokyo, Canberra, Wellington—where he subdued the objections of one government after another and persuaded them to accept the American position on the treaty before submitting the document to an international conference. He even began bilateral talks with the Soviet representative at the United Nations, Jacob Malik, but the Russian soon ended the discussion.

By the end of the year 1950 Dulles had accomplished the main purpose of his mission. Everything was set for the conference and for a series of security treaties to accompany the entry of Japan into the community of free and independent states. President Truman, greatly pleased, on January 10, 1951, designated him Special Representative of the President with the personal rank of ambassador.[12]

After this intricate negotiation—domestic, political, and then international—all else in connection with the Japanese Peace Treaty was anticlimactic. The Peace Treaty was a document of international reconciliation to which participating nations adhered over protests and threats by the Soviet Union and its satellites. In the preamble Japan indicated the intention to apply for membership in the United Nations and to adhere to the UN's principles. The recently defeated and occupied nation emerged as a fully sovereign state with the right to arm in self-defense, alone or through a coalition.[13] As Volume XVI in the present Series (on Secretary Acheson) will show, several security treaties accompanied the Peace Treaty of September, 1951: the United States concluded alliances with the Philippines and Japan, and worked out a tripartite arrangement with Australia and New Zealand (the ANZUS Treaty).

Together, the Japanese Peace Treaty and the security treaties represented an American determination to strengthen the peace and security in the Pacific against the ambitions of Red imperialism. The security treaty between the United States and Japan was in essence an alliance, allowing for the maintenance of American troops in Japan for the foreseeable future. Neither power could withdraw by itself, of course, and the assumption, stated explicitly in the treaty, was that the terms would last until affairs in the Far East, with the Soviet Union and Red China, had settled down. The Philippine security treaty was a bilateral mutual-defense treaty, an interesting acknowledgment by both nations of the fears for Philippine independence which had marked United States-Japanese relations for so many years. The ANZUS Treaty, also a security arrangement, was similar to the Philippine-American treaty except in two respects: it recognized British Commonwealth responsibilities of Australia and New Zealand; it provided for a council of foreign ministers, in the manner of the Rio Treaty of 1947.

At the Conference for the Conclusion and Signature of the Treaty of Peace with Japan, held at San Francisco from September 4 to 8, 1951, Dulles saw the culmination of this diplomacy. He was pleased when President Truman in an opening address gave him great credit for what had happened: "Mr. Dulles has performed this task faithfully and well, guided by the highest traditions of statesmanship."

Acheson said he agreed with Dulles that the treaty partook of the fundamental moral principles of the great spiritual teachers and leaders of all nations and of all religions, and this latter endorsement especially pleased Dulles.[14] Shortly thereafter he would recall that representatives of the Christian countries at San Francisco had found "that the treaty was a Christian peace," and representatives of Buddhist and Moslem lands saw a reflection of the truths of their religions. The gathering at the City of St. Francis, he said late in April, 1952, "was in many respects like a prayer meeting, and indeed, it closed with the benediction often pronounced in churches." The San Francisco Conference, he believed, showed the value of moral law—it invoked forgiveness, humanity, fair play, not vengeance, hatred, fear, greed, arrogance. It was a perfect example of magnanimity based on power.[15]

The Peace Treaty of San Francisco did not end Dulles' responsibility, as he continued to hold his special post as ambassador until the Senate consented to the treaty in March, 1952. He resigned on March 21. President Truman commented on Dulles' good work. "I am most grateful to you," the President wrote, "as indeed the whole country is."[16] Truman then told him he had earned the greatest of all satisfactions, knowledge that in a task of the utmost importance he had served his country well.

CHAPTER FIVE

DETERRENCE AND LIBERATION

THE presidential campaign year, 1952, marked a critical period in Dulles' life. The Republican Party was about to nominate a candidate for President of the United States, and it looked like a winning year. Twice before, in 1944 and 1948, the defeat of the party had frustrated Dulles' ambition. He was advancing in age, and 1952 might be his last opportunity. The party was torn between two factions gathered around Senator Robert A. Taft and General Dwight D. Eisenhower. Whom should he support? A wrong choice, or premature timing of his decision, could prove politically fatal. Taft was an old friend, Eisenhower a comparative stranger. Dulles had known Taft since youth, and relations had always been good. He had seen Eisenhower on several ceremonial occasions, and had a few private sessions, but did not know the man well. Least of all did he understand the General's political and diplomatic opinions; for that matter, few of his countrymen knew them. Eventually Dulles came to see that Taft's international views were too conservative. Eisenhower's opinions, tentatively elaborated, were more congenial: the General supported Western European unity, freer world trade, a strong Anglo-American alliance, the mutual security program, and even economic contacts with the communist nations.

1

Dulles first had met the General in 1948, and the initial encounter did not produce a strong enough impression for Eisenhower to recall it. The General's earliest recollection of a meeting was during the autumn of 1949 when Dulles asked support in the New York senatorial campaign. Eisenhower, then president of Columbia University, declined on the ground that his military status and university position precluded participation in politics. He did inform Senator Dulles that he was a Republican and, indeed, was critical of the Democratic Party.[1] For some time thereafter, relations between the two men were casual.

After the autumn of 1951 Dulles was under pressure from Republican presidential aspirants, particularly from the Taft and Eisenhower forces, the so-called isolationist and internationalist wings of the party. Upon his resignation as adviser to President Truman in March, 1952, the pressure for commitment to one or the other candidate increased. Following a series of discussions with Senator James Duff of Pennsylvania, General Lucius D. Clay, and Governor Dewey, Dulles decided to support the General, but not yet publicly. At the suggestion of Clay, Dulles early in May, 1952, journeyed to Paris ostensibly to address the French National Political Science Institute, but also "to plumb for himself the mind and personality of . . . General Dwight D. Eisenhower."[2]

He had prepared two memoranda for Eisenhower: one on Taiwan; the other a long essay on American foreign policy. Before leaving he showed these to Clay who forwarded them to the General. In the foreign policy essay Dulles developed twin strategic doctrines to place the United States on the offensive in the cold war and weaken and eventually disintegrate the Soviet empire. He had been thinking about these ideas for some years, mulling them over, trying to find their exact justification and consequences.[3] He had a clear understanding of the importance of what he was doing. He was now the undisputed Republican spokesman on foreign affairs, and with the death of Senator Vandenberg in 1951 the Republican trustee of bipartisan foreign policy. He was the foremost candidate for the office of Secretary of State, no matter who won the Republican nomination.

The twin-doctrines memorandum involved a long philosophic preamble. Dulles saw American postwar policies as dangerously inadequate, despite such courageous and well-developed actions as the Truman Doctrine, Marshall Plan, North Atlantic Alliance, and the decision to go to war in Korea. All these worthy policies, he claimed, failed to end the communist peril. At home the Administration's security policies were perilously costly, having led to unbalanced budgets, cheapening of the dollar, and expansion of military control. Abroad Europeans found them "too militaristic, too costly, too erratic and too inconclusive." The "far-flung, extravagant and surreptitious military projects" disillusioned and frightened allies and friends, who believed the United States was conducting a feud with the Soviet Union "rather than performing a public service for peace." All major policies since the end of the Second World War, he wrote, involved emergency measures to contain Soviet communism—all were negative, unable to end the communist threat or bring relief from the tremendous exertions of the American people, exertions which devoured their "economic, political and moral vitals."

To end the futile policy of containment he suggested a better way. The United States, as the greatest power in the world, must stop misusing its strength. The only commodity in which it was deficient was faith. Materially and morally the United States was far stronger than the Soviet Union. The presence of fifteen million prisoners in Soviet labor camps, suppression of liberty in satellite countries, constant disputes, suspicions, and purges among leaders of the Soviet Government—all reflected weakness and corruption, not strength. "The free should not be numbed by the sight of this vast graveyard of human liberties. It is the despots who should feel haunted. They, not we, should fear the future."

The first step on the road to victory was to solve the military problem via a policy of deterrence. Here was the first of the twin concepts. The American military establishment, Dulles said, must defend not only Europe but all areas of the world: the Middle and Far East, as well as Africa. This was impossible with a 20,000-mile Maginot Line, matching the Red Army man for man or gun for gun, or by answering the Soviet challenge at the time and place of their choosing. "There is one solution and only one: that is for the free world to develop the will and organize the means to retaliate instantly against open aggression by Red Armies, so that, if it occurred anywhere, we could and would strike back where it hurts, by means of our choosing." Capacity to counterattack was the ultimate deterrent. He recalled that as Senator he had supported the North Atlantic Pact because it did not commit the United States to the land defenses of any particular area but to action of America's own choosing rather than action that an aggressor could dictate. Creation of "a community punishing force," ready to retaliate in event of aggression, with weapons of its choosing, targets of its choosing, times of its choosing, would provide the West with an "enlightened and effective" deterrent until international disarmament would make the deterrent obsolete.

Then came the second concept, liberation. With an effective military defense and strategy, the United States and the free world could undertake a political offensive based on principles of the American Revolution and what Dulles called several truths: dynamic forces always prevail over static, active over passive; nonmaterial forces have a more powerful effect than material; and moral or natural law, not made by man, determines right or wrong, and in the long run only those nations conforming to this law escape disaster. He restated themes from earlier speeches, articles, and books. Vigor, confidence, sense of destiny, belief in mission, all had led to the growth of the American Republic from feeble and humble origins to great power. American dynamism had its roots in moral and intellectual forces rather than military or material power. By conduct and example the United States could project its political, social, and economic ideas, which were "more explosive than dynamite." America was once the conscience of mankind, and the Soviets were bidding to replace it. This must not happen. America, he urged, must return to the historic qualities of its people and recapture the spirit of the American Revolution. It must become dynamic, use ideas as weapons, and never forget that ideas have to conform to moral principle. Containment or stalemate were alien to American experience. As the historic leader of the forces of freedom, the United States had to abandon alien policies and substitute a positive concept, and that was liberation. Dulles urged the government of the United States to indicate publicly that it wanted and expected liberation. The goal would be peaceful, to bring "genuine independence in the nations of Europe and Asia now dominated by Moscow." The United States would not be party to any "deal" confirming Soviet rule over the satellites. Such a public statement would electrify the captive peoples, and put the Soviet Union on the defensive. Dulles was hopeful that separation could occur peacefully, and for an example he pointed to Tito's Yugoslavia.[4]

The doctrine of liberation especially appealed to Dulles, because of its kinship to Woodrow Wilson's principle of self-determination. Like Wilson, he would encourage peoples in Eastern Europe and elsewhere to look to the United States for political freedom. It would be Dulles' fate, as it was Wilson's, that the peoples of many of these subjugated nations and their relatives in the United States would blame him when he did not achieve these high resolves and promises.

General Eisenhower read Dulles' memoranda with interest. Deterrence, rather than liberation, attracted him most. He was excited, the General recalled later, by theories "similar to those I had long been pondering, regarding the conservation of our national military power and influence through a policy which has commonly come to be called 'massive retaliation.'" In late March he wrote General Clay indicating his appreciation for Dulles' memoranda. Later, on April 15, Eisenhower wrote Dulles that he "felt highly privileged to read these papers and was as deeply impressed as ever with the directness and simplicity of your approach to such complex problems." While in substantial agreement, he did feel that the New Yorker had oversimplified. In case of serious aggression, say in Berlin, the United States and the West had pledged to retaliate with an all-out attack. What of local minor aggressions? internal subversion? One point in the long paper bothered him. "What should we do," he asked, "if Soviet *political* aggression as in Czechoslovakia, successively chips away exposed portions of the free world? So far as our resulting economic situation is concerned, such an eventuality would be just as bad for us as if the area had been captured by force. To my mind, this is a case where the theory of 'retaliation' falls down." The long- and short-range purpose of military forces, General Eisenhower wrote, "is to convey a feeling of confidence to exposed populations, a confidence that will make them sturdier in their opposition to Communist inroads." The Supreme Commander of Allied Forces in Europe reminded Dulles that military as well as economic strength would produce "the atmosphere in which *internal* aggression can be defeated." This, he explained, led to the conclusion "that, along with all other means and matters of opposition, we have an added reason for producing a respectable defensive posture as rapidly as possible." He asked Dulles to accept his criticism in the spirit he gave it. "I have been living so close to the problem of confidence and national morale—and it has been so fundamental to our operation here—that I neglect no opportunity to talk about it."[5]

Eisenhower made no comment on the policy of liberation, about which he later had misgivings.

The letter was formal: addressed to Senator Dulles, and signed Dwight D. Eisenhower.

2

Now came the Dulles-Eisenhower meeting. The two men were together on Saturday, May 3, 1952, and again on May 5. During the three-hour luncheon at SHAPE headquarters, attended by General Clay, they discussed issues and problems in the Far East and Europe. It pleased Dulles that Eisenhower shared many of his ideas. Both men agreed on the need of policies to oppose communism, on the NATO principle of collective defense, and on the efficacy of sustained pressure to promote Western European unity through the European Defense Community. Dulles told Eisenhower he would support his candidacy for the Republican nomination, but would hold off public announcement until he had seen Senator Taft.

Two days later, May 5, Dulles delivered to the French National Foundation of Political Sciences what the American and European press described as a major address. The speech was timely, at a moment when Frenchmen and Americans were discussing action to prevent the Chinese Communists from entering the Indochina war, and how to meet entry should it occur. French officials knew that although Dulles had severed relations with the Truman Administration he had shown his speech to Under Secretary of State David K. E. Bruce and to John Allison, now Assistant Secretary for Far Eastern Affairs, and that neither felt that Dulles' ideas would embarrass the American Government. They interpreted his remarks as an indication of State Department thinking. Moreover, he was a well-known advocate of bipartisanship, the Republican spokesman on foreign affairs, and a possible future Secretary of State.

The Paris speech gave Dulles the first opportunity

to recommend his doctrine of "peace through deterrence" in a foreign forum, apply it to a specific area, and test its acceptance. He spoke before an attentive French audience of about eight hundred persons. The threat of air and naval bombardment of the Chinese mainland, he suggested, could keep Chinese Communists from direct intervention in Indochina. The Soviets also would hesitate to commit aggression if it became clear that they would lose their ports and lines of communication in Siberia. Dulles identified this strategy as the doctrine of "peace by deterrent power" and urged that it be "openly and unashamedly organized on behalf of the community of free nations." In the vast regions of Asia the Western powers, he told his listeners, could not possibly create the kind of local defense which prevailed in Europe. The cost was prohibitive. As long as the Soviet and Chinese Communists picked the time, place, and method of aggression, anywhere in Asia, the United States and its allies would continue at a disadvantage which could be fatal. The only answer was to warn a potential aggressor that aggression would bring retaliation at times, places, and with weapons "of our fashioning." Dulles recalled that he had preached this doctrine of peace by deterrent power in Japan when he pointed out that security arrangements between the United States and Japan meant that an open attack on Japan would bring an American strike of overwhelming power. He was sure his doctrine would not only neutralize the external menace to exposed Asian nations but make internal revolutionary problems of some of them more manageable. This strategy, he felt, had been demonstrated in Japan, and the Philippines, and could apply to Indochina.[6]

The reaction to his address was pleasing. The French press and officials liked it because it offered hope of stopping communist aggression through a common Western policy in the Far East. Dulles had suggested deterrence within the framework of the UN Charter and perhaps with help of the Peace Observation Commission. "If it were done that way, it would, on the one hand, impress more strongly the potential aggressors and, on the other hand, give reassurance that no single free-world nation would recklessly take action which might have grave consequences for many." The French press interpreted this as a reassurance to Europeans that no nation, not even the United States, would or could without consultation and approval set in motion the retaliatory power, which if necessary all would undertake together.[7]

At home the press gave Dulles' speech a wide coverage. John Foster Dulles, so read a New York *Times* editorial, "is providing us with much food for thought these days. . . . His ideas must be respected and mulled over, for they are based on deep religious convictions, long diplomatic experience and careful thought. He preaches a gospel that represents America at its best. It can be mistaken at times, but it is never superficial and never materialistic or mercenary or selfish." The *Times* recalled the "unusual consistency" of Dulles' views, and welcomed his ideas which "go to the very heart of the problems" and "call for such a profound—and even daring—assumption of dynamic leadership." The *Herald Tribune* echoed its rival, and advised attention to Dulles' strategic position within the Republican Party, particularly as "one of the master-builders of our bi-partisan tradition." It endorsed Dulles' deterrence doctrine as leading to the reestablishment of bipartisanship, ending "many of our present confusions and weaknesses in foreign policy."[8]

As the master builder of bipartisanship Dulles had hoped to advance his ideas. He had maintained bipartisanship during the presidential campaigns of 1944 and 1948. Would he be able to do so in 1952? "I look forward," he had remarked at the time of his resignation, "to the possibility of expressing my views about foreign policy under conditions which will not risk embarrassment either to the administration or to any presidential candidate. In so doing, I shall seek to avoid doing anything that might hinder the possibility of bipartisan accord on basic foreign policy issues, for I believe that, under present conditions, this is necessary to save our nation from mortal danger."[9] Unfortunately these hopes were not to materialize. His twin doctrines of deterrence and liberation, reiterated in addresses and articles, became planks in the Republican platform of 1952: when supporters of both Taft and Eisenhower asked him to write the foreign policy planks in the platform he incorporated his doctrines, particularly liberation. These two concepts which he offered Dwight Eisenhower and the American people with such conviction and fervor came under sharp criticism, much of it generated by the campaign, and damaged the bipartisanship which he had supported for almost a decade.

CHAPTER SIX

AMBITION FULFILLED

1

AFTER seeing Eisenhower, Dulles returned to the United States and began a busy schedule. It started off at what was then Idlewild Airport where he learned about "a fake interview" broadcast from Shannon where his plane had stopped on the way. A dispatch had quoted him as saying: "There seems no doubt that Gen. Eisenhower will be elected," and that Dulles considered himself the "obvious" choice as Secretary of State. He attributed its origin to passenger gossip.[1] Within a few days he began a series of speeches, the most notable on May 12, 1952, at the annual award dinner of the National Conference of Christians and Jews. Here he restated the thesis expressed in his Paris speech. A few days later *Life* magazine with minor changes published the memorandum he had sent Eisenhower under title of "A Policy of Boldness." Again the American electorate became aware of Dulles as a potential Secretary of State.[2]

The most interesting development since return, he wrote Eisenhower on May 20, had been a call from "Bob" Taft asking to meet with him in Washington. Dulles knew what Taft had in mind. So he first had "talked the situation over" with Herbert Brownell, Jr., and General Clay, who agreed that Dulles if at all possible should lead the discussion "so as to promote a foreign policy plank in the Republican platform which would avoid an open battle between the so-called 'isolationist' wing and the so-called 'internationalist' wing." He was also to prevent the adoption of planks on which Eisenhower would have difficulty. The meeting took place on May 16. Taft asked Dulles to support his candidacy or at least indicate neutrality, saying that both could work together on foreign policy. Dulles answered that he intended to come out in public support for Eisenhower as soon as he had completed his present series of articles and speeches.

He was pleased to report to Eisenhower that Taft agreed with him that everything possible should be done to prevent the Republican Party from being "rent asunder" at the convention in Chicago, and that the Ohio Senator felt the New Yorker's recent speeches and writings "had developed a large area of possible agreement." Taft asked Dulles to prepare a draft of foreign policy planks for the Republican platform, on behalf of both him and Eisenhower. Dulles answered that he could not accept without approval from Eisenhower, but did indicate he favored the suggestion. Both men assumed that in event Dulles did undertake the task he would avoid public support to Eisenhower while working on the platform and "as long as it seemed that a constructive outcome was possible."

Dulles reported to Brownell and Clay who "seemed gratified at the way the situation had developed." Clay got in touch with Eisenhower who approved that Dulles should work on foreign policy planks. Dulles then informed Taft he "had cleared his proposal with Paris," and was ready to assume his new responsibility. But he was not sure he would succeed, despite Taft's sponsorship. Taft "may not be able to control his followers and it may be merely or partly a ruse to keep me tied up for the time being." He felt the goal "sufficiently important" and "worth going after," provided Eisenhower agreed. "I do not want," he informed the General, "any possible doubt in your mind . . ."[3] In a month the Republican National Committee announced Dulles as the chief foreign policy adviser to the platform committee. Taft assured reporters that Dulles' planks "would be acceptable to both himself and to General Eisenhower" and would remove the only dangerous obstacle to party harmony. "I believe," he told the press, "he can get the factions of the party together." The Ohioan saw no difference on principle: "Eisenhower possibly puts more emphasis on Europe than I do, but it is a difference in methods, not in principle."[4]

Not all Republicans were happy with Taft's endorsement of Dulles. Taft's statement that forthcoming planks on foreign policy, to be written by Dulles, would be of a kind which both Taft and Eisenhower could support, confused Eisenhower supporters. The *Herald Tribune* called attention to unbridgeable differences: the General had been emphasizing that "our defense lies in Europe" and the need to strengthen the Western coalition, while Taft who had voted against NATO stressed retirement from Europe and reliance on American air power.[5]

Eisenhower worried over the planks. He had previously summarized his thoughts to Dulles and the resolutions committee, but now thought it necessary to ask Dulles for a draft of proposals before the convention adopted them. He was anxious that the final statement call for leadership to promote collective security. The General disliked empty phrases based on begrudging approval, and warned against ideas of "retiring within our own borders" which he believed would lead to national disaster. He recalled again that he had been devoting his fullest energies to convince the allies that America could not live alone. The United States must trade freely with nations or areas from which it had to obtain raw materials, and could not allow the loss of territories to communism by armed aggression or political means. The only way to stop communist expansion, he wrote Dulles, was collective security. Such actions encouraged weak, threatened nations to build economic, political, and spiritual strength. Once more he reminded Dulles that reliance on retaliation was not a sufficient and workable deterrent to "broad" Soviet threats. The only acceptable strategy was a public warning that the United States would not allow any nation to cut off areas in the world necessary to America's power. He had not entered the presidential race for personal reasons, but because of belief that ideas he had outlined were important. To the limit of his strength he was prepared to fight isolationism. He realized that Dulles' task in writing a foreign policy platform that would accommodate widely divergent views would not be easy, but was certain the New Yorker would be "equal to the burden of carrying forward" his ideas.

To bring divergent ideas within the Republican Party into a program for foreign policy was no easy task. Internationalist views were not established. Many Republicans in Congress had resisted foreign aid, NATO, and large military spending. Some advocated high tariffs and unilateral actions in the Far East. This group of Republicans had set the tone for the convention in Chicago, and wanted Taft. When Eisenhower was nominated on the first ballot on July 11 it did not nullify their opposition. Conservative Republicans would go on believing that vote-getting appeal as a war hero had nominated Eisenhower, not his internationalist ideas. Their behavior in regard to the platform, the campaign, and the subsequent Eisenhower Administration revealed that their marriage to the General was one of convenience, not love.

Dulles' planks on foreign policy were a combination of Eisenhower's views with Taft's conservatism. Dominant ideas were the very ones he had developed in his memorandum of March, 1952, later published in *Life*, which singled out the imperative need for the unification of Western Europe, but gave only a moderate support for NATO and the United Nations.

The platform spoke of "expansion of mutually advantageous world trade," and thoughtfully emphasized exports over imports. It mentioned collective security, to which Eisenhower was committed, and managed to stress air power coordinated with land and sea forces supplied with abundant weapons including expansion of the nuclear arsenal "to deter sudden attack." And then there was the promise of liberation—the freeing of captive nations—instead of the policy of containment which, so the platform said, abandoned countless human beings to a despotism. The new doctrine of liberation was in tune with the popular mood of impatience with the cold war in Europe and hot war in Korea. It may not have swung the election in favor of the Republicans, but it did set the tone of the campaign. It was a tone congenial to most Republicans, but not to Eisenhower who accepted liberation with misgiving.[6]

The platform reflected an earlier decision of the Republican high command to make foreign policy a major issue. This meant rejection of bipartisan restraints which had characterized the presidential race of the twice-nominated and twice-defeated Governor Dewey. Convinced that Dewey had met defeat in 1948 because he had not used the "sequence of diplomatic decisions at Teheran, Cairo and Yalta," Republican strategists urged the party to go on the offensive. Eisenhower took no pleasure in those portions of the platform written "in purple 'prosecuting-attorney' style" which indicted the "twenty-year record of Democratic stewardship." As a political novice he believed that "it was habitual in both parties to do so." "In any event," the General would recall, he "was interested primarily in the platform's pledges, not its charges."[7]

2

The Republican blueprint for the future condemned the Truman Administration for losing the peace "so dearly earned by World War II." It described Teheran, Yalta, and Potsdam as "tragic blunders" which left such friendly nations as Latvia, Lithuania, Estonia, Poland, and Czechoslovakia to "fend for themselves against the Communist aggression which soon swallowed them." It promised to "repudiate all commitments contained in secret understandings such as those of Yalta which aid Communist enslavements," and anticipated "genuine independence of those captive peoples," adding:

> We shall again make liberty into a beacon light of hope that will penetrate the dark places. It will mark the end of the negative, futile and immoral policy of "containment" which abandons countless human beings to a despotism and godless terrorism, which in turn enables the rulers to forge the captives into a weapon of our destruction. . . .
>
> The policies we espouse will revive the contagious, liberating influences which are inherent in freedom. They will inevitably set up strains and stresses within the captive world which will make

the rulers impotent to continue in their monstrous ways and mark the beginning of the end.[8]

One should have no question who wrote the above. The style, tone, ideas, hope—all pure Dulles.

As mentioned, Eisenhower showed little enthusiasm for liberation. After much prodding from the Republican National Committee he spoke in favor of the liberation policy, always careful to add the phrase "by peaceful means." The candidate did not go as far as expected of him. Not so Dulles. As the campaign went into full swing, Eisenhower became concerned with Dulles' speeches and found it necessary to criticize him personally for failure to couple the statement "by peaceful means" when speaking of liberation. Many years later President Eisenhower recalled that only twice had Dulles vexed him, the first time related to the episode just mentioned, the other to Suez Canal policy in 1956.[9]

The National Committee embraced liberation, for the fate of East European peoples offered an opportunity to appeal to ethnic groups of Americans whose origins lay behind the Iron Curtain. As Republicans increased their activities to capture the hyphenated vote, liberation hopelessly entangled itself in domestic politics. The more the Republicans associated it with the nationality vote, the less likely became its realization. To the National Committee it meant liberation of ethnic Americans from Democratic containment. To some Republicans it meant a grand new strategy to disintegrate the Soviet empire; to others it meant a reduced national defense budget, an end to national anxiety, ultimate victory without economic strain or danger of war. To many ethnic leaders it meant restoration of prewar governments in native countries, and Republican political patronage in the adopted land.

To Dulles liberation meant positive foreign policies. After attacks on his doctrine he emphasized that it did not mean a war of liberation led by the United States, nor need or desirability that America "try to foment violent revolution." The latter "would mean only the exposure and massacre of those who most cherish freedom."[10] He could not understand why liberation frightened people—made them think it meant war. This fear, he said in December, 1952, after President-elect Eisenhower had chosen him as Secretary of State, "illustrates the degree to which even free people have come to think in governmental and military terms." The United States, he told a nationwide radio audience, "from its beginning, has stood for liberation." Dulles quoted Lincoln's interpretation of the Declaration of Independence as "liberty not alone to the people of this country, but hope for the world for all future time." That idea had never frightened anyone—until recently. Dynamic foreign policy was not military policy but a moral and spiritual force. As long as the American people lacked faith, mission and purpose, so said the Secretary-designate, forces of despotism would continue to threaten and subjugate mankind.[11]

Reaction to the idea of liberation was not generally

favorable; leaders of the Democratic Party, bothered by the strong Republican indictment, were critical. Secretary of State Acheson warned that liberation of Soviet-dominated territories or people was "a positive prescription for disaster." He chided the Republicans that "it is something of a new experience to be urged to be more positive, dynamic and bold by many whose chief contribution until now has been holding back. They have their hands on the horn, and their feet on the brakes."[12] Adlai E. Stevenson, the Democratic candidate, termed liberation a "cynical and transparent attempt, drenched in crocodile tears, to play upon the anxieties of foreign nationality groups in this country." President Truman without mentioning Dulles accused him of willingness, despite knowledge of the "precarious situation the world is in . . . to have the Republican Party, and the Republican candidate, say things that increase the risk of war, simply in order to get votes."[13]

Dulles was incensed when leaders of the Democratic Party, notably Senator Paul Douglas of Illinois, attacked him personally, stating that he had shared in many of the policies he was now calling futile, mistaken, and negative. Angrily he wrote Douglas, with copies to Acheson, Truman, and the press, accusing him and the Democratic leadership of wrecking bipartisanship, and expressed doubt that two-party unity could continue under a Democratic Administration.[14] A heated public exchange followed. Concerned about bipartisanship, Dulles proposed a "high-level council" with representatives of both parties, to make long-range plans for unified foreign policy, and offered a code of ethics to cover political debate on foreign policy.[15] Eisenhower, describing himself as a Vandenberg Republican, promised to revive and extend bipartisanship. Vandenberg, he said, had "ended once and for all" the old American belief in isolationism, led the Republican Party to collective security, and produced a desire for national unity in foreign policy.[16]

3

On the first Tuesday after the first Monday of November, 1952, the American people elected General Dwight D. Eisenhower to the presidency, and this decision produced Dulles' appointment. The overwhelming vote of confidence in the popular war hero, and hoped-for peace hero, brought the Republican Party to power and responsibility after twenty long years. The election was one of several presidential campaigns in American history in which foreign policy dominated. Among leaders and adherents of both parties it was to leave a residue of ill will and strained or broken friendships. Abroad, some of the extreme attacks on the foreign policies of the Truman Administration coupled with promises of new orientations, such as deterrence and liberation, produced bewilderment. But Eisenhower was the choice of the people, the newly dominant figure in the Republican Party.

It was not at first clear what part Dulles would

take in the new Administration, and there was a possibility that he might not be Secretary of State. The General was known to have a list of candidates which included Henry Cabot Lodge, Paul Hoffman, John J. McCloy, and even Allen Dulles. Most people thought Dulles would be the appointee, but it was not certain, and the very fact of his being the front-runner, so to speak, tended to focus opposition. Not since William Jennings Bryan was the principal choice for Woodrow Wilson's top Cabinet post had there been so much objection. There was one difference between Bryan and Dulles: most of Dulles' opposition came from abroad.

The trouble abroad was that Dulles was "the great enigma of every capital city, from Moscow to Washington." Many Europeans, so wrote the syndicated columnist Joseph Alsop, saw a "fire-breathing war-monger who would obliterate Europe with hydrogen bombs in order to free Poland and so gain votes in Hamtramck."[17] The British press was sure that Dulles, as the *Economist* said, would "take the wraps off Formosa" and encourage the bombing of airfields and communications in Manchuria and on the Chinese mainland.[18] Long before the Republican Party nominated Eisenhower there had been solicited and unsolicited advice on appointees for Secretary of State. Some statesmen tried to prevent the appointment of Dulles through off-the-record interviews with journalists in which they indicated their fear of Dulles. Others were more direct. Early in June, 1952, when Eisenhower stopped in London on the way home from Paris, Anthony Eden "expressed the hope" that he would not appoint Dulles. This was a most uncharacteristic remark from the British Foreign Secretary. "From anyone else," Eisenhower recalled, "I would have resented such a suggestion as an unwarranted intrusion in America's affairs. But my long association and friendship with him during war and peace, involving the frankest kind of exchanges between us, made such a remark understandable." The General did not reply. The British statesman thought him taken aback. Sometime later, when Eden visited the President-elect after he had appointed Dulles, the General beckoned him aside to assure him his fears would prove groundless.[19] The immediate cause of Eden's extraordinary attempt to influence Eisenhower's decision resulted from Dulles' negotiations for the Japanese Treaty. Eden believed Dulles had violated an agreement with Herbert Morrison, then Foreign Secretary of the Labor Government, that neither man would press the Japanese Government to recognize one or the other China. He was incensed when the government of the United States permitted publication of a letter of the Japanese Prime Minister, Shigeru Yoshida, before ratification of the treaty, indicating that Japan would recognize Nationalist China. Eden claimed the British Government was not notified beforehand, and blamed Dulles. This was an unfortunate misunderstanding, not due to bad faith on the part of Dulles. Existence of the Yoshida letter detailing the Japanese position had been known to the British Ambassador in Washington, Sir Oliver Franks, and to Morrison, and Dulles mistakenly thought they had informed Eden.[20] The controversy over the Yoshida letter unfortunately aggravated relations between Dulles and the future Prime Minister of Great Britain.

For whatever reason, for some time after the election Dulles' position in the new Administration remained uncertain. When President Truman invited the President-elect and Eisenhower's closest associates to meet with him to facilitate the orderly transfer of duties, Dulles was not among those chosen. Absence of the Republican spokesman and drafter of the foreign policy planks in the platform was conspicuous.

That meeting of November 18, 1952, at 2:00 P.M., held in the cabinet room of the White House, was an interesting conference between the outgoing and incoming Presidents and their aides. Neither man looked forward to it. Truman's invitation was dictated by what he conceived the national interest, and Eisenhower accepted reluctantly. The General arrived at the White House accompanied by Joseph M. Dodge and Senator Henry Cabot Lodge. Truman, seeing Eisenhower unsmiling and tense, invited him to meet privately in his office. He hoped to put the victorious Republican nominee at ease. After twenty minutes of attempted pleasantries he outlined the purpose of the conference and then escorted the General to the cabinet room where Acheson, Secretary of the Treasury John W. Snyder, Secretary of Defense Robert A. Lovett, Director of Mutual Security W. Averell Harriman, Senator Lodge, and Dodge were waiting for them.

Truman opened the meeting by indicating his desire to facilitate an orderly transfer of government by supplying Eisenhower or his aides with all necessary information, without trying to shift responsibility for actions taken until January 20, 1953. He invited Eisenhower to express his views on foreign policy. The General declined. Truman turned to Acheson to brief the assemblage on current problems. The Secretary, taken aback by Eisenhower's austere and formal acknowledgment of his presence, reviewed major trouble areas, emphasizing those requiring action during the interregnum.

Acheson discussed Korea, particularly the current debate in the United Nations on whether to use force to return prisoners to their native lands. The United States opposed forceful repatriation, outright or through an international commission or political conference, and was attempting to align the British, French, and others. He hoped Eisenhower would give public support. The President-elect did not commit himself but said he soon was to see Foreign Secretary Eden and would discuss Korea.

Acheson mentioned the British-Iranian dispute over oil. Both sides had been unreasonable, he felt. The Iranians were emotional, and the British unable to understand. The government of Great Britain believed economic pressure would force Iranian leaders to act rationally. The result had been the opposite. The United States was considering independent steps to solve the problem.

The Secretary alerted the incoming Administration

to two immediate problems in Europe. The first concerned the forthcoming meeting of the North Atlantic Council which could not delay beyond the first two months of 1953 without defeating military progress that year. The second related to the treaty with Germany and the European Defense Community (EDC) treaty. Both treaties were in great difficulty, and neither had any chance of immediate ratification. Internal French attacks on EDC, and the recent defeat of the government of Chancellor Konrad Adenauer on a motion to take up the treaties, had produced a crisis in Western European cooperation.

Acheson turned to Indochina. The situation in that part of Southeast Asia had concerned the government, he said, for a long time. In France he noted increased opposition to the war which lessened the possibility of French-German equality in European defense. The French had lost the will to fight. The peoples of Indochina were fence-sitting, unwilling to move until assured of who would win. The United States had helped France in the financial burden, one third to one half of the cost. The French Government, Acheson said, sought a political solution, and the new Administration must prepare for that eventuality.

The session concluded at 3:15. After General Eisenhower and his aides left, Truman was troubled. "There was something about his attitude during the meeting that I did not understand." He speculated that until this encounter Eisenhower did not grasp the responsibilities of a President and was "awestruck" by the multitude of problems. Truman noted

Eisenhower's "frozen grimness" through the conference. Or was it a sudden realization that politics during the campaign had "badly distorted" the achievements of the Truman Administration. "Whatever it was," Truman later wrote, "I kept thinking about it." Eisenhower's recollection differed. The meeting "added little to my knowledge, nor did it affect my planning."[21]

It was two days after the conference that Eisenhower summoned Dulles to the Hotel Commodore in New York and offered the post of Secretary of State. Dulles accepted, saying something approximately as follows: "With your prestige and respect and my knowledge and experience in diplomacy, we should make an excellent combination." In the presence of the President-elect he wrote out in longhand on yellow paper a statement of acceptance, which he later sent Eisenhower as a memento: "General Eisenhower has asked me to be his Secretary of State and I have accepted. The nomination is, of course, subject to Senate confirmation. General Eisenhower is a great and purposeful leader. His desire for our nation is a just and durable peace. I shall gladly serve in that cause to the best of my ability."[22]

And so he was in, at last. He was aware that apprehension remained about him. He determined to dispel this concern, as rapidly as possible, for he could hardly be a good diplomat, not to mention statesman, until the American public and leaders of the other nations were receptive to his policies and perhaps his leadership.

CHAPTER SEVEN

THE FIRST ACTIVITY

JOHN FOSTER DULLES assumed office having pledged himself to recapture the initiative in American foreign policy, to adapt the best of America's Revolutionary heritage to the revolutionary movements of the twentieth century. After a long diplomatic tutelage he had obtained responsibility. The newly elected President gave him full power to run the Department of State and recognized him as ranking member of the Cabinet.

Dulles guarded jealously his relations with the President. It was crucial to have Eisenhower's confidence. Throughout his tenure as Secretary he kept the President fully informed. Some time after retirement from the presidency, Eisenhower recalled Dulles' vast knowledge and capability and that he knew of no occasion when Dulles had made an important decision without discussing it.[1] While in Washington, Dulles saw the President almost daily, in addition to talking by telephone. After each conversation, vis-à-vis or phone, he wrote out a memorandum for the files. When away the Secretary, particularly if negotiating abroad, cabled long dispatches to the White House detailing and analyzing the positions of foreign statesmen, giving his own opinions, often requesting guidance. Frequently Dulles' dispatches to the President were accompanied by reports from ambassadors and other members of the Department not always agreeing with his views or recommendations.

Once Dulles became sure of Eisenhower's confidence, the relations between the two men became close and even intimate. Eisenhower enjoyed Dulles' company. He enjoyed his humor. "You know," the President recalled years later, "some people doubted, because of his austere manner, that Foster had a sense of humor. But I remember him often throwing back his head and roaring with laughter and delight which were quite contagious."[2]

1

On the eve of the first trip to Europe after taking office, Dulles gave his initial radio and television address as Secretary. Enlightened self-interest, he said, was his guide in American foreign policy. Often used by Eisenhower, this phrase made it obligatory for the United States to have friends and allies. American involvement in world affairs was necessary because the enemies, Russian Communists and their allies, plotted to destroy the United States. By outright control of nearby governments, by political warfare and indirect aggression, the Soviet Union had extended its rule over eight hundred million people and was "hard at work to get control of other parts of the world"—Korea, Japan, Indochina ("the

Asian rice bowl"), the Middle East, Africa, Latin America. He reaffirmed his determination to expedite Western European unity, particularly the European Defense Community. He was concerned that some French and German leaders "want again to go in their separate ways." The main reason for a tour of Western Europe was to find out firsthand "whether this trend to unity is on the upgrade or is on the downgrade." The United States in postwar years had invested over thirty billion dollars in Western Europe, hoping to help unify the region. "If, however, there were no chance, and that I just refuse to believe, but if it appeared there were no chance of getting effective unity, and if in particular France, Germany, and England should go their separate ways, then certainly it would be necessary to give a little rethinking to America's own foreign policy in relation to Western Europe." Here was the first expression of what would be known as the policy of "agonizing reappraisal." This plain speaking by an American Secretary of State, so akin to the shirt-sleeves diplomacy of American envoys in years gone by, was new in the short history of the Atlantic partnership. It suggested that the Administration if resolved to work in concert with its European allies was not bound to support them if they did not live up to American expectation.

The Secretary repudiated any thought of preventive war, and reiterated his belief in creating in other peoples "such a love and respect for freedom that they can never really be absorbed by the despotism, the totalitarian dictatorship, of the Communist world." The Russians had "swallowed" nearly a billion people and were showing signs of indigestion which "will become so acute that it might be fatal." Drawing on the *Federalist Papers* he emphasized "our own enlightened self-interest by demonstrating by our own performance, by our own examples, how good freedom is and how much better it is than despotism." He promised to restore trust in the Department by cleaning it of communists and sympathizers and, reminiscent of President Wilson, pledged that his diplomacy would be open, simple, moral. "These principles of openness, simplicity, and righteousness—these principles are those which are in accord with what used to be the great American traditional foreign policy."[3]

Dulles began as Secretary with a tour of Western capitals. Accompanied by Harold E. Stassen, Director of Mutual Security, he left for Europe on January 30. He took with him documents on British policy towards ANZUS, new policies toward the Middle East, a copy of his statement of November 14, 1947, before the Senate Foreign Relations Committee, a dossier on John Carter Vincent whose loyalty an Acheson-appointed committee of distinguished Americans had reviewed, a briefing paper for talks with the French relating to Indochina, and memoranda prepared by Under Secretary of State Walter Bedell Smith concerning British requests for delays in arms aid to Egypt and for American oil technicians in Iran.[4]

The tour of Western capitals—Paris, London, Bonn, The Hague, Brussels, Luxembourg, Rome—lasted until February 9. The Secretary timed it to coincide roughly with Eisenhower's State of the Union message of February 2, giving an opportunity to gauge the reaction. The President's address set out specific intentions, such as action in Asia, eventual liberation in Eastern Europe, unity in Europe, and wresting the initiative from the Soviet Union. It included the dramatic announcement that Eisenhower had ordered the Seventh Fleet to withdraw from the Straits of Formosa, a reversal of President Truman's order of June, 1950, which had charged the Seventh Fleet with preventing either a Chinese Communist attack on Taiwan or Nationalist Chinese military operation against the mainland.[5]

On arrival in Paris, Dulles received a briefing by the American Embassy, and learned that a majority of French officials including Premier René Mayer and Foreign Minister Georges Bidault supported an "Atlantic policy" of safeguarding peace through NATO. The French also had determined to push what they called a "European policy" within the Atlantic policy: the Russians would interpret any weakening of the European policy as a weakness of the Atlantic policy. Dulles' talks with Mayer and other offiicials encouraged his belief that they would break the opposition to EDC. He reported to Eisenhower that the road ahead was hard but ultimate success was possible. He cabled the President of a good reception for the State of the Union message, that the initial concern over withdrawal of the Seventh Fleet had disappeared.[6]

It was far otherwise in Britain, where Dulles arrived at the height of official and public criticism of Eisenhower's order—fear that large-scale American operations against Communist China were about to begin, a Third World War in the making. The day before arrival Eden had informed an aroused Commons that the British Government had learned of the revocation of Truman's directive three days in advance and immediately counseled against it, fearing it "would have unfortunate political repercussions without compensating military advantages." He did not have any information whether action was to follow the presidential decision, and advised the House to avoid "extremist views."[7]

Dulles met Prime Minister Winston Churchill and Eden on February 4, 1953, his first session with them as Secretary of State. It went off well. In Dulles' opinion the discussions were highly satisfactory. He believed he had established cordial relations and allayed distrust of American policy in the Far East which, he felt, the Labor Party and the British sensationalist press had stirred up. The day following the meeting Eden pleased the Secretary by assuring the House of no reason for panic over Far Eastern policy, that the President's order did "not mean that grave events will necessarily follow," and that Her Majesty's Government felt that no step would occur without London's having an opportunity of expressing views beforehand. He made this statement on his own responsibility, Eden told the House, because Dulles and Stassen had said before leaving Europe that they would make no commitments on their journey.[8] Gratifying too was the British view that EDC was indispensable. Other matters Dulles discussed with Churchill and Eden related to Egypt, Iran, and economic problems.

The visit to Bonn turned out equally useful. Chancellor Adenauer was certain he could push ahead with EDC despite the opposition. Adenauer's determination impressed Dulles.

Only in Brussels did the Secretary find a lukewarm attitude toward EDC, but he remained optimistic.

Trips to the other capitals were uneventful and seemed encouraging.

What had come from this preliminary West European reconnaissance? What, at least, had Dulles concluded? Upon return home he gave his second formal address to the American people. He told them on February 12, 1953, that he and Stassen had found "good will and friendliness," but "some fear that the United States is not qualified to give the free world the kind of leadership which it needs at this critical moment." Europeans conceded America's material power, he said, but questioned "the accumulated wisdom to make the best use of that power."[9]

A week later he addressed the Foreign Service officers of the Department and offered a candid, confidential appraisal of the world situation. Never before, he claimed, had the United States and Western civilization been under greater peril. The old civilization dominated by Judeo-Christian ideas of the nature of man was confronting an atheistic, material force which believed man "a sort of domesticated animal," to be driven out to pasture by a few leaders, and then taken back to be milked in the barn. Approximately a third of the world had gone to communism, and the rest was in danger, particularly in Asia's peninsular and insular areas which the West could hold with difficulty; should those places fall, communist despotism would inundate Asia. The Middle East likewise was an area of burdens: he recalled that Stalin had broken with Hitler and accepted the risk of invasion because the German dictator refused Stalin's demands in the Middle East. The present Soviet leadership's anti-Semitic tactics, after a period of neutrality between Israel and the Arab world, showed readiness to achieve the goal in the Middle East denied to Hitler. Africa also lay in turmoil, revolution spreading like wildfire. South America, a region long taken for granted, was not safe because seeds of communism and anti-Americanism "are planted and growing vigorously as weeds." The general world picture, Dulles told the Foreign Service officers, was not pleasant.

The Secretary was convinced—a feeling, he said, Eisenhower shared—that the aggressor should not have an uncontested initiative. America could not continue to sit tight, a policy against the character of the American people. The Secretary restated his belief that without risking war it was possible to take immediate action to enlarge unrest within the zones of Soviet conquest. In the twenty nations subjugated by the Soviet Union, indigestion was visible. American policy might produce "some regurgitation."

The Far East had tied down important American and French land forces at a time when Soviet armies remained an uncommitted central reserve. The Russians did not want an armistice in Korea. Indochina he also considered a serious problem, particularly because of its effect on Western European unity. Eisenhower's announcement about the Seventh Fleet was the first step in putting the communists on the defensive.

The Secretary turned to the Middle East where he thought it entirely possible, without abandoning "worthy policies" which had led to establishment of the State of Israel, to improve relations with the Arab states "obsessed" with the view that the United States was a prisoner of Israeli policy. The government had an opportunity to bring the Arabs and the Israelis closer together.

In relations with allies, America had the responsibility of leadership—delicate and dangerous—requiring a forward pace, but not too far ahead so that "you haven't got anybody to lead." The talk about going ahead with the allies "arm in arm in happy and jovial fellowship" was a pretty picture, but not reality. In the free world only one great power was capable of leadership, the United States. Some of the nations and leaders were exhausted. To follow their paces in foreign policy would reduce the initiative of the Western world to the slowest possible progress—a snail's pace—if, indeed, there would be any pace.

Dulles would not be rash, not give ultimatums to friends and allies. He denied he had been "indulging in that." Those who accused him did not "know what they have been talking about." He recalled that the recent meetings with the heads of state and foreign ministers of Western Europe were cordial, the atmosphere friendly, exchanges unmarked by the "slightest semblance" of an attempt at dictation, "although there was a very frank presentation of certain facts of life which are better known than ignored." But he wanted the allies to know it was impossible for him to say that the United States would do nothing unless all the allies approved. Such a tactic would tie the free world in such knots as to make it incapable of action, as compared to the enforced unification imposed on the Soviet block by Russian leaders. Providence, Dulles said characteristically, had therefore entrusted responsibility to the United States.[10]

2

While the new Secretary was trying to win confidence abroad he was attempting to set his own house in order. He was aware of the fragile morale of the Foreign Service and anxious to raise it. He had come to office in the midst of a raging emotional controversy about the Department of State, which the Republican victory had not assuaged. Out of control of the presidency for twenty years, Republicans were influenced by views of such men as Senator McCarthy who were certain that incompetent and even disloyal personnel had infiltrated the Department. Voices from the capital and newspaper offices had spoken of reorganizations, cleanups, transfers, a reduction in force (the "rif"), dismissals.

Dulles' first published statement as Secretary of State had been bland and inauspicious. Within fifteen minutes after he had been sworn in at the White House at 5:30 P.M., on January 21, he had issued a press release addressed to his new associates in the Department and Foreign Service. "We are," it read in part, "front line defenders of the vital interests of the United States which are being attacked by a political warfare which is as hostile in its purpose and as dangerous in its capabilities as any open war. . . . The peril is of a kind which places a special responsibility on each and every member of the Department of State and the Foreign Service. It requires of us competence, discipline and *positive loyalty* to the policies that our President and the Congress may prescribe. Less than that is not tolerable at this time."[11]

Shortly after returning from his European tour he had met, as mentioned, with the Foreign Service officers. At this closed luncheon meeting on February 19 he told them they were a group of highly competent and thoroughly loyal Americans on whom the President and he would depend for facts and evaluation. "You are," he said, "to a very special degree, the eyes, the ears, the voice of the United States in relation to foreign policy and in the making of foreign policy." He recognized that they were going through a difficult period demanding replacement of twenty years of loyalty to one administration with loyalty to another, much more painful because of a presidential campaign that had involved policy issues and the competence of the service. It was not easy, Dulles had noted, to shift loyalties from persons and policies. Still, this was part of the American system of government. The Secretary commended to the Department a motto of the late Senator Vandenberg, "This, too, shall pass." He promised to make the transition as rapid and painless as possible.

But the phrase "positive loyalty" reverberated from desk to desk in the Department and elsewhere. Dulles attempted to temper his ill-chosen phrase by asking that it should not be misunderstood, "that loyalty does not . . . call for any one to practice intellectual dishonesty or to distort his reporting to please superiors." Requesting that positive loyalty not be misunderstood stressed its presence. He had spoken of loyalty at the wrong time, to a group harassed and oversensitive. It was just the sort of phrase the press liked to set in bold type. In the sickly era of hunts for evil motives it could produce an evil result.

Conditions of early 1953 did not lend themselves to a rapid and painless reorganization of the Department. The inauguration of Eisenhower did not quiet the tremendous concern and fear of the American people of communist subversion. For several years they had watched the cold war, seen the televised disclosures of espionage, and listened to the fantastic oratory of McCarthy who relentlessly accused the Department and other government agencies of harboring communists, subversives, and perverts. The recent presidential campaign had convinced many people that the Truman Administration had misconceived the national interest. Even after the inauguration of Eisenhower many Republicans, despite the party's ascendancy, went on claiming that the government was full of disloyal Americans.

In this atmosphere Dulles attempted by "orderly processes" to correct "the accumulated errors of the last 20 years," and for many employees at home and in the Foreign Service the transition period was a nightmare. Acheson and Truman had protected them; now protection seemed gone. To be sure, the designation of an individual such as Bedell Smith as Under Secretary of State was reassuring. Not so the appointment of Donold Lourie, president of the Quaker Oats Company, as Under Secretary for Administration, a new position which Dulles hoped would relieve him of administrative duties. Dulles was naive in believing that a Secretary could divorce himself from administrative problems. Lourie was a kind and personable man, but totally inexperienced in public service. Entrusted with responsibility for personnel security, he turned those touchy matters over to a man he did not know at all—Robert Walter Scott ("Scotty") McLeod, a former FBI agent and member of the senatorial staff of Styles Bridges of

New Hampshire, friendly to the McCarthy wing of the Republican Party. At first Dulles welcomed the McLeod appointment. He had not forgotten his disillusioning experience with Alger Hiss, whom he had recommended to head the Carnegie Endowment for International Peace. The subsequent conviction of Hiss for perjury, and the grave question of whether Hiss had been traitorous, had shattered the Secretary's confidence in judging people. "I'm not going to be caught," Dulles was quoted as saying to Department officers, "with another Alger Hiss on my hands."[12]

The new security officer, who had limited experience in international affairs, began his duties with an excess of zeal. His staff compiled a list of Department officers who read "communist" publications, including those who read the liberal magazine *Reporter*. Most disturbing was the way McLeod used the presidential directive authorizing a reduction in force. The "rif" was a weapon in the hands of the security officer. In seven months, from February to August, 1953, the roster of personnel of the Department dropped from 42,154 to 20,321, partly through transfer to other agencies (16,000) but partly through outright termination (5,000). Incidentally, only 306 citizen employees and 178 aliens with no indication of active disloyalty were dismissed on the basis of revised security regulations. The accelerated reduction—terminations, dismissals, forced retirements, accompanied as they were with investigations, reinvestigations, and almost contemptuous disregard for the feelings of those involved—shattered the morale of the Department for many months. McLeod's zeal came to an official end when he tried to interfere in the appointment of Charles E. Bohlen as ambassador to the Soviet Union. Dulles asked McLeod to concentrate his main effort on supervising the refugee relief program. Later McLeod became ambassador to Ireland.[13]

Dulles' own decision to terminate if for differing reasons the careers of John Carter Vincent, John Paton Davies, George F. Kennan, and Paul Nitze increased the sensitivities of his associates. After studying the voluminous file on Vincent, whose record of diplomatic service in the Far East the Republicans had attacked, he found neither disloyalty nor a security risk but questioned Vincent's competence. Meeting with Dulles on March 21, 1953, Vincent submitted his resignation effective the end of the month. Dulles took the same position on Davies, forcing him to retire on full pension. The question of disloyalty or security risk did not weigh against Kennan or Nitze; Dulles believed both men had only committed themselves to policies with which he did not agree. He hoped that Kennan, whom he retired from the Foreign Service by not reassigning him within a specified period, would remain available for consultation. Dulles recommended Nitze's transfer to the Department of Defense in charge of policy planning there; the Administration was willing, but pressure from McCarthy and other Republicans blocked the shift.[14]

It was clear that Eisenhower's overwhelming victory at the polls had not united the Republican Party, and here was some of the reason for hesitant or plainly maladroit administrative actions within the Department. Conservative Republican leaders were in a highly critical mood also because many of them had believed that Eisenhower and Dulles intended to repudiate the Yalta and Potsdam Agreements, a prelude to liberation of the Soviet satellites, and the new Administration had failed to do so. Events during the first weeks of January, 1953, pointed to an early realization of such campaign pledges. Three House joint resolutions and two concurrent resolutions of House and Senate demanding repudiation were introduced within hours after opening of the Eighty-third Congress. Senator Taft said publicly that Congress would support the President should he decide to abrogate these wartime agreements by executive action. Senators Alexander Wiley, Karl Mundt, Homer Ferguson, Representative Walter H. Judd, and Vice President Richard M. Nixon agreed. Secretary-designate Dulles during hearings on his nomination was friendly to liberation. He told the Foreign Relations Committee that the enslaved peoples deserved to be free, and that, "from our own selfish standpoint, ought to be free because if they are the servile instruments of aggressive despotism, they will eventually be welded into a force which will be highly dangerous to ourselves and to all of the free world. Therefore, we must always have in mind the liberation of these captive peoples."[15] Then the broad general principles of the President's inaugural address dampened the spirit of the repudiators and liberators. His State of the Union message revived and encouraged them, but only briefly. "We shall never acquiesce," Eisenhower said, "in the enslavement of any people in order to purchase fancied gain for ourselves." He informed Congress that at a later date he would ask it to join in an "appropriate resolution" making clear that the government would not recognize the kind of commitment "contained in secret understandings of the past with foreign governments which permit this kind of enslavement." Three weeks later he sent a draft resolution to Congress asking both Houses to support him in a declaration accusing the Soviet Union of destroying international agreements made during the war and thereby subjugating free peoples in Eastern Europe and elsewhere. There was no call for a declaration voiding the Yalta and Potsdam Agreements—for such a repudiation was now recognized as more in the interest of the Soviet Union than of the United States. The wartime agreements were the only contractual arrangements the United States had with the Soviet Union permitting protests against Russian action in Eastern Europe: the Yalta Declaration on Liberated Europe had pledged the USSR to good democratic behavior in that area, and gave the United States the right to criticize violations. To the disappointed it seemed that Eisenhower now had asked the Republican Congress to absolve his predecessors, Roosevelt and Truman, of all blame. The President's draft resolution was introduced as House Joint Resolution 200, and Dulles went up to Capitol Hill to urge its adoption instead of the six resolutions then before Congress which demanded immediate repudiation. In the end, not one of the resolutions, including the President's, was reported out of the House Foreign Affairs Committee. The Senate thereupon dropped the matter.[16]

Dissatisfaction within the Republican Party reached its height when Eisenhower nominated Bohlen to the critical post of ambassador to the Soviet Union. Earlier apointments had not produced controversy. Party leaders were pleased that all major diplomatic posts fell to Republicans, although the absence of Democrats marked a departure from the bipartisan appointments of Truman. Henry Cabot Lodge, Jr., went to the United Nations (Dulles had offered the post to the defeated Democratic candidate, Stevenson, who had refused), Winthrop W. Aldrich to London, C. Douglas Dillon to Paris, Mrs. Clare Booth Luce to Rome, and President James B. Conant of Harvard to West Germany. Eisenhower and Dulles wanted to retain Chester Bowles as ambassador to India, but pressure from conservative Republicans was too strong. The appointment of Bohlen, a career diplomat and authority on the Soviet Union, split Republican ranks. To many Republicans, Bohlen who had accompanied President Roosevelt to the Teheran and Yalta Conferences was a symbol of FDR's diplomacy. Bohlen did not help matters when during the hearings on his nomination he upheld the Yalta Agreement. In the end his nomination went through, but the Republican furor in Congress revealed unmistakably that in the future a section of the party might not support its leader in the White House and, indeed, might oppose him by the same methods used during the Truman Administration.[17]

Appointment of Bohlen also signified an end to the idea of liberation, or so it seemed to those who had urged this policy upon the Administration. The East Berlin uprising on June 17, 1953, marked a flicker of hope for the policy. Many observers agreed with the prominent journalists, the Alsop brothers, that the Berlin uprising was a test of Eisenhower's campaign pledge. Dulles hailed the revolt in Berlin as proof of his long-held belief that the Soviet Union had overextended itself and that "it could be shaken if the difficulties that were latent were activated." The Secretary did not promise American intervention.[18] Nor was there any move some years later, in 1956, during the massive intervention of Soviet troops in the Hungarian Revolution. The denouement to liberation came after the death of Dulles when Congress on July 17, 1959, passed the so-called Captive Nations Resolution, asking the President to designate the third week in July as Captive Nations Week and "to issue a similar proclamation each year until such time as freedom and independence shall have been achieved for all the captive nations of the world." This resolution had started in the Senate Judiciary Committee, without consultation of the Foreign Relations Committee. Thus the Captive Nations Week was added to the long list of other national proclamations designating days, weeks, or months to honor veterans, mothers, crippled children, athletes, and just about anything.[19]

Finally, there was for Dulles and his Administration colleagues, the President not least, the problem of Senator McCarthy. The Republican victory had increased McCarthy's power by making him chairman of the Committee on Government Operations, and its Permanent Subcommittee on Investigations. Unhesitant and with apparently unlimited power he undertook to examine all phases of State Department activity. His first challenge was in connection with the Bohlen nomination. Despite Dulles' extraordinary assurance that he personally had studied all files made by investigative authorities, including the FBI, and concluded that Bohlen was loyal, highly competent, and needed in the Soviet Union because of the recent death of Stalin, McCarthy was not satisfied. The Senator charged that Dulles had overruled the findings of the Department security officer, "Scotty" McLeod, and also given false testimony. He actually demanded that Bohlen take a lie detector test! This, happily, did not occur. But McCarthy bounced back from defeat in the Bohlen matter with a widely heralded investigation of the Department's Voice of America and the International Information Administration. The world watched with dismay as two of McCarthy's assistants, Roy Cohn and G. David Schine, ran amuck through the libraries of American embassies in Europe searching for the thirty to forty thousand books which McCarthy claimed communists and fellow travelers had written. Some scared officials disposed of books, possibly by burning them. The world press likened this truly un-American behavior to the book burning of the Nazis.[20] President Eisenhower who might have stopped such antics admonished Americans not to join the book burners. Not until late summer of 1954, after McCarthy had turned on the US Army and tried to humiliate a war-decorated brigadier general, did the Senate in accord with a fully aroused American public bring an end to McCarthy's fanaticism by formally condemning him. McCarthy died in 1957.

3

Other Republicans, notably Senator John W. Bricker of Ohio, advocated means to protect the country from "internationalism," "world government," and possible betrayal of the national interest by the President. Within a few days after inauguration of General Eisenhower, Senator Bricker supported by sixty-three Senators of both parties had introduced a joint resolution, the latest version of the so-called Bricker Amendment to the Constitution. It proposed to limit the agreements to which the United States could be a party, and introduced novel controls on presidential power to negotiate treaties and executive agreements. The intent was to limit the jurisdiction and power of international bodies like the United Nations in what the amendment's supporters considered matters of domestic interest, such as the UN-sponsored draft of an international covenant of human rights, and to prevent the President from making international agreements which were not in harmony with Congressional opinion. The first four sections of the resolution read:

> Section 1. A provision of a treaty which denies or abridges any right enumerated in this Constitution shall not be of any force or effect.
>
> Section 2. No treaty shall authorize or permit any foreign power or any international organization to supervise, control, or adjudicate rights of citizens of the United States within the United States enumerated in this Constitution or any other matter essentially within the domestic jurisdiction of the United States.
>
> Section 3. A treaty shall become effective as internal law in the United States only through the enactment of appropriate legislation by the Congress.
>
> Section 4. All executive or other agreements between the President and any international organization, foreign power, or official thereof shall be made only in the manner and to the extent to be prescribed by law. Such agreements shall be subject to the limitations imposed on treaties, or the making of treaties, by this article.[21]

During and immediately after the 1952 campaign Bricker was certain his proposal would pass. Dulles in April, 1952, had indicated publicly that modification of constitutional provisions regarding the treaty power of the President was desirable under modern conditions. He had warned of the "great dangers" inherent in executive powers.[22] Within a few days after the election Bricker called on Eisenhower for public support of an amendment. The President-elect asked Bricker to telephone him in a few hours, so as to give opportunity to discuss the issue with Dulles. Dulles called in Herman Phleger, his future Legal Adviser in the Department, and both men agreed that Eisenhower should not endorse the Bricker Amendment. Bricker never forgave Dulles for this advice to Eisenhower.[23]

The Senate Judiciary Committee began hearings on the Bricker Amendment in the spring of 1953, and Dulles was asked to appear, which latter exigency led to an exchange of views between him and Eisenhower. The Administration had determined not to allow the amendment's passage. Even less welcome to Dulles was a substitute text, subsequently incorporated into the Bricker Amendment as the "which clause," offered by Senator Arthur V. Watkins of Utah, specifying that treaties or executive agreements would become effective "only through legislation which would be valid in the absence of a treaty."[24] Before testifying against these propositions Dulles wrote out a long draft statement which he sent to Eisenhower for comment. The President's reply showed both concern and political astuteness. Eisenhower had made an intensive study of the Bricker Amendment, consulting distinguished lawyers and professors of law: John W. Davis, Judge John Parker, Judge Orie Phillips, and Professor Edward S. Corwin.

He agreed with Dulles' view but not with the supporting arguments. The President doubted the appropriateness of telling Congress that the Bricker Amendment and other similar resolutions would make the President the servant of Congress. A better argument would be that the proposed amendment would stifle necessary action in international relations. And even if one conceded that the resolutions before Congress would upset the traditional relation between executive and legislative branches, such a contention should be used in a place other than a Congressional hearing. Eisenhower was critical of a statement that Dulles was ready to submit at the hearing that under a different Administration the Bricker Amendment might be desirable. The President thought this a wrong argument; indeed if Dulles did believe that future Presidents might be unwise and dishonest he should support the Bricker Amendment.[25]

Senator Bricker and supporters were unmoved by Dulles' subsequent testimony and Eisenhower's pleas. There followed months of discussion and hearings producing a voluminous record. Finally pressure for adjournment of Congress prevented a vote on the Bricker Amendment, the Knowland substitute (Senator Knowland had taken over Republican leadership in the Senate following the death of Taft), and other texts. The more Eisenhower and Dulles studied the Bricker Amendment, the more determined they were to prevent passage. Anticipating reintroduction, Eisenhower early in January, 1954, asked Dulles about the international effect of the Ohioan's proposal.

The Secretary responded that adoption of the amendment or any of the other alternatives would damage the Administration's effort to cooperate with the Soviet Union in diverting atomic energy into peaceful channels; undermine NATO and the hoped-for European Defense Community; endanger security in the Pacific and Asia; perhaps fatally affect America's capacity to act with allies.[26]

Soon after the 1954 Congressional session began, the Bricker Amendment was reintroduced. It then was defeated, by vote of 31 nays against 60 yeas—one "nay" had prevented a two-thirds majority. Against were 14 Republicans and 16 Democrats and 1 Independent; in favor had been 32 Republicans and 28 Democrats. Eisenhower was relieved. He told Republican legislative leaders that the Bricker Amendment was "a thing of the past," that they "could turn to the work of moving forward the administration's legislative program."[27] But the Bricker Amendment was not a thing of the past. In successive years—1955, 1956, 1957—it would be reintroduced and defeated, always a threat to the Administration's foreign policy.

CHAPTER EIGHT

AGONIZING REAPPRAISAL

1

SOMETIME during the first week of March, 1953, Joseph Stalin had died, and news of the death of the ruler of the Soviet empire and chief of the communist world coincided with arrival in the United States of Western statesmen who came to continue discussions begun with Dulles during his recent tour of Western Europe. Talks centered around NATO and the European Defense Community, the Far East, and generally the future of American economic and military assistance. But the fact of Stalin's demise, which marked the end of an era, lay in the background of the conversations, producing thoughts of a high-level meeting with the new leaders of the Soviet Union. The change of regime in Russia had opened avenues for a *rapprochement*.

First were the British, headed by Eden and Richard A. Butler, then Chancellor of the Exchequer, who spoke of trade and currency convertibility. They feared an American return to protectionism. Eden also was apprehensive about American policy in the Middle East.

Next came the French represented by Premier Mayer and Foreign Minister Bidault. If the French fretted over their position as a European and world power, jeopardized by a resurgent Germany and heavy involvement in Indochina, the topic of discussion was the European Defense Community, the treaty signed by six nations (France, Germany, Italy, Belgium, the Netherlands, Luxembourg) in May, 1952, not yet ratified by all their parliaments. EDC was to integrate their armed forces with existing European institutions: NATO, the Coal and Steel Community, and a proposed Political Community, as well as consenting to the so-called Contractual Agreements giving full sovereignty to the German Federal Republic. Dulles was an ardent supporter of this grand design. He, Jean Monnet, and other European statesmen viewed it almost as a solution for European difficulties, a symbol of European regeneration, promise of a secure future.

Its very simplicity intrigued Dulles. The European Defense Community would safeguard Western Europe against Soviet ambition and the ambitions of member states, eliminating what he often described as "the world's worst fire hazard." He saw a perfect solution to two difficult problems: the military defense of Western Europe, and a resurgent industrial Germany. West Germany tied to the Atlantic Alliance would not only allay fears of its neighbors, but by helping in the common defense would brake its fantastic economic growth which was rapidly creating an industrial plant surpassing that of the other Western European nations. There was possibility, if not certainty, that with unification of Western Europe and with German rearmament the United States might recall some of its divisions and reduce its economic aid.

Naturally, French failure to act on EDC disturbed Dulles, already annoyed by the lukewarm British attitude. To the visiting statesmen he pointed out that rejection could mean collapse of the hopes that inspired the Marshall Plan, North Atlantic Treaty, and the Mutual Security Program. The Secretary was dismayed when Mayer and Bidault, while willing to establish EDC "with minimum delay," insisted that a settlement of the long-standing Franco-German dispute over the Saar must precede French ratification. Dulles dismissed the French condition as having no legal basis.

Discussion on other matters produced better results. The French and British delegations pledged to stop shipments of strategic goods to Communist China, and the United States endorsed the French contention that the struggle in Indochina was part of the same pattern as the Korean War, requiring frequent consultation between governments. Anticipating an armistice in Korea, both the French and British warned Communist China not to use released military forces against Indochina and Southeast Asia.

The meeting of Adenauer with Eisenhower and Dulles during the first week of April, 1953, indicated official reconciliation with the former enemy nation and acceptance of Germany as an ally "in superior standing." No basic difficulties marred the talks. Unlike the Chamber of Deputies, the Bundestag had approved EDC. The Chancellor left Washington pleased by American pledges of military and economic aid, a renewed promise to aid Berlin, and assurance that Germany's adherence to the Western community would not in any way alter American interest in reunification of Germany "by peaceful means and on a free and democratic basis."

Through these discussions Dulles emphasized EDC. He told the visiting dignitaries that he could not commit his government to future economic aid until American policy had been realigned according to Republican philosophy. The Secretary also stressed coordinating the interests of the allies into a positive policy toward the Soviet Union, Eastern Europe, and Communist China. He fought off suggestions from the British and French for a summit conference with the new Soviet leaders. He appreciated Adenauer who, too, said that such a meeting was premature.[1]

It was not surprising that the Washington gatherings did not produce full agreement. The talks were preliminary, to bring out differences.[2] French and British statesmen left with a belief that despite the death of Stalin the United States had determined to step up resistance to the Soviet Union by offensive strategies, at the same time slowing down rearmament and economic assistance to the allies.

Sentiment meanwhile increased for fairly drastic changes in American foreign policy. The French and English press feared the United States was taking the allies toward war with Russia, objected to American leadership, recommended European freedom of action; some newspapers suggested that their governments negotiate independently with the Soviet Union. In the United States an important element of the Republican Party led by Senators Taft and Knowland urged Americans to rely on their own strength, emphasized the Far East over Europe, expressed fear of the Soviet Union, wanted freedom of action, at the same time advocating reduction of federal expenditures. Ominous was Taft's so-called "go it alone" speech of May 26, 1953, which challenged Eisenhower's foreign policy. The Ohio Senator, so physically stricken as to be unable to deliver his address in person, advocated abandonment of the United Nations, if not the Atlantic Alliance. He noted that the French and English "are more than anxious to settle with Russia, and resume as much trade as possible," and doubted the value of cooperating with them in a world-wide alliance against the Soviet Union.

Eisenhower was greatly concerned about the "go it alone" doctrine. He assured his press conference of May 28 that "no single free nation can live alone in the world. We have to have friends. Those friends have got to be tied to you, in some form or another." Taft's ideas on foreign policy were unworkable. "If you are going to go it alone one place, you of course have to go it alone everywhere." The President restated his belief that a coalition of free nations demanded recognition of individual and common interests as well as willingness to compromise. He concluded: "I earnestly believe we cannot desert the great purpose for which we are seeking—for which we are working." The President sobered the responsible conservatives of his party. A few days later Dulles informed him that Taft had called to explain that his speech had not indicated any break with Eisenhower's foreign policy. Taft on June 5 issued a clarifying statement: he had not used the phrase "go it alone" in his remarks; the United Nations served a purpose as a town meeting of the world.[3]

Meanwhile the death of Stalin had encouraged Eisenhower to find ways to convince the new Soviet leadership to start "toward the birth of mutual trust founded in cooperative effort." On the very day he heard of Stalin's death he was anxious to address the Russian people. Dulles cautioned that "it might be read as an appeal to the Soviet people in mourning to rise against their rulers." This was interesting advice from a man often characterized as a fire-breathing warmonger ready to unleash war to liberate captive peoples within the Soviet empire. The President overruled his Secretary of State and broadcasted a message.[4]

Late in March, 1953, the President had begun work on a foreign policy address setting forth the intent of the United States to improve relations with the Soviet Union, leading to reduction or elimination of tension throughout the world. He hoped it would also ease, if not end, opposition among the allies. Eisenhower felt it important at this period, the end of the Stalin era and beginning of his own Administration, that people of the world know he was "deadly serious," that he was ready with acts and not phrases. Dulles counseled that American readiness to improve relations should follow deeds by the Soviet Union. As a starter he suggested (quite a prescription!) that the President insist on such deeds as an Austrian treaty, release of German prisoners of war, Soviet influence to bring a truce in Korea and peace in Asia, and that nations in the Soviet orbit should have freedom to choose their governments. Eisenhower nonetheless proposed a modest and, he hoped, workable program.

The President sent drafts of his speech to Churchill, Mayer, and Adenauer. He did not want to say anything publicly until he knew the allies were in agreement. He was anxious to have Churchill's reaction. All of the allied leaders thought the statement excellent, but only Adenauer gave unqualified support.

The French Premier applauded American initiative on the peace front and favored pressure on the Soviets to make agreements. He felt Soviet acceptance of an Austrian treaty followed by evacuation of troops from Austria, Hungary, and Rumania would give evidence of readiness to consider other problems. Mayer opposed a summit conference, which pleased Dulles. The only comments of substance related to Germany and Indochina. The Premier feared a reunited Germany, which he assumed would be a neutral and disarmed Germany, before reaching an agreement with the Soviet Union. A reunited Germany might deal with the Soviet Union and Eastern Europe. France, he said, could not permit this unless with a simultaneous general disarmament. He supported EDC and rearmament of Germany as a means of convincing the Soviet Union of the desirability of general disarmament. The Premier requested the President to couple the demand for a Korean settlement with an end to the war in Indochina.

Churchill questioned some of the proposed address's assumptions. He felt that a change in Soviet mood and perhaps in policy had become apparent with the death of Stalin, and that the time was ready for informal, private conversation among a few leaders of the major powers. The Prime Minister doubted the wisdom of too many conditions as a means of testing Soviet intentions. It would be a mistake, Churchill would say publicly on May 11, "to assume that nothing can be settled . . . unless or until everything is settled," evidently fearful that an American or NATO policy failing to take account of Stalin's death might "impede any spontaneous and healthy evolution which may be taking place inside Russia."[5]

Eisenhower delivered his speech before the American Society of Newspaper Editors on April 16. The night before he suffered a painful attack of ileitis—a condition corrected surgically in 1956—and his doctors advised postponement of the address. With great physical effort, hiding discomfort from his listeners, he extended an offer to the new Soviet leaders. "The world knows," he said, "that an era ended with the death of Joseph Stalin," and now the dead leader's followers had a precious opportunity. "We are only for sincerity of peaceful purpose attested by deeds," and opportunities for deeds were many. "Even a few such clear and specific acts, such as the Soviet Union's signature upon an Austrian treaty or its release of thousands of prisoners still held from World War II, would be impressive signs of sincere intent." The President urged disarmament, control of atomic energy, and prohibition of atomic weapons under safeguards by the United Nations. It was a dramatic speech, well received. Churchill hailed "a massive and magnificent statement of our case." The new Soviet hierarchy even allowed *Pravda* and *Izvestia* to print it in full. Dulles described the President's address as "a fact which will inevitably influence the course of history."[6]

Initial favorable response was soon marred by negative reaction from Russia and Britain. Soviet leaders, professing approval of peaceful settlement, objected to both the manner and content of the proposals. Churchill's address in the Commons on May 11, calling for a summit conference and questioning United States demands for Soviet deeds, badly damaged Eisenhower's hopes.[7]

2

Eisenhower thereupon sent Dulles to Paris to the April meeting of the North Atlantic Council, to converse with Western statesmen. This move became particularly important as the new Soviet Premier, Georgi Malenkov, had launched a peace offensive aimed, so the President believed, at gaining time for consolidation of power at home, preventing the constitution of EDC, and slowing rearmament of the United States and the West.[8] Dulles expressed the Administration's view on the Soviet peace offensive, NATO, and related matters. He recalled Eisenhower's close association with NATO, as well as his own leadership in the Senate which helped to ratify it. The death of Stalin, he told the European ministers, had not altered Soviet aims. Russian moves were tactical. It might prove otherwise, but so far Soviet deeds had not satisfied optimistic expectations. Soviet Communism, he lectured, frequently had practiced the art of advance and retreat. Both Lenin and Stalin taught that. Dulles warned his audience not to reach for crumbs recently dropped by the Soviet leadership: a few visas, a handful of prisoners released. The United States would always be receptive to a change of heart.

The Secretary advised watching for three facts which so long as they existed would spell danger to the West: the Soviet Union is a totalitarian state with immense military and economic power; this dictatorship distrusts any noncommunist government; Soviet leaders deny the moral law and are not bound by morality where violence will serve their purpose. The West must not lower its guard, but prepare to meet the Soviet peril not "at some year, 1954-1955-1956, which can be assumed to be the year of maximum peril," but "ten years from now as well as a year or two from now." This short- and long-range effort should reflect a balance between military and economic strength. The allies, Dulles continued, must not make a military effort so exhausting that it destroyed the freedoms it was to protect.

Dulles was aware that some European leaders thought the Administration would concentrate on Far Eastern matters. Operations in the Far East closely related to defense of Europe. He quoted Stalin as having said that "the road to victory over the West lies through revolutionary lines with the peoples of the East." Western Europe could not become safe by isolating it from the rest of the world, particularly Asia. The United States would continue "to make very considerable effort" in Asia. As long as there was no peace in Asia the United States stood ready to increase rather than decrease its contribution—military in Korea, financial in Indochina. It would not disregard Europe or NATO. The first to benefit from these efforts would be Western Europe. Dulles reiterated his plea for ratification of EDC.[9]

The Secretary left Paris believing the NATO meeting a "solid if not spectacular accomplishment." The allies had agreed to strengthen NATO by concentrating on quality—making it "compact and hard rather than . . . big and soft"—and on policies which would "preserve and not exhaust" their economic strength. He was delighted with the meeting's resolutions which stressed the need to ratify EDC quickly, importance of Soviet deeds over words, that the West "must not be sucked by any phony peace campaign," but go on building its strength and move toward greater European unity. The conference, he informed the President, was an achievement.[10]

Dulles was mistaken, for Soviet utterances encouraged Western Europe to think more of its own policy. In France, EDC was becoming less urgent; in Italy resistance to EDC increased; in Great Britain, Churchill supported by the French urged a summit conference. Increasingly the European press described American policy as inflexible.

Eisenhower was unhappy, and in late May asked Dulles to invite the French Premier and British Prime Minister to meet him at some quiet place. There was need to show friendship, regardless of the public press which, he was sure, gave a contrary impression. Churchill, anxious to see the President, immediately agreed, as did the new Premier of France, Joseph Laniel. The place chosen, Bermuda; the time, the first week of June, 1953.

Now it was Dulles' turn to be unhappy, for he did not like the idea of this first joint meeting of chiefs of state since Potsdam. It could demonstrate unity among the allies, but could end unity. A dramatic failure, he advised, would increase isolationism in the United States. The Secretary was disturbed by Churchill's "incipient tendency" to mediate. Churchill's overtures of friendship toward the Soviet Union, derived perhaps from a desire to close his public career with a grand coup, threatened to weaken American leadership, and placed the United States, Dulles believed, in the position of roadblock, a situation well suited to Soviet propaganda. Certain that precise agreements would not be reached at Bermuda, he recommended that discussion center on a few general topics: acceptance of United States action in Korea; support of the American position that the USSR was seeking to prevent European unity; recognition that unity would create a new balance on the Continent which would not only deter Soviet expansion there but in the Middle East; common policy toward colonial areas; finally, the feasibility of a four-power summit meeting including the Soviet Union.

The Bermuda Conference scheduled for June, 1953, was not held, for on its eve Churchill was struck down by a paralytic stroke. Eden, who had been ill, was unable to replace him.

A month later, July 10, the Marquess of Salisbury, Lord President of the Council and acting Foreign Secretary, together with Bidault, retained as Foreign Minister in the Laniel government, visited Dulles. The abortive uprising of the people of East Berlin in June, and the fall of the Soviet secret police chief Lavrenti P. Beria, strengthened Dulles' belief that the Soviet Union would back down. He thought that the major cause for Soviet conciliatory moves was increasing unrest in the satellite nations. Events offered confirmation "that the Soviet Communist leaders would come to recognize the futility of trying to hold captive so many peoples who, by their faith and their patriotism, can never really be consolidated into a Soviet Communist world." On the opening day of the so-called "Little Bermuda" conference (held, of course, in Washington), Dulles took note of Beria's disgrace as a sign that "freedom is again in the air. A new convulsion is underway. The old system may remain and may continue to threaten, but inherent weakness is disclosed."[11] Neither Salisbury nor Bidault was as optimistic.

The main conversation was Churchill's proposal for a four-power summit meeting "with a fluid or flexible agenda." During his last talk with President Truman and Secretary Acheson in January, 1952, Churchill had thought the central factor in Soviet foreign policy was fear of the West. Now, a year later, Churchill offered a different analysis. Prior to the meeting the Prime Minister had informed Eisenhower that Adenauer (perhaps as a result of the Berlin uprising) now spoke with approval of a four-power conference. Churchill took note of Senator Alexander Wiley's recent statement analyzing Soviet policy as due to fear "among a trembling remnant of gangsters and felons." The Soviet leaders, the Prime Minister now said, were not "cringing" people. They could reach the Rhine in a month, and the sea within two months. If they did not wish to march alone they could without difficulty stir or bribe armed Chinese to throw Indochina, Burma, and Thailand into a holocaust. These concerns made him anxious not to reject all hopes of a Soviet change and do everything possible to convince people everywhere that the West had done its best. He had no intent of being fooled by the Russians, and recalled his Fulton, Missouri, speech of 1946. A change in the world balance of power had occurred since his famous warning of Soviet purposes, largely through American action and rearmament, also because of the ebb of communist philosophy and the death of Stalin.

Churchill's plea for a four-power conference, supported by Salisbury, did not win Dulles' approval, and there was a compromise, to hold a conference of foreign ministers of the four nations, with agenda limited to German and Austrian questions. The Washington meeting ended with reaffirmation of Western unity. Dulles was pleased that the final declaration pledged a desire "to see true liberty restored" in the countries of Eastern Europe, a first acknowledgment of his principle of liberation by London and Paris.[12] But this expressed unity was based more on phrases than objectives. And as Salisbury and Bidault departed they indicated publicly that a four-power conference on a higher level was still open.[13]

President Eisenhower was disappointed that talks did not end the disarray among the allies, and his concern increased as he studied the European press. He sent Dulles a memorandum enclosing a critical editorial presenting "a sorry picture of American prestige and America's position in the world," and asked him to get busy explaining more effectively the Administration's policies and determination. Dulles answered that the editorials reflected bewilderment about American foreign policies because for more than twenty years foreigners had feared a Republican Administration as "isolationist." While they knew that neither the President nor he was isolationist, they believed that neither man could counter the tendency of the party. The fact that the Administration, with overwhelming support of Republicans in Congress, had been cutting expenditures abroad confirmed that American policy was moving toward isolationism.

Congress had been dominated by such persons as Taft, long known as an isolationist, and other Republicans like Knowland who apparently wanted general war in Asia against Red China. He called to the President's attention that American columnists and writers had been skeptical about American policies and that their views were reflected abroad. Dulles nevertheless felt that once new policies were "firmed up" they would command respect.

3

During the closing months of the year 1953 Dulles through deeds and words, mostly words, tried to strengthen the American position abroad, but was not successful. Churchill pressed for unlimited informal discussion with the Soviet leadership, while Dulles kept emphasizing a conference of foreign ministers limited to Germany and Austria, to be followed—should it prove successful—by a summit meeting. Dulles met with Churchill in London in October, 1953, to explain again American opposition to a high-level meeting. He offered two reasons: one was the many responsibilities of Eisenhower as head of state, the other the Secretary's fear that such a meeting would prejudice passage of EDC. Churchill, who never had cared for EDC, grudgingly agreed it was important for the French to make up their minds. Dulles insisted that only if EDC were ratified could the allies talk with the Soviets. Churchill indicated that he might meet alone with Malenkov. His position as Prime Minister, he said, was different from that of Eisenhower who was chief of state. Dulles recognized that Churchill was free to do what he wanted, but expressed concern that such a meeting would create the impression that Great Britain was a middleman between the United States and USSR, undermining the historic Anglo-American partnership. Churchill was irritated. The United States, he told Dulles, could trust him not to be entrapped in Moscow. Dulles answered that he was sure Churchill would not be trapped, but since he hardly could go to Moscow as an American representative, American public opinion would almost inevitably characterize him as a middleman. Dulles left London believing that neither Eden nor Salisbury, who were present, shared Churchill's ideas.

Adenauer was the only European statesman who gave Dulles comfort. The West German Chancellor felt that Churchill was in precarious health; because of this, the British Government was in a position similar to the French in that neither was capable of a European policy. Adenauer thought it would be "suicide" for the three allies to see the Russians in the near future, and suggested a three-power meeting (France, Britain, United States) at the end of the year before gathering with the Russians.[14]

Eisenhower, Churchill, and Laniel finally met in Bermuda in December, 1953, but this conference produced little. The declaration restated allied policies: unity, NATO, EDC. The leaders agreed that aggression appeared less imminent and attributed this fact to the increased strength of the free world and firmness of its policy. All nations in the world "have no cause to fear that the strength of the West will be invoked in any cause of wrongful violence." The allies, they announced, intended to "lose no opportunity for easing the tensions that beset the world." In this spirit they were ready to meet the Russians on Germany and Austria. No word about a summit conference. Behind the facade it was apparent that the American power of decision and capacity to influence the allies had weakened—and so, too, the will of the allies to work in unison. Each had determined on more freedom of action because of the perplexing uncertainties created by Stalin's death.[15]

If fear of the Soviet Union was no longer the cement of European unity, perhaps fear of an isolationist United States would be: so Dulles thought as he surveyed Europe at the end of 1953. In peacetime unity could not come through reason, because only fear forced nations together. "We have concluded," he told the December, 1953, meeting in Paris of the NATO ministerial conference, "that Soviet armed aggression in Europe is less likely today than it seemed several years ago." In great part that was because of NATO. The Soviet threat remained. Much had been done to make Western Europe a cooperative area, but Europe must move ahead "to more complete and organic forms of union." EDC was essential. There was no reason to fear that once EDC were established the United States would abandon military support of Europe. He recalled that at the recent Bermuda Conference, Eisenhower, Churchill, and Laniel had indicated that if EDC were created within the Atlantic Community "it will ensure intimate and durable cooperation between the United Kingdom and United States forces and the forces of the European Defense Community on the Continent of Europe." Should the French reject EDC, and Germany and France again become enemies, continental Europe could never be safe. That, Dulles warned, "would compel an agonizing reappraisal of basic United States policy."[16]

He had said it! The threat of agonizing reappraisal, repeated at a press conference in Paris, raised a storm. It was not the first time Dulles had said this. Now he wanted to jolt French public opinion, and he succeeded. Eden saw the "strength of the argument," but would have preferred different timing. At a secret meeting of the French cabinet several members protested the strong language. Paul Reynaud, the Vice Premier, dismissed their arguments: he thought Dulles "perfectly justified"; it was not important that the Secretary was undiplomatic; he "spoke the truth." Foreign ministers and representatives of Belgium, the Netherlands, and Luxembourg felt Dulles was right. Sir Pierson Dixon said in presence of Eden that the warning was "timely and useful." Underneath the smoke around the Secretary's bombshell, wrote the correspondent of the Columbia Broadcasting Company, David A. Schonbrun, to his chief, Edward R. Murrow, "there is solid evidence Secretary Dulles took calculated political risk which is his trademark, with good chance it might pay off in forcing early French action on EDC." He thought it important that the French press, including several usually anti-American papers—*Combat* and *Le Monde*—conceded that Dulles was justified, although they deplored his language. Schonbrun's "best informed sources" told him that Dulles' remarks to the French people and parliament were clear, blunt, and necessary.[17]

Dulles had been "a very sober and shaken man" when Eisenhower asked him to be Secretary of State. So recalled a future Secretary, Dean Rusk, as he recounted a meeting with Dulles on the day the President-elect offered the post. "I remember at the time I thought that this was rather extraordinary, because here was a man who had been in foreign policy matters all his life—since he was 19 years old, in fact."[18] By the time Dulles took office he had regained his composure and believed in his ability to reorganize the Department so as to free himself from administrative and ceremonial chores, and to strike out on new paths in foreign policy. Despite support from the President this latter hope proved illusory. He found that foreign policies do not begin or end with incoming or outgoing administrations; that he, and for that matter the President, did not have freedom. He would admit in September, 1954, that before he became Secretary he had proposed many answers to cold war tactics, but in practice his solutions were not as available or effective as he had hoped. He thought that in large part his frustration derived from the cumbersome nature of the American form of government, the limits on action of the executive. What was needed, he reflected, were "war powers." The cold war could not be won, he feared, as long as he had to operate on a ponderous peacetime basis, an intolerable handicap in the face of increasing problems in all corners of the world.

CHAPTER NINE

MASSIVE RETALIATION

JOHN FOSTER DULLES prefaced his tenure as Secretary of State with a call for liberation, and ended his first year with a threat of agonizing reappraisal. Liberation sought to put the Soviet Union on the defensive; agonizing reappraisal to strengthen Western European unity. Both slogans were simple and to the point, if not simple of execution. Each raised an uproar. The press, of course, welcomed the bold prose, tailor-made for headlines. But perhaps the Secretary should not have been a phrasemaker. Dulles seldom wavered in belief in the rightness of his policies. Individuals who knew him felt a sense of mission, drive, and greatness. Many who knew him only through the written word and the camera saw a man of rigidity, a preacher, a Wall Street lawyer. He did not seem to have the charisma, the external style highly valued by some journalists and commentators.[1]

The Secretary did not hesitate to take a stand and, in the course of it, coin a phrase. Eisenhower in the closing days of the first presidential year took note of the "vast amount of survey activity" which he thought had characterized the Administration. "As the new year begins," the President wrote Dulles, "much of this exploratory work is behind us; the time has come for clear-cut determined action in setting this Nation on a moderate but definite course."[2] It was two weeks later, on January 12, 1954, when Dulles announced before the Council on Foreign Relations that in the future the United States would "depend primarily upon a great capacity to retaliate, instantly, by means and at places of our choosing."

The third slogan! The American military establishment, he had said, would coordinate its operations with foreign policy "instead of having to try to be ready to meet the enemy's many choices." This decision already taken by the President with approval of the National Security Council would give the United States and other free nations "a maximum deterrent at a bearable cost." Local defenses could not turn aside the land power of the communist world; local forces needed "the further deterrent of massive retaliatory power." Aggressors must know that they could not prescribe battle conditions that suited them where they had superiority in manpower. Dulles restated his belief in the need of allies and the importance of collective security—factors made "more effective, less costly" by "placing more reliance on deterrent power, and less dependence on local defensive power."[3]

Dulles first had introduced deterrence in Paris in the spring of 1952 when he related it to Korea and Indochina. French statesmen and the French and American press then had hailed his pronouncement.

Fear of massive retaliation had forced the Chinese Communists, he believed, to prompt the North Koreans into the Korean armistice in July, 1953. At the outset of the new Administration, Mao Tse-tung had frustrated all efforts to end the Korean conflict, certain that China could exact more favorable terms from Eisenhower because of campaign promises to end the war. Sometime in early 1953 the exasperated President had authorized Dulles to drop the information that "in the absence of satisfactory progress" the United States would not be inhibited from using its atomic arsenal and "would no longer be responsible for confining hostilities to the Korean Peninsula." The Secretary relayed the statement, probably through Whitehall, to Prime Minister Jawaharlal Nehru of India, to a "contact" in Hong Kong, and to another "contact" present at truce negotiations at Panmunjom. Dulles was certain the warning got through and that it had achieved the Korean armistice.[4]

Would the threat of massive retaliation work again? The idea, he told members and guests of the Council on Foreign Relations in January, 1954, "has been applied to foreign policy." In Korea in 1953 the Administration had "effected a major transformation" and ended the fighting "on honorable terms" because the aggressor faced "the possibility that the fighting might, to his own great peril, soon spread beyond the limits and methods which he had selected." New aggression by the Red Chinese army in Indochina, he said, would produce "grave consequences which might not be confined to Indochina."[5]

The timing of Dulles' speech seemed favorable. So, too, were first reactions. During early 1954 the United States had nuclear superiority over the Russians. The USSR had exploded a hydrogen-type nuclear device in August, 1953, but the Defense Department was certain the Soviets did not yet have the means of delivery. Dulles was about to leave for a conference in Berlin with the foreign ministers of Britain, France, and the Soviet Union—the first such meeting in five years. He wished to negotiate from strength, wanted the communists to know the United States had the will as well as capacity to use atomic weapons. There also was a domestic reason, involving finances: increased reliance on air power and atomic weapons (the "new look") would give the United States a military force commensurate with a balanced budget. "More bang for the buck," publicists were saying.[6]

Unfortunately the Secretary's well-laid plans went awry. Shortly after the address a series of sensational events dramatized the phrase "massive retaliation," distorting it, causing dismay among the allies and apprehension throughout the world.[7] First came some hair-raising revelations of thermonuclear explosions carried out by the United States at Eniwetok in November, 1952. A five-megaton force had ripped a mile-wide crater in the ocean's floor, devastating an area six miles in diameter. The world had scarcely assimilated this fact when the United States on

March 1, 1954, detonated a huge hydrogen bomb, the destructiveness of which far exceeded the expectation of scientists who had developed it. The Soviet Union would need seven years to explode a bigger weapon. These disclosures and sophisticated public speculations on radioactive fall-out caused shudders, and led to questioning of the theory of massive retaliation. The March, 1954, explosion, especially, brought trouble. A little Japanese tuna trawler, the *Lucky Dragon,* had wandered into the fall-out area, and its crew received a near-fatal dose of radioactivity; one crew member died of after-effects. The United States Atomic Energy Commission shamefacedly had to lower its "maximum permissible dosage" for exposure. The American Government made monetary payments to the injured crew members or their relatives. When all this information became public there was a great to-do, a flood of polemics, a tide of books mixing sociology, politics, religion, and foreign policy.

World reaction to the American nuclear explosions was not lost on Soviet leaders, and Stalin's successors shrewdly put themselves forward as advocates of a "relaxation of international tensions." Here was opportunity to capitalize the fear of war, to increase distrust of Washington, undermine the will of the West, protect the Soviet Union against hostilities in Europe and elsewhere while accelerating efforts in the nuclear arms race where the Soviets were lagging behind the United States.

Questions increased in a near-deafening crescendo.

Where, when, and under what circumstances, would the United States use its massive retaliatory power? Indochina? inside the Iron Curtain? who would decide—the United States, the allies? what, exactly, was "by means and at places of our choosing"? Speaking within a week of the Bikini explosion, Adlai Stevenson asked almost the same points Eisenhower had raised in May, 1952. How would the United States react to covert aggression, or to Soviet threats to Berlin? The so-called new look in foreign policy, said the titular head of the Democratic Party, was no new look at all. Massive retaliation left the United States with the "grim choice of inaction or a thermonuclear holocaust," inviting Peking and Moscow to devour us with a series of small bites. Former Secretary of State Acheson thought Dulles' policy would lead to nuclear war. Strategic bombing, he said, should be a last resort, not a first. He feared his successor's theories would weaken the Western coalition, strengthen Russian leadership in the communist world, and alienate the uncommitted nations. In allied capitals many people questioned anew the reliability of the United States. Would America aid its allies and risk destruction of its own cities?

Dulles had to explain, and beginning with his press conference of March 16, 1954, he repeatedly attempted to clarify. He did not intend to brandish nuclear weapons or suggest that the United States would drop atomic bombs on Russia in reprisal for "the outbreak of small-scale conflicts anywhere in the world" or turn every local war into a holocaust.

His purpose was to make clear that an aggressor could not count on superior conventional military power to overwhelm areas like Western Europe. The purpose of the Administration's new policy was not massive retaliation but deterrence. The allies should know that America would consult them, that it was not moving away from collective security, and did not intend to pull forces out of Europe. Deterrence was in large part dictated by desire to encourage "European allies, some of whom hesitated to believe that the United States would risk destruction to come to their assistance if they were attacked." Massive retaliation, Dulles held, was militarily correct "because it enables the United States to concentrate its forces at the points of greatest danger, particularly in Western Europe, the Formosa Strait and the United States." To disperse American forces would be a grave mistake: "Nothing could be more dangerous than . . . to scatter our forces in many areas." The Administration did not intend "to rely wholly on large-scale strategic bombing as the sole means to deter and counter aggression." Small tactical nuclear weapons, recently tested, had made possible "less reliance upon deterrence by vast nuclear power." At the end of 1954, Dulles summarized his defense of massive retaliation in milder tones. The greatest contribution the United States could make to the peace of the world, he said in November, was "to be ready to fight if need be, and to have the resources and the allies to assure that an aggressor would surely be defeated." This "does not mean being truculent or provocative or militaristic. It does mean seeking peace not only with the heart but also with the mind."[8]

In all the discussion of atoms and peace, laced with talk of massive retaliation and lucky dragons and radioactive fall-out, surrounded by speeches, articles, pamphlets, and books, there was a more quiet development toward the end of the year 1954 when the UN General Assembly approved the President's "atoms for peace" plan. The endorsement set a course which promised a more serene future for mankind. Secretary Dulles must have observed this action with relief.

When Dulles in January, 1954, had warned the Chinese Communists to stay out of Indochina, threatening them with massive retaliation, he was sure they would not miss his meaning. Then the month of March began with a thermonuclear bang heard round the world, prompting an historic controversy over massive retaliation. Dulles became less sure of the Chinese. It was in the same month that a decision proved necessary over Indochina which set the scene for the military intervention of a decade later.

CHAPTER TEN

INDOCHINA

1

WITH the end of the war in Korea, the French military and political position in Indochina continued to deteriorate. All of Southeast Asia lay in peril. Should America fill the vacuum created by French military blunders in Indochina and political weakness in Paris? If so, by what means? What was the nature of the American commitment, if any, in Indochina? Secretary Dulles reviewed the record of his predecessors and concluded that the fundamental blunder had come in 1945 when the United States, victorious over the Japanese empire, allowed France to return to Indochina. President Roosevelt had been against it. At the conferences in Cairo and Teheran he had urged that Indochina become an international trusteeship, against strong opposition from Churchill and General Charles de Gaulle but with concurrence of Generalissimo Chiang Kai-shek and Stalin, so Dulles understood.[1] But the Truman Administration, overwhelmed by problems of the Chinese civil war, allowed the French to restore the French colonial position. Unable to win the loyalty of the native population, the French tried to preserve their position by military force. This offered a popular issue against which the French could not easily prevail, and led to uprisings.

During the first year of his presidency Eisenhower, like Truman before him, offered financial and military aid to French Union forces to help surmount communist threats and deter Chinese Communist aggression as in Korea. No suggestion had come from the French or from any other quarter that the United States should intervene militarily. When Eisenhower began his second year, conditions in Indochina became critical. France looked for a way out—either through direct American military involvement or through capitulation. This was the grim situation as Dulles readied himself for the Berlin Conference of Foreign Ministers scheduled for January 25, 1954. There was to be no agenda at the conference; the purpose was to discuss problems of Austria, Germany, and Korea. The Secretary expected the Soviet delegation to use the occasion to disrupt allied unity, to frustrate the proposed EDC, and prevent Franco-German reconciliation.

Indochina offered an excellent opportunity at the meeting for the Soviets to drive a wedge between the United States and France, and Foreign Minister Molotov lost no time in trying to woo France away from the United States. Aware of pressures on the Laniel government to achieve a settlement in Indochina, he hinted to Bidault during the second day of the conference that peace might be possible for the price of French rejection of EDC and concessions on Germany. According to information given to Dulles,

Bidault refused. But at the end of the first week Bidault began to weaken, ready to accept the suggestion that at the hoped-for Korean Political Conference, called for Geneva on April 26, 1954, "the problem of restoring peace in Indochina" would also be discussed. Supported by Eden, Bidault urged Dulles to agree.[2]

The Secretary counseled against discussion of Indochina at Geneva. He tried to convince Bidault that any suggestion to negotiate would place France and the United States on slippery ground, leading to deterioration of French morale and adverse effects in the United States. The communist Vietminh forces, Dulles cautioned, would intensify their efforts to gain a military success prior to the Geneva Conference.

While Dulles labored at dissuasion, he learned of Congressional lack of confidence in French military activity in Indochina and fear of American concessions to Communist China at Geneva. He felt concern when Under Secretary Smith informed him and the President that the Congressional mood stemmed from an interview the French Minister of National Defense, Pleven, had granted five senior American correspondents. Pleven had said that only Communist China could resolve the Indochina problem, and that in return the Chinese would demand recognition and an easing of the trade embargo. The key nation to make concessions was the United States. Smith felt that Pleven was extremely free with the American position. Angered by Pleven's injudicious statement, Eisenhower reacted by saying that if such were French thinking why did they not withdraw their request for military aid?[3]

Dulles' opposition to discussing Indochina at the conference had no result. Bidault, pressed by Pleven and manipulated by Molotov, refused to change his position. Bidault said he had to do something to end the war in Indochina, else "the bottom will fall out" in France. Dulles was conscious of the close relation of EDC to Indochina, and knew that Molotov had been trying to take advantage of it. For months Dulles had been blunt with the French over EDC, warning that if EDC failed it would be impossible for the United States to maintain that France was a major European or world power. The Secretary threatened to revert to bilateral cooperation with Great Britain as during the war years. But too much pressure might destroy hope for EDC and an honorable settlement in Indochina. American exhortation against a conference might carry a moral obligation to sustain French military operations on a much larger scale. Moreover, displeasure over the French military effort and French desire to negotiate might lead Congress either to end financial and material support or attach conditions which the French would reject as inconsistent with their sovereignty. Should this happen, Dulles wrote Eisenhower, anti-American reaction in France would be severe, and almost certainly defeat EDC. Dulles agreed to a compromise proposal for a restricted four-power conference on the Far East in Geneva on April 26, 1954. He found it necessary to assure the French that the Americans would carry out their agreement to continue aid. By that time American aid had amounted to a billion dollars in supplies and equipment.[4]

As Dulles predicted, after the Berlin Conference the Vietminh forces undertook a drive for military success prior to the Geneva Conference. Activity began on March 13 with the siege of the French fortress at Dienbienphu, a tactic which opened a new chapter in Indochina. With disaster imminent, France hoped for American intervention, and three times in 1954, twice in April and once in May, the French asked for direct involvement.[5]

The President and Secretary of State repeatedly had warned Communist China that the United States would take a grave view of open Chinese aggression in Indochina. In autumn of 1953, after discussion with French Ambassador Henri Bonnet, Dulles publicly singled out Communist China as the nation that was training and supplying communist forces in Indochina and was ready to send its armies into that area. "The Chinese Communist regime," he said on September 2, "should realize that such a second aggression could not occur without grave consequences which might not be confined to Indochina." The Secretary repeated the warning in his massive retaliation speech in January, 1954.[6]

The Chinese did not attack openly. Their troops were not in the trenches around Dienbienphu. They did furnish artillery, emplaced on the surrounding hills.

The Eisenhower Administration had anticipated

French military reversals and considered intervention, but long before the battle of Dienbienphu it had decided that the United States would intervene only if the war were international, if there were a clear invitation from the native population, and only if the French would agree to independence of the Associated States of Indochina, namely, Laos, Cambodia, and Vietnam. French leaders had learned that American forces would never go into action "where it would be logical or possible to describe such intervention as an effort to perpetuate colonial rule." Two weeks after the siege began, the French Chief of Staff, General Paul Ely, stopped in Washington on his way back to France from Indochina, and accompanied by Admiral Arthur W. Radford, Chairman of the Joint Chiefs of Staff, he called on Dulles to discuss military problems. He asked whether the United States would intervene with air power if Communist China's air force attacked French planes bringing supplies to Dienbienphu. Dulles replied that "if the United States sent its flag and its own military establishment—land, sea or air—into the Indo-China war, then the prestige of the United States would be engaged to a point where we would want to have a success." The United States could not "suffer a defeat which would have world-wide repercussions."[7] If the French wanted American participation they must realize it would require greater partnership than hitherto, notably in relation to independence for the Associated States and for training indigenous groups. Nothing came of this proposal, perhaps because there was no intervention by Communist China. Presence of the French chargé d'affaires during the talks nonetheless had alerted Dulles to the certainty that a French Government request would follow. At suggestion of the President he reviewed for Congressional leaders the situation in Indochina and possible American action He told them the Administration was considering a public call for united action in Indochina and would appreciate their endorsement. Pleased with their favorable response, the Secretary drafted a memorandum. Obtaining Eisenhower's approval and showing the memo to leaders of both parties, he submitted it to ambassadors of nations closely involved in Indochina.

Dulles incorporated the memorandum in his speech of March 29, 1954, in which after describing the worsening situation and the steps the United States had undertaken to assist the French, he apprised the nation of the Russian and Chinese threat in Southeast Asia. "The United States feels that that possibility should not be passively accepted, but should be met by united action. This might mean serious risks. But these risks are far less than those that will face us a few years from now, if we dare not be resolute today."[8]

A week later, April 7, 1954, Eisenhower in a press conference described Indochina's position as similar to one piece in a row of dominoes: if one falls it upsets the rest.

Dulles on April 3 apparently had asked Congressional leaders to meet with him and Radford at the

Department. The sense of the gathering was that the United States should not intervene in Indochina alone, but attempt to secure cooperation of other free nations in Southeast Asia, and that Congress then probably would authorize participation.[9] Next day Dulles and Radford saw the President. The decision was to invite Britain and France to cooperate in "united action" in Indochina and Southeast Asia. Eisenhower wrote Churchill urging support of a new coalition to check communist expansion in Southeast Asia—the United Kingdom, France, the Associated States, Australia, New Zealand, Thailand, the Philippines. "If I may refer again to history," the President explained, "we failed to halt Hirohito, Mussolini and Hitler by not acting in unity and in time. That marked the beginning of many years of stark tragedy and desperate peril. May it not be that our nations have learned something from that lesson?"[10] The allies immediately requested that Dulles come to London and Paris. Before leaving, the Secretary consulted diplomatic representatives of Great Britain, France, Australia, New Zealand, the Philippines, Thailand, and the Associated States. He informed other Asian governments. The ambassadors of Thailand and the Philippines showed willingness to join in action; other envoys thought their governments would be sympathetic.

On the very day (April 4) of the White House meeting of Radford and Dulles and Eisenhower, Laniel and Bidault through the American Ambassador in Paris, Dillon, requested prompt American intervention in Dienbienphu. Dillon reported to Dulles who, consulting the President, replied he had explained to Ely, in the presence of Radford (March 23), that the United States could not become a belligerent without full political understanding with France and other interested countries and without Congressional approval. Eisenhower had prepared to consider united action in Indochina based on a coalition of nations including British Commonwealth countries.[11]

The Secretary accompanied by Walter Robertson thereupon left for London and Paris on April 10. Talks with Churchill and Eden lasted two days. Dulles was certain he had succeeded in bringing the British to the American view of the need to do something before the Geneva Conference. The final communique, which pleased him, said among other things:

> We deplore the fact on the eve of the Geneva Conference the Communist forces in Indochina are increasingly developing their activities into a large-scale war against the forces of the French Union. . . . We realize that these activities not only threaten those now directly involved, but also endanger the peace and security of the entire area of Southeast Asia and the Western Pacific. . . .
>
> Accordingly we are ready to take part, with the other countries principally concerned, in an examination of the possibility of establishing a collective defense, within the framework of the Charter of the United Nations, to assure the peace, security

> and freedom of Southeast Asia and the Western Pacific.[12]

Dulles' report to the President was optimistic: the British accepted the American view of danger in Indochina, and the need for united action.

Nevertheless he left with an uneasy feeling, for his conversation with Churchill and Eden had revealed that the British had determined to oppose use of their ground forces in Indochina and had rejected the theory that loss of northern Vietnam would mean loss of the entire area. Churchill evidently did not share Eisenhower's domino theory. British leaders, Dulles told the President, were more interested in a buffer state in the north which in conjunction with a South Asian NATO-type alliance could stem Chinese Communism. Dulles was satisfied that he had taken a big step toward winning over the British. Friendliness of the London press gratified him, as did the *Daily Worker*'s compliment that he was the most unwelcome guest since 1066.[13]

Accompanied by Robertson, Dillon, Douglas MacArthur II, and Lieutenant Colonel Vernon A. Walters (interpreter), Dulles met Laniel and Bidault in Paris on April 14. The Secretary told them he had persuaded the British to come close to the American and French position and showed the text of the joint British-American communique. Laniel congratulated him on doing a difficult chore. Before discussing Indochina, Dulles talked at length on the importance of EDC. Events in Indochina and elsewhere had made

EDC more important for the United States. Americans could not stand still while France made up its mind. Laniel said he intended to announce next day the date of opening parliamentary debate on EDC though he realized the risks. Dulles said he was ready to issue a declaration thirty-six hours afterward, which he believed would have a good effect on French public opinion. It was imperative that France demonstrate a capacity to act; there was no weakness greater than indecision. Dulles was certain that once the French deputies realized the position France would occupy in EDC, they would appreciate that there was no alternative way to augment France's power and prestige in Europe and the world. There was much more at stake than a mere signature ratifying a treaty: the fraternity of nations was in danger. Should France choose to go it alone, American public opinion might move toward isolationism, which would be a calamity. French leaders had opportunity not only to save France but the free world, including the United States. At this point Reynaud, who had come late to the meeting, expressed concern over reports that some American generals doubted French ability to win the war in Indochina. France's greatest disappointment, Reynaud said, was the Vietnamese army. Dulles answered that he saw no difference between the people who made up the Vietnam forces and those of the Vietminh, just as there was no difference between the peoples of North and South Korea. Training and inspiration could instill energy and will to victory. Laniel and Reynaud regretted that no Syngman Rhee led the Vietnamese. The Frenchmen assured Dulles that the Paris government would grant full independence to the Associated States within the French Union, thus removing the Asian accusation that France was a colonial power. At the end of discussions Laniel and Dulles prepared a joint statement which read in part:

> We recognize that the prolongation of the war in Indochina, which endangers the security of the countries immediately affected, also threatens the entire area of Southeast Asia and of the Western Pacific. In close association with other interested nations, we will examine the possibility of establishing, within the framework of the United Nations Charter, a collective defense to assure the peace, security and freedom of this area.[14]

2

Dulles returned home and within a few days proposed—to Washington representatives of France, Great Britain, Australia, New Zealand, the Philippines, Thailand, Laos, Cambodia, and Vietnam—a meeting on April 20, 1954, to examine "the possibility of establishing a collective defense, within the framework of the Charter of the United Nations, to assure the peace, security and freedom of Southeast Asia and the Western Pacific." It was shortly thereafter that he heard from the British Ambassador, Sir Roger Makins, that the latter had instructions not to attend. The British

Government thought such a meeting premature. Privately, later publicly, Churchill and Eden showed reluctance to organize action until the Geneva Conference was more clear. The American plan for collective action collapsed. The allies faced the Geneva Conference divided.[15]

Under such a pall of confusion the foreign ministers of France, Britain, and the United States met for the NATO ministerial council on April 23, 1954, their last opportunity to bind the allies. In the middle of the afternoon on opening day Bidault beckoned Dulles aside to show him a message from General Henri-Eugene Navarre to Laniel which described the situation at Dienbienphu as desperate. The French commander in Indochina saw only two alternatives: a massive B-29 bombing from American bases, or an immediate cease-fire. Bidault asked Dulles to meet with him that evening, and the Secretary consented, but added that B-29 intervention was out of the question "under existing circumstances." He promised to pass Navarre's assessment to the President, and discuss it with Radford. Dulles felt sorry for the Foreign Minister: "Bidault gives the impression," he wrote Eisenhower, "of a man close to the breaking point . . . it has been painful to watch him presiding over the council. . . . He is obviously exhausted and is confused and rambling in his talk."[16]

Eisenhower replied to Dulles' message that he understood these feelings of frustration. He recalled efforts to get the French to internationalize the war, and attempts to convince the British of the seriousness of a French defeat. He asked Dulles to try again to awaken the British who must not shut their eyes and later plead blindness for failure to propose a program. Churchill, he informed the Secretary, had cabled asking for a meeting in Washington on May 20; he saw no profit in it and wanted to refuse.[17]

Accompanied by MacArthur and Dillon, Dulles met that evening with Laniel and Maurice Schumann. Laniel analyzed the French military situation as grave. Dienbienphu, symbol of resistance and prestige, might fall any day. He feared the morale of the Vietnamese; there was the possibility of mass desertions. In France the loss of Dienbienphu would overthrow his government. These prospects forced him to ask for direct American military assistance. The Secretary answered that the United States had done everything to help France, short of belligerency. Military action required approval of Congress. He would seek Congressional approval on condition that Britain agree to join the military defense of Indochina, and that the states in Indochina achieve true independence. The latter point presented no difficulty, for France had agreed. The key was Britain, and Dulles would do what he could to convince the British. Meanwhile France must hold firm should Dienbienphu fall, France should not panic. Sure that his government would go down, Laniel remained silent.

On the following day, April 24, 1954, Dulles and Radford met Eden, Bidault, and Laniel, and the Secretary opened discussion by asking the French their position if Dienbienphu fell. Laniel and Bidault answered they would like the fighting to go on, but were not sure of other members of the government or of French opinion. Dienbienphu had become a symbol. They acknowledged that trying to hold Dienbienphu was a mistake. Dulles asked if France would agree to a cease-fire before the Geneva Conference. Bidault answered no, he wanted to go to Geneva with his hands free. At this point Eden threw in a bombshell. Referring to the communique of April 13 he said the United Kingdom was not committed to intervention in the Indochina war; he wanted no misunderstanding. He said that if France wished to ask his government for action with respect to Indochina, he would be glad to take this request to London. He was not, he said, suggesting this; he thought it would be a mistake. Bidault made no reply except that France was war-weary and that he was not proud. He would appreciate anything to strengthen the French force in Indochina. Dulles spoke of Navarre's belief that the alternative to a cease-fire was immediate and massive American air power, and showed Bidault a draft letter he had dispatched to Washington for consideration, and asked whether such a letter would help. The gist of the draft was that while time perhaps had run out for the garrison at Dienbienphu, the United States was ready to intervene provided France, Great Britain, and other allies joined. Bidault thought it would be useful; it disturbed Eden, who glanced at it. The Secretary asked Bidault whether the joint communique issued in Paris still stood. The Foreign Minister replied it did, and he also understood that Great Britain did not have to intervene in Indochina, despite the London communique. Dulles left believing Bidault would do his best to limit the loss of Dienbienphu. Eden thought Britain would have to make a "decision of first-class importance," whether or not to go along with the American plan, and decided to return to London to discuss it with the cabinet.[18]

Next day Dulles flew to Geneva, and at ten that evening he called on Eden who had just arrived from the London meeting with Churchill, the cabinet, and the Chiefs of Staff. Britain, he told Dulles, opposed intervention. The British Chiefs were sure it would have no effect. Evidently they were confident they could hold Malaya. After discussion with the British Chiefs, Radford concluded they saw no relation between Indochina and EDC and NATO. Their approach, he thought, was narrow—local British interests, without regard to other areas in the Far East such as Japan. While Eden regretted bringing news which was not what Dulles would like to hear, he did have some proposals. The communists, he said, knew the allies were considering united action. His proposals would in no way remove that advantage, since the communists would be guessing as to what the allies would do if Geneva failed to yield an honorable solution. The Foreign Secretary outlined the British position: Her Majesty's Government would give the French all possible diplomatic support at Geneva to assure satisfactory settlement in Indochina; after such settlement Britain would join the United States and interested countries of Southeast Asia in guaranteeing the settlement; and would work with the United States on military measures to defend Thailand and the rest of Southeast Asia—but not Indochina—should France capitulate at Geneva. Without a settlement the British Government would examine united action with the United States.

Dulles saw nothing in the British proposals that could possibly help the French at the conference or on the battlefield. The British had increased the prospect of capitulation, if not unconditional surrender, he told Eden. He had reservations about immediate air intervention at Dienbienphu; it could not save the fortress, and would involve the United States in an unsound political and military venture. The important thing was to give the French hope, so as to take the loss of Dienbienphu. It would be a mistake, Dulles thought, to write off all Indochina and Southeast Asia. Thailand, Malaya, and Indonesia would fall, even Japan might go. Eden acknowledged the gap between the American and British positions. He had explained the British position to Bidault earlier that evening; the Foreign Minister had not raised questions and seemed resigned.

Now the United States stood alone; the British refused to fight in Indochina, and were not willing to have any conversation which assumed participation. Should the United States intervene to lift the siege? Would this strengthen French will? Dulles did not think so. American involvement could not save Dienbienphu. The Secretary was not certain that if the jungle outpost fell France would continue, even if the

United States entered the conflict. There was a strong possibility that a new French government might repudiate American participation, leaving the United States in an embarrassing position in the Western Pacific. Time was short to arrange a military and political understanding with France. Some French leaders might think the United States had intervened to prevent France from making peace. The United States might have been asked to replace French troops with American ground forces; refusal would confirm the view that the United States merely tried to keep France in the fight. Moreover, American action without British concurrence would affect relations with the Commonwealth. Direct American intervention might result in Chinese and Russian involvement, and general war in Asia.

With the Geneva Conference about to begin, the Laniel government made every effort to hold Dienbienphu, hoping the United States might convince the British to overcome internal political problems and find some means to allow military assistance. Laniel understood that British concurrence was a requisite for American action, but thought the United States might not hold to that condition. Dulles despaired of ability of the allies to act in unison. The decline of France, the impotence of Italy, and weakness of Britain created a situation, he believed, which required the United States to set out a right course, keeping in mind its own long-range interests and the importance of the allies. Resolute leadership would bring the allies to follow the United States, if not immediately then ultimately. But first a solution in a very troubled area.

Dulles again attempted to win over the British, on the last day of April. At high noon he met alone with Eden and told the latter he was greatly distressed over the British stand and its effect on American-British relations. He had believed the British Government had agreed to work out with other countries a common defense for Southeast Asia. In accord with the joint communique of April 13 he had called a conference for that purpose. The British Government now refused to attend, and indicated unwillingness to go ahead with the agreement he and Eden had signed in London. There were other reasons Dulles felt indignant. Not a single Western European power had answered recent vicious attacks on American policy in Korea by Molotov and the Communist Chinese Foreign Minister, Chou En-lai. Only South Korea, Colombia, and Australia had supported the United States. It was annoying for the United States to receive the label of "imperialist" when, following American tradition, it had been eager to sponsor nationalism in independent colonial areas, thus beating the communists at their own game. Washington had refrained from doing so in North Africa, the Middle East, and Asia, out of desire to help Britain and France. Geneva was presenting a pathetic spectacle of drift and indecision.

Dulles cautioned Eden that if efforts in Southeast Asia collapsed, the United States might follow its own policy: closer collaboration with Syngman Rhee and Chiang Kai-shek, who had defects but were willing to stand up. Aware that British reluctance to follow American leadership in Southeast Asia stemmed from fear of an atomic war with China, Dulles attempted to quiet these apprehensions and told Eden the United States did not seek war with China or even a large-scale invasion of Indochina.

At this point Eden, no doubt dazed by Dulles' frankness, handed him an eight-point memorandum of British views. It said that military means could not check communism in Asia, that the allies had to win the backing or at least benevolent neutrality of all countries in the area. To secure such support demanded preparation, not contrivance. The British did not share the American fear that French collapse in Indochina was imminent, but were ready to begin immediate and secret examination of a collective defense system for Southeast Asia.

Dulles did not think the memorandum useful. The United States had invited Thailand, the Philippines, Australia, and New Zealand to share in a Southeast Asian defense organization. The first two nations had agreed and the others showed interest. The North Atlantic Treaty, Dulles reminded Eden, had developed from the Brussels Pact, with addition of the United States and Canada, the Scandinavian countries (excluding Sweden and Finland), Portugal, Italy, and most recently Greece and Turkey. Surely any Southeast Asian arrangement would have to include Thailand, the Philippines, Australia, New Zealand, the United States, the United Kingdom, France, and the Associated States. Why could not a Southeast Defense Treaty begin with that nucleus and develop through natural progression? Eden did not reply.

In the afternoon of that same day, April 30, Dulles and Eden met Bidault who said that the tactical position of France had deteriorated as a result of the confusing positions of Britain and the United States. French interpretation of Eisenhower's press conferences, coupled with Churchill's recent speech, the obvious British repudiation of the Eden-Dulles communique, and lack of support in Paris, had removed communist uncertainty as to Western intentions. France had no bargaining position with the Vietminh. There was nothing to prevent a communist victory, no means to stop or moderate communist ambitions. The fall of Dienbienphu would mean loss of all Indochina, sure defeat of EDC, a possible threat to NATO. Dulles tried to encourage Bidault, and said he hoped Britain and other nations could revive communist doubts as to Western intentions, and perhaps the military situation would improve. Something could prevent total surrender and continue the war so as to reduce the drain on French manpower without involving American and British troops. Would it not be possible to hold some places with indigenous forces trained to resume the struggle? Bidault thought there was some merit in Dulles' ideas. After Bidault left, Dulles told Eden they should announce the beginning of discussions on what to do if the conference failed to produce a solution. The Foreign Secretary was not enthusiastic. He would think about it, he told Dulles.[19]

CHAPTER ELEVEN

THE GENEVA CONFERENCE OF 1954

1

DIENBIENPHU fell on May 7, 1954. Next day the Geneva Conference held its first plenary session on Indochina. That same day Ambassador Bonnet called on Dulles in Washington to ask that the United States "internationalize" the war. The French Government could not wait until conclusion of the Geneva Conference; by then all Indochina might have gone. The French were aware that the United States would not intervene unilaterally, that Australia could not decide until after the May 29 elections, that Britain—probably because of fear for Hong Kong, pressure from Nehru, and other reasons—would not help. But it was imperative that France know what the United States was willing to do. Dulles told Bonnet the United States was prepared to talk, but not until after the vote of confidence in the French Assembly scheduled for the next day, May 9. Meanwhile he would discuss the request with the President and Congressional leaders.

Three days later, on May 11, Dulles made his decision. He felt it no longer feasible to internationalize the war. France might decide to internationalize or surrender, and might well do the latter. He told Bedell Smith to inform Laniel that Eisenhower would ask Congress for authority to use armed force to support friendly, recognized governments against aggression or subversion, under certain conditions. As summarized by Dulles on June 11 in Los Angeles these latter were: (1) an invitation from local authorities; (2) independence for Laos, Cambodia, and Vietnam; (3) evidence of concern by the United Nations; (4) collective effort of other nations in the area; and (5) assurance that France would not withdraw until after winning the battle.[1] Dulles believed France wanted to use the United States as a lever to obtain better terms at Geneva. He saw no objection, so long as France did not commit him to action incompatible with the above conditions. Without independence to Vietnam and the other Associated States, the Philippines and Thailand would not join a collective defense system in Southeast Asia, and, of course, the United States did not want to lead a white Western coalition which all the Asian states would shun. Dulles insisted that France keep him informed before reaching any decisions so that he could express his views, and if the French then ignored his views he could dissociate the United States from the French position.

In the middle of May, Maurice Schumann, after seeing Bidault in Geneva told the American Ambassador in Paris that a successful settlement was impossible without American military involvement. Perhaps the United Nations could come in, as Thailand had suggested. Bidault had been against bringing in the United Nations because of fear of the Arab block, but was now more hopeful, especially because the United States considered participation by the United Nations important. France was ready to accede and promised to be helpful if the matter went before the United Nations, provided that Laos and Cambodia joined Thailand in support. Meanwhile, as preparations continued to involve the United Nations, Schumann urged that America commit ground troops in Vietnam, say 20,000 Marines. (France did not use conscripts in Indochina, and could not ask for American draftees.) He warned that France could not keep its forces indefinitely in Indochina. Parliament would not ratify EDC so long as France had an obligation to retain men in Indochina for an indeterminate period. Schumann presented the United States with a sort of ultimatum: France would ratify EDC only if it had the right to decrease and then withdraw troops from Indochina.

With agreement at Geneva in the offing, Dulles wondered how to avoid a commitment contrary to American principles. What should be the American response to possible Soviet demands that the principal powers including the United States guarantee the settlement? Such a guarantee might well prevent the United States from liberating these peoples from communist captivity. He had pledged never to acquiesce in subjugation of Eastern European peoples. A promise to sustain communist domination of Vietnam, Laos, and Cambodia would be out of the question. Eden and Bidault, he thought, should know this. Perhaps Molotov. It was disquieting that Russia might advance a proposal which would salvage something for the French, contingent on American guarantees. And should the United States decline, the communists could use the refusal as an excuse to deny France even minimal face-saving. The United States would have to be careful not to fall into this trap, certain to cause anti-American feeling in France, with effects on EDC and NATO.

Western disunity raised communist hopes. "They have a big fish on the hook," Bedell Smith reported to Dulles on May 20, "and intend to play it out." Communist negotiators at Geneva expected as a maximum to obtain control of all Indochina; as a minimum, parts of Vietnam, Laos, and Cambodia. Indications were that Chou En-lai and Ho Chi Minh trusted British pressure to restrain the United States from intervention.The continuing weakness of the French Government, on the edge of survival, coupled with Churchill's statement on May 17, 1954, that Britain would make no commitment prior to a Geneva settlement, reassured Asian communists that time was on their side. It was to their interest to prolong the meeting by not making concessions. Indochina was falling into their hands.

When the Geneva meeting seemed bound to become a drawn-out affair, another Panmunjom, Molotov suddenly took initiative toward an early settlement. At the end of May he invited Bedell Smith, Walter Robertson, Herman Phleger, and other top American officials for dinner and discussions. Molotov,

Gromyko, Smith, and Robertson met privately, and the Soviet Foreign Minister asked for Smith's view on Vietnam, Laos, and Cambodia. The Under Secretary replied that conditions differed in each. He acknowledged that in Vietnam the forces of Ho Chi Minh were well-organized, disciplined, and controlled large parts of the country, and that two hostile ideologies did exist. Solution of the problem required an armistice and withdrawal to specified areas, followed by a political settlement supervised by neutral authorities. Laos and Cambodia, plagued by small dissident elements, were viable states. Molotov agreed with Smith's analysis, but not with his estimate of the size of the dissident elements. Smith suggested that a neutral committee sent into the area could ascertain the truth, but Molotov countered that such a survey would delay the conference.

Molotov wanted to bring France, Vietnam, and the Vietminh together. Smith did not know if France would respond, nor could he recommend that the French do so. The American position on Indochina was not the same as that on Korea. The United States was not a belligerent although it assisted France and the Associated States. France was an ally, and Great Britain, another ally, was in Malaya. The United States had a treaty with the Philippines, as well as other historic and recent commitments in the Pacific. Molotov understood but was disturbed about reports that the United States did not want an end to the fighting. The Under Secretary denied this, adding that Washington wanted an honorable cessation of hostilities but would never accept any capitulation by force of arms.

Molotov was frank, pleasant, self-confident, objective, and detached. His attitude, so drastically different from his behavior during the Stalin regime encouraged Smith to bring up American-Russian and American-Chinese relations. The Soviet Union, Smith said, was surely aware that the United States wanted peace and friendship. After a long era of name-calling the United States and Russia had sat down at a conference table to seek solutions to world problems. He could not say the same for Russia's associate. Communist China, Molotov answered, was a young country and would always be Chinese—never European. The USSR, he asserted, had worked out its relation with China; why could not the United States? Smith reminded Molotov that China and the Soviet Union shared an ideology, which helped understanding. Molotov implied that this was not entirely true and that the United States was not the only worried nation.

The Under Secretary asserted that United States intervention in Korea stemmed from deep-rooted moral principles. When the Chinese moved into Korea, the United States could have dealt with them easily, had it been willing to use all available resources. This it had not done. America had suffered thousands of casualties rather than commit its prestige and possibly that of the Soviet Union. There was a line beyond which compromise could not go. The

United States was ready to promote an honorable peace in Indochina. Molotov said he understood the American position, and hinted that someday it would become known that the Soviet Union had restrained the Chinese during the Korean War! Was he implying he was doing the same at Geneva?

2

If Molotov's decision to expedite the Geneva Conference encouraged the American delegation, optimism proved illusory, for the government of Joseph Laniel fell on June 12, 1954. Four days later Prince Buu Loc, Prime Minister of Vietnam, gave way to Ngo Dinh Diem, then in Paris. Next day Pierre Mendes-France, a Radical Socialist leader, promised that if elected to head a new French government he would end the war within four weeks, by July 20, or resign. The National Assembly endorsed him as Premier (419-47) on June 18. He also assumed the office of Foreign Minister.

Mendes-France indeed had determined to end the war in Indochina. A quick settlement, he believed, would revive French spirits and unite the country. Under no condition would he accept peace based on surrender or a disguised capitulation. As for EDC, the Premier favored it, but did not think the time ready, as long as the war in Indochina prevented French forces from returning home. An end to hostilities surely would enhance his prestige, enabling him to ask the Assembly to make a decision on EDC.

Mendes-France met Chou En-lai on June 23, and the Chinese Communist leader was conciliatory, recognizing for the first time the existence of the state of Vietnam; he accepted the French proposal that a cease-fire should lead immediately to a political settlement; agreed to a division of Vietnam into two states eventually unified by direct negotiations; agreed to postpone a plebiscite; promised to press the Vietminh to speed negotiations in Geneva. The National Assembly, pleased with Mendes-France's activity, gave him a larger vote of confidence (433-23).

Steady Vietminh advances in Indochina marred the progress at Geneva. By the first week of July, French Union forces were ready to begin armistice talks. At this point Mendes-France asked that Dulles or his Under Secretary return to Geneva to head the American delegation, downgraded since June 19 to an "observer" mission. Dulles did not want to go to Geneva, but finally agreed to meet the Premier in Paris. Here was opportunity to restate the American position and obtain, firsthand, views of the new French Government. For some time Dulles had felt that the French were increasingly confused by columnists and commentators, presidential press conferences, as well as their own interpretations of American policies.

In Paris on July 13 the Secretary opened by saying he wished to review the American position, and do so frankly. Mendes-France liked the suggestion, volunteering that he was a neophyte; his ambition had been the ministry of finance and perhaps the premiership, but not the ministry of foreign affairs. Dulles then stressed three themes. First, the United States had confidence in Mendes-France and appreciated his new approach. Hitherto French indecision and political weakness had created major obstacles in relations with the United States and the allied nations. France had agreed repeatedly to take certain decisions, only to abandon them. French procrastinations and recent signs of unwillingness or inability to honor commitments concerned Dulles. Mendes-France's forthright promise to press for immediate decisions was encouraging. Secondly, the United States, the Secretary said, knew that France had overextended in Indochina. Dulles did not want the Premier to think the American Government had been pushing France to make impossible pledges. It had always been aware of the gap between French responsibilities in Europe and Indochina, and capability to meet them. The United States had given France billions of dollars and this aid, in fact, had increased French dollar reserves.

Dulles' third point related to EDC and Germany. The Soviet objective, he said, was to keep Germany and France apart, to prevent European unity, and deny Germany partnership with the West. Exposed and neutral, Germany might fall into the communist orbit. So long as there was no unity in Europe, Russia would continue to harass France in Europe, Indochina, North Africa, and elsewhere. The United States together with the allies wanted to begin negotiation with the Soviet Union but only from strength. Dulles referred to the recent Eisenhower-Churchill talks in Washington (June 25-29, 1954) in which the two leaders had drawn up a protocol to restore sovereignty to Germany. The time had come to permit Germany full participation in Western European defense. Recent conversations had alerted him that the next Congress might not appropriate a single dollar for NATO unless France agreed to include Germany in a European defense system. France must act, or damage would be incalculable.

Mendes-France responded that he had always been a staunch supporter of European unity. There was no clear majority in the French parliament for EDC. Outright defeat, or passage by a slim majority, would be a victory for Russia, defeat for France, and a threat to NATO and European unity. Perhaps modification of the existing treaty might help passage by a substantial majority. Dulles explained this was unacceptable for it would reopen debate among the other nations, particularly Germany. It was essential to ratify EDC, however slim a majority. Mendes-France thought the probability for passage by even one vote was negligible. Long-term interests of the allies demanded that he delay, to find a proper formula to assure a reasonable majority.

Later that evening Dulles, accompanied by Phleger, Dillon, and Douglas MacArthur II, met with Mendes-France, and with Eden. The Premier reviewed the latest negotiations at Geneva. France had proposed roughly the 18th parallel as the partition line in Vietnam. The Vietminh countered with an S-shaped line in the vicinity of the 13th parallel; but after learning that Dulles was about to meet Mendes-France they suggested the 16th parallel. The Premier thought this shift attributable to Dulles' arrival. With respect to Laos the communists now admitted to Vietminh forces there, and agreed to withdraw them. They had insisted on elections within six months after hostilities, preceded by evacuation of French forces from Vietnam, but under pressure from Mendes-France agreed that the two political regimes of Vietnam should decide the election date later.

Dulles then gave a detailed comment on the American position. The objective of the Soviet Union at Geneva was to disrupt allied unity and prevent ratification of EDC. The Far East was a secondary object, a means to split France from the United States. Neither he nor Bedell Smith would return to Geneva. This decision he based on two fears: the communists might press for proposals conditional upon American guarantees, and should the United States turn these down France might charge Washington with failure to achieve peace in Indochina. At some point during the final stages of the negotiation France might inform the American delegation of need to accept a bad settlement, unless the United States entered the war on brief notice.

Mendes-France did not think he could avoid the dilemmas presented by Dulles even if high officials did not represent the United States. The communists did not want Dulles at Geneva. They would interpret his absence as a rift among the allies. The Secretary's or Smith's presence would force more reasonable terms. Eden said it could tip the balance in favor of the West. Dulles commented that he wanted to do everything in his power to end the Indochina war. Had the allies agreed to act three months ago, some naval and air power and a small ground force might have resolved the situation. Now it was too late. If the war resumed it might force the allies into a major war against a third-rate communist team in the Far East—a colossal military blunder.

The Secretary handed Mendes-France a seven-point memorandum outlining the American position for settlement of the war. It corresponded roughly to an agreement by Eisenhower and Churchill during their talks in Washington, calling for independence of Laos and Cambodia and division of Vietnam at approximately the 17th parallel. South Vietnam, Laos, and Cambodia were to have the right to maintain forces for self-defense, receive aid from the West, and employ foreign advisers. There were to be no political provisions which might lead to communist control of South Vietnam, and no hindrances of any kind to ultimate unification of Vietnam by peaceful means. The people of Vietnam were to have free migration north and south. The last point suggested international supervision. Mendes-France accepted the memorandum, promised to try to obtain such a settlement, and again asked Dulles to return to Geneva.

Satisfied with Mendes-France's reaction, the Secretary recommended to Eisenhower that Smith return to the conference, and Smith, though ill, agreed. Dulles departed Paris on July 15, leaving Mendes-France five days to secure a truce. The Geneva Conference concluded on July 21 with armistice agreements for Vietnam, Laos, and Cambodia—agreements dated July 20, which was Mendes-France's self-imposed deadline.

3

The settlement came remarkably close to the American seven-point memorandum. It partitioned Vietnam along the 17th parallel; prohibited foreign bases; allowed neither North nor South Vietnam to join a military alliance; provided for country-wide elections leading to unification by July 20, 1956; and established an International Control Commission to supervise the agreements. It was an accord between the French and Vietminh, the contestants in the war. They were to administer their respective territories until free elections. Both were to help people who wished to leave one zone for the other. This provision of approximately one year's duration led to a large refugee migration under American supervision, and had much meaning for later American policy in Vietnam. Neither the United States nor South Vietnam signed the document. As expected, Smith issued a unilateral declaration that the United States would "refrain from the threat or the use of force to disturb" the Geneva agreements, would view with grave concern any renewal of aggression, and would seek to achieve unity through free elections, supervised by the United Nations.[2]

The Geneva accords suspended the war in Indochina, but did not eliminate the sources of conflict in the Far East. They gave the communists a respite for the next phase, and the West opportunity to establish a collective security arrangement to meet the inevitable challenge. Vietnam joined the other divided nations of the world—residues of the cold war, sources of hot wars: Germany, Korea, China.

The communists hailed the Geneva Conference as a great victory, another defeat of the bankrupt policy of the United States. The Vietminh gained control of North Vietnam and opportunity to establish a communist state under Ho Chi Minh. Communist China, whose presence at Geneva increased its status as a power in the Far East, acquired a friendly and what seemed a dependent state on its border. Russia improved relations with the United States without losing face in the communist and nonaligned world, and managed for a while to restrain the Chinese Communist challenge to Soviet leadership. There was no escape from the fact that North Vietnam represented the first territorial gain for the communists since Mao Tse-tung's seizure of Tibet in 1950-51. They could have gotten much more had it not been for the United States, and perhaps the Soviet Union. Until the last day of the conference the communists were not sure the United States would intervene. Russia, concerned with Europe, pressed the Vietminh and Chinese Communists to agree on a formula acceptable to France. But regardless of differences between the two communist colossi, their object remained the same: to fortify control over areas held and to bring about gradual elimination of American influence from Europe and Asia. The Chinese reached the first stage of their strategy at Geneva; their second was about to begin. And when France rejected EDC on August 30, 1954, the Soviets too would gain.

What effect did the Geneva accords have in the West? Mendes-France announced that while the armistice was cruel it was the best available in the "present state of affairs." The British agreed. Prime Minister Nehru and other noncommunist statesmen felt relieved. The end of the war pleased the majority of Americans, the first world-wide peace since the early 1930s. Forgotten was the fact that the conference had failed to bring a political settlement in Korea—it would not come during Dulles' tenure, nor has it come as of this writing (1966).

What lessons did Dulles draw?Difficulties within the Western alliance had come into view. It had been a ticklish business to combine pleas for unity with warnings to each of the allies; to hide the gaps among them and warn communists of united action; to urge local populations to ignore the Vietminh cry for self-rule and cooperate with the French forces; to press France to grant independence and continue the war; to proclaim a pacific intent and willingness to deter aggression. Dulles saw communists take success from their identification with social progress and nationalism, preempting and perverting the historic tradition of the United States. He thereafter sought to disengage the United States from French and British colonial involvements. "The important thing for now," he said two days after the conference, "is not to mourn the past but to seize the future opportunity to prevent the loss in northern Viet-Nam from leading to the extension of Communism throughout Southeast Asia." One of the lessons, he said, was that "resistance to Communism needs popular support."[3]

CHAPTER TWELVE

SECURITY FOR THE FAR EAST: SOUTH VIETNAM, SEATO, AND THE BRINK AT TAIWAN

WOULD Communist China and North Vietnam honor the spirit and intent of the Geneva accords of July, 1954? One day after the signing of the armistice Ho Chi Minh announced that the Geneva agreements would not hamper him in unifying Vietnam. "The struggle," he broadcasted, "will be long and difficult; all the peoples and soldiers of the north and the south must unite to conquer victory." Two weeks later Chou En-lai called for liberation of Taiwan and liquidation of "the traitorous Chiang Kai-shek group."[1]

Something had to be done, and Dulles was ready. The Secretary wanted to support strong nationalist governments, and thwart the communist threat in Southeast Asia and Taiwan with the probability of repercussions in Africa and the Middle East.

1

The first concern was Vietnam, Laos, and Cambodia, where Dulles believed that French presence was a liability—France must not reestablish influence in South Vietnam. The French had failed in the past and would fail again. The infant triplet states of Indochina had to be independent. He would have to offer them American economic and military aid.

Within a few weeks after the Geneva Conference he informed Mendes-France that the United States had readjusted its policies to meet new conditions. From now on Washington would deal directly with the Indochinese governments (with exception, of course, of North Vietnam). He notified Prime Minister Ngo Dinh Diem that he was ready to give economic and military aid. President Eisenhower acknowledged this policy; the purpose of American aid, the President wrote Diem, "is to assist the Government of Viet-nam in developing and maintaining a strong, viable state, capable of resisting attempted subversion or aggression through military means."[2] American direct aid to South Vietnam and the other states of Indochina suggested French withdrawal from that area, and so the French departed and the United States moved into the vacuum. If France still had responsibility for carrying out political provisions of the Geneva agreements, including free elections in 1956, authority now belonged to the United States, though it had not ratified the Geneva treaties and was not bound by them.[3]

The important problem for Washington was viability of the government of South Vietnam. Should the United States support Bao Dai, the erstwhile French puppet who was Chief of State? Or work with other groups? Dulles decided to help Diem, who had the makings of a Chiang Kai-shek or a Syngman Rhee. Diem also had support of such Americans as Francis Cardinal Spellman. Diem's promises to remake Vietnamese society, implant a national spirit, centralize authority, and fight communism, impressed the Secretary. The French advised Dulles to limit Diem's power. The Secretary took the recommendation seriously and resisted schemes and suggestions to build up Diem; he did not wish to tie America's prestige to Diem's grandiose plans for making South Vietnam a Western-style nation in Southeast Asia. On appropriate occasions he would tell the allies that he did not want to make it seem that Diem was an American protégé, or that the United States irrevocably had committed itself to him. But the policies of the Vietnamese leader—his stands on communism and nationalism—had, so it seemed to Dulles, the necessary ingredients for success. There was no other comparable leader in sight. And so Diem came eventually into an almost monarchical control of South Vietnam.[4]

American aid to Diem strengthened his control over army and administration. Soon the Prime Minister defeated and weakened the influence of various sects, and finally supplanted Bao Dai as Chief of State: South Vietnam became a republic in 1955 with Diem as its first President. When in 1956 North Vietnam invoking the Geneva agreements asked for free elections, Diem refused. A plebiscite might have united Vietnam under communist rule—this despite an exodus from North Vietnam of approximately one million people, most of them Catholics.[5] At a London conference Russia and Great Britain, two signatories of the Geneva agreements, issued a halfhearted appeal for elections. The Soviet Union was not anxious to establish a precedent for East Germany and the other satellites. Both powers knew that South Vietnam would not alter its stand, any more than North Vietnam would agree to reduce its military force illegally built up, from twenty divisions down to seven.[6]

Despite pessimism about the motives and abilities of Diem, the South Vietnamese leader for a while maintained a state described by many observers as "the miracle of Vietnam." Dulles thought of South Vietnam as a success, and his opinion of Diem improved with each meeting. But in the summer of 1959 the government of South Vietnam faltered. Ho Chi Minh had hoped to take control of South Vietnam within a few years after 1954; by 1959 these hopes had withered. The Hanoi government therefore decided to unite all of Vietnam through guerrilla raids and acts of terror. The Vietcong (communist-led insurrectionists in South Vietnam) grew from roughly 3,000 well-trained soldiers to over 12,000. Their activities ended the miracle of South Vietnam, opened a new chapter in the bloody history of Indochina, and eventually led to large-scale American military involvement.

The future of South Vietnam did not postpone Dulles' decision to establish a collective defense system in Southeast Asia; preparatory work for a security arrangement began before the end of the

Geneva Conference, under direction of military leaders of the United States, France, Great Britain, Australia, and New Zealand—subsequently by an Anglo-American group set up after the Eisenhower-Churchill meeting in Washington during the last week of June, 1954. These nations, together with the Philippines and Thailand, were to be the backbone of the Southeast Asia Treaty Organization (SEATO).

SEATO appeared at a time when solidarity among the allies had become strained, and coincided with emergence of the ideas of noncommitment or nonalignment. With Nehru's India in the vanguard, newly independent nations in Asia, the Middle East, and later Africa began or hoped to play an increasing role in world affairs. With patriotic fervor they declared themselves free from any affiliation, insisted on political and economic independence, and in the same breath requested economic and military aid (for internal security, of course) from both sides of the East-West struggle. They were not at all reluctant to play one side against the other.

Dulles did not question the desire of these nations to be neutral, and indeed he welcomed it. He did object to their lack of concern about communist motives and threats. Disturbing were their unrestrained attacks on the West and their branding of the United States with the epithet of "colonialist." Dulles thought that such behavior smacked of immorality, and lectured the offending statesmen on mistaking neutralism for neutrality as practiced by Switzerland and Sweden. The resulting talk about the true meaning of neutrality as opposed to the immorality of neutralism was confusing; at times it confused Dulles himself, or so it seemed.

As the Secretary prepared to bring the Western allies into a system for the Far East he was aware of their reluctance. The Europeans, he thought, did not wish Far Eastern problems to preoccupy the United States. European statesmen had been telling him that American involvement in the Far Pacific would weaken if not end American responsibility in Europe. They were fearful that the Republican Administration would prove Far-Eastern minded. "If we are weak in situations in the Far East," Dulles recalled later, ". . . we may get pressures elsewhere, for instance in the Persian Gulf and Berlin." The United States had to look on the world as a whole; to be weak anywhere meant danger. "The Europeans need to remember that our power is primarily nuclear and would not be engaged in a local conflict in the Far East. Nothing would be more foolish than for us to invade the Chinese mainland with 650 million inhabitants." This did not say that the United States should retreat from any of the areas it had committed itself to defend. Were America to step back before Communist China, "no matter how we rationalize it, the nations of the area will say: 'One side retreated, one side advanced.' "[7]

Preliminary negotiations for SEATO revealed differences between the Americans and British, for Great Britain was anxious to be in the treaty, to counter the damage to its position in the Far East by exclusion from ANZUS. London hoped to obtain an American commitment to safeguard Malaya and Hong Kong. Moreover, the British wanted India as a member and pressed for the five Colombo powers (India, Pakistan, Ceylon, Burma, Indonesia). They thought India an important link with Communist China, and argued in its behalf even at risk of offending Dulles who was not enthusiastic. The Secretary thought Nehru naive, politically unrealistic in assessment of Communist China's motives, attitudes, and policies. He resented Nehru's "impartial" and moralistic lectures. To British advocacy of India he countered by supporting Nationalist China, which London did not appreciate. But British pleas for India turned out to be academic. Believing the proposed treaty would do more harm than good, Nehru refused to join. So, too, did the governments of Ceylon, Burma, and Indonesia. Only Pakistan accepted.[8]

On the opening day of the SEATO conference, September 2, 1954, Dulles indicated that SEATO was not a replica of NATO—the United States would not commit substantial forces. Indeed he shied away from the popular term SEATO, trying to substitute MANPAC, the Manila Pact. He did not wish to tie the United States with weak nations. In Southeast Asia there was no fixed line between communists and anticommunists. The nations were unstable, with no local initiative or will to resist. The Manila Conference, Dulles told the eight-nation gathering, was to make clear that "an attack upon the treaty area would occasion a reaction so united, so strong, and so well placed that the aggressor would lose more than it could hope to gain." The United States could best serve "by developing the deterrent of mobile striking power, plus strategically placed reserves." Perhaps some delegates who recalled the fate of Indochina were not impressed with reaffirmation of this "new look," nor happy when Dulles insisted that the treaty single out communists as the threat to security in the Pacific.[9]

The United States, Britain, France, Australia, New Zealand, Philippines, Thailand, and Pakistan signed the SEATO Pact at Manila on September 8, 1954. All powers excepting Britain and France were represented by their foreign ministers. The treaty resembled ANZUS in that it was an indefinite commitment, but differed drastically from the Rio and NATO treaties which had obligations. Each party recognized that "aggression by means of armed attack" in the designated areas "would endanger its own peace and safety," and agreed in event of aggression to "meet the common danger in accordance with its constitutional processes." In case of indirect attack the signatories agreed to consult immediately "on the measures which should be taken for the common defense." The specified area was Southeast Asia and the Southwest Pacific not including the area north of 21 degrees 30 minutes north latitude—which excluded Hong Kong, Taiwan, and all territories to the north. A special protocol attached to the treaty included Cambodia, Laos, and South Vietnam, assuring them protection without requiring any obligation, but no action except by invitation or consent. Appended was an American pledge to take action only in case of communist aggression and armed attack, although the United States would consult the allies in event of indirect attack.

Other provisions called for a council at Bangkok to consult on military planning and cooperate on political and economic institutions. At the request of the Philippines a separate declaration known as the Pacific Charter, signed on September 8, pledged signatories to disassociate themselves from colonialism. Each nation promised to "prevent or counter by appropriate means any attempt in the treaty area to subvert their freedom or to destroy their sovereignty or territorial integrity." Dulles suggested afterward that this "ringing" declaration might prove "the most momentous product of the Conference."

The communist nations and India said SEATO was against peace, security, and national independence of the Asian peoples. Dulles countered that it was "against no government, against no nation, and against no people," but "only against aggression." The treaty had created a deterrent power which "can protect *many* as effectively as it protects *one*."[10]

SEATO seemed to stop armed overt aggression in the areas under its protection. The communists received a warning, this time by a coalition of five Western and three Asian nations. From then on the communists tended to resort to nonmilitary means. But would the SEATO Treaty stand the test of time? Would the allies stick together against the new type of subversion and guerrilla warfare, the danger of which so worried President Eisenhower?

2

The moment Dulles arrived in the Philippines for the Manila Conference, Mao Tse-tung as if by prearrangement started to "liberate" Taiwan. At 1:45 A.M., E.S.T., September 3, 1954, Communist Chinese troops began heavy artillery bombardment of selected targets on the island of Quemoy. The initial attack killed two American soldiers. At dawn on the following day reports indicated an assault was imminent. Deputy Secretary of Defense Robert B. Anderson directed the commander-in-chief of the Pacific Fleet to move carrier forces into position to rescue Americans, and await orders. The shelling of Quemoy brought a critical period in American diplomacy. Through the next nine months the question of Taiwan and offshore islands such as Quemoy threatened to split the United States from nearly all its allies and bring the world to the brink of nuclear war. To Eisenhower and Dulles the Straits of Formosa were a test of leadership and diplomacy.[11]

Taiwan was not in the defense perimeter of the contemplated Manila Pact. There was no security treaty with Chiang Kai-shek.

Eisenhower read the ominous message from Anderson relayed to his summer White House in Denver at 7:00 P.M., September 3, 1954. The chairman of the Joint Chiefs of Staff together with Chiefs of the Air Force and Navy recommended a change in policy to permit naval and air forces to assist in defense of ten selected offshore islands, including Quemoy. Anderson concurred. Majority opinion, so Anderson informed the President, held that while the islands near the Chinese mainland were not essential to defense of Taiwan, their loss would have adverse psychological and political effects on Chiang Kai-shek's troops and on other Asian countries. Moreover, there was great concern for the many Nationalist troops on the offshore islands. The Joint Chiefs thought that in all probability American military support would not be effective unless Eisenhower gave permission to attack selected targets on the mainland. Only General Matthew B. Ridgway, the Army's Chief of Staff, disagreed, arguing that it was not within the province of the Joint Chiefs to base recommendations on their assessment of psychological and political prospects.

While Eisenhower in Denver was preparing an answer, Dulles in Manila pondered communist motives. He had just read the confidential report of a British Labor Party member who had visited Russia and China and interviewed leaders of both nations. It so impressed him that he accepted most of the conclusions. Communist China and the Soviet Union, despite mutual distrust and inevitable future friction, pursued the same aim: to split the Western alliance. The wedge of the moment was Taiwan. The attack was not a prelude to invasion, but a stratagem to lure the United States into engaging its forces against a small contingent of Chinese Communists. When the "invasion" began and the United States fell into the trap, the Soviet Union would call an emergency session of the Security Council to accuse the United States of being a threat to world peace. Communist parties throughout the world would start massive propaganda depicting the United States as imperialist. The Soviet Union and Communist China were confident that neither France nor Britain would go to war over Taiwan. Isolated from allies and world opinion, the United States would have to retire from Europe and Asia, opening the way for Chinese Communist absorption of Taiwan and Soviet domination in Europe and elsewhere.

Concurrently Chinese leaders were shocking Western visitors with statements that an atomic attack would not awe them. The deaths of several hundred million Chinese would still leave several hundred million. Some Chinese suggested that such an eventuality would ease the food shortage.

Within a few days of return to the United States, Dulles journeyed to Denver for a special meeting of top foreign policy and military advisers. It was here on September 12, 1954, that the Administration decided on what he called a horrible dilemma. Admiral Radford, supported by Admiral Robert B. Carney and General Nathan F. Twining, urged that the United States defend the offshore islands and bomb the mainland. Eisenhower disagreed: "We're not talking now about a limited, brush-fire war. We're talking about going to the threshold of World War III. If we attack China, we're not going to impose limits on our military actions, as in Korea." The President reminded his advisers that "if we get into a general war, the logical enemy will be Russia, not China, and we'll have to strike there." Dulles spoke, and stressed the complex nature of the problem. The Chinese Communists were probing American intentions; they had to be stopped or the United States would face disaster in the Far East. But if the government drew a line and committed itself to defend Quemoy and Matsu, it might find itself at war with China without allies. He suggested an alternative: take the question of the offshore islands to the Security Council "with the view of getting there an injunction to maintain the status quo and institute a cease fire in the Formosa Strait. Whether Russia vetoes or accepts such a plan, the United States will gain." Here was a way of wresting initiative from the communists and nullifying their combined strategy outlined in the confidential report. Eisenhower approved Dulles' suggestion.[12]

The Chinese Communists continued to shell offshore islands but did not attempt invasion. The situation remained tense. As Washington prepared to carry out the decision reached at Denver, American political leaders and foreign statesmen urged conflicting courses. Clement Attlee, the British Labor Party leader, wanted Chiang Kai-shek retired; Anthony Eden desired Quemoy and Matsu neutralized; Senators Lehman of New York, Wayne Morse of Oregon, and John F. Kennedy of Massachusetts, along with India's spokesman Krishna Menon, urged abandonment; Admiral Radford recommended military action—bombing of the mainland; Senator Knowland suggested a blockade of the Chinese coast and hinted at preventive war; Syngman Rhee pleaded with the United States to join him and Chiang in a "holy war of liberation."

The attack alerted Dulles to the need of reexamining American policies toward both Chinas within America's world strategy, discarding policies which were obsolete and introducing new ones. The policy of the United States, as Dulles saw it, had been to defend vital interests; not to provoke war; to pursue peace but not at expense of principles. The Secretary in mid-autumn of 1954 did not think there was a need for a change in policy toward the Chinese problem but for some adjustment to bring it closer to principles and constitutional requirements. He suggested a mutual security treaty with Nationalist China to cover Taiwan and the Pescadores but not the offshore islands. The alliance with Chiang Kai-shek should be defensive. Under no circumstances should Taiwan be a "privileged sanctuary," used or abused by Chiang for direct or indirect operations against the mainland. American policy toward Nationalist China, Dulles thought, should be as toward Germany and Korea: Adenauer had renounced force to unite Germany; Rhee, under constant pressure from Dulles, had promised to refrain from renewing the war in Korea. Dulles had determined to prevent any of the partitioned nations from involving the United States in a war. Eisenhower agreed.

Preparations began to bring the offshore islands problem before the Security Council, and Dulles proceeded with negotiations for a security treaty with Nationalist China. Preliminary discussions were difficult. Finally, on December 2, he signed a mutual defense treaty with Foreign Minister George K. C. Yeh. Both nations agreed that an armed attack on either would endanger the peace and safety of the other. The treaty covered a direct attack on Taiwan and the Pescadores. In substance this treaty, and an exchange of notes of December 10, 1954, recognized that the Chinese Nationalists would not use force from Taiwan, the Pescadores, or the offshore islands without consent of the United States.[13] Several weeks later Chiang urged logistic support for defense of the offshore islands. The President refused.

This bilateral mutual defense treaty with the Republic of China supplemented agreements with Japan and South Korea, and together with SEATO raised the total of American alliances to forty-two, not counting the commitments in the United Nations Charter.

Communist China ushered in the new year 1955 with a stepped-up offensive in the Formosan Straits. On January 10 hundreds of MIG planes attacked the Tachen Islands. A week later Red Chinese troops seized the island of Ichiang, seven miles north of the Tachens. Eisenhower decided the time had come "to draw the line." At a meeting in the White House on January 19, Dulles argued that although not one of the offshore islands was defensible without American help the communists should not be able "to seize *all* the offshore islands." The Secretary suggested modification of policy: "We should assist in the evacuation of the Tachens, but as we do so should declare that we will assist in holding Quemoy and possibly the Matsus, as long as the Chinese Communists profess their intention to attack Formosa [Taiwan]."[14] Eisenhower approved a special message to Congress asking authority to use United States forces to protect "Formosa and the Pescadores and related positions, if necessary, in defense of the principal islands." Less than two weeks later, on January 28, 1955, the Senate passed, by vote of 83 to 3, the so-called Formosa Resolution, signed by Eisenhower next day, which authorized the President "to employ the armed forces of the United States as he deems necessary for the specific purpose of securing and protecting Formosa and the Pescadores against armed attack, this authority to include the securing and protecting of such related positions and territories of that area now in friendly hands and the taking of such other measures as he judges to be required or appropriate in assuring the defense of Formosa and the Pescadores."[15]

The Formosa Resolution and the mutual security treaty with Nationalist China indicated American determination to protect Taiwan and the Pescadores, but not necessarily Quemoy and Matsu. The future of these latter islands was unclear. Early in February, 1955, the United States assisted in evacuation of the Tachens and the nearby small islands of Yushan and Penshan. Communist China rejected the invitation of the Security Council to join in discussion of a New Zealand proposal for a cease-fire.

3

The Formosa Resolution threatened to widen the split in American-British relations. Churchill urged evacuation of Quemoy and Matsu. The United States, so he wrote Eisenhower, should give Chiang "its shield but not the use of its sword." Again Dulles had to explain American policy to Eden. During their long meeting on February 24, 1955, he reviewed the latest American attempts to prevent hostilities in the Taiwan area. The United States had made a mutual security treaty with the Republic of China which excluded all areas except Taiwan and the Pescadores, had obtained assurance of no offensive actions against mainland China except by joint agreement, had pressed Chiang to surrender the exposed Tachens, well to the north of Taiwan, and restrained the Generalissimo from attacking the communist marshalling areas on the mainland during recent attacks on the offshore islands. Despite an aroused Congress and public opinion which demanded retaliatory action against Chinese Communists for continuing to imprison some American airmen captured in the Korean War, the Administration had limited the Congressional resolution to Taiwan and areas deemed important to defense of Taiwan. Moreover, the United States had clearly accepted a United Nations cease-fire and worked hard to secure Chiang Kai-shek's acceptance.

In face of all these temperate actions, the Chinese Communists had become more intemperate. Abandonment of the Tachens whetted their appetite. They were exuberant, almost hysterical, as a result of successes of their revolution, and the momentum which had propelled them from conquest of the mainland to victories in Korea and Indochina and Tibet, now perhaps Taiwan. The United States, Dulles told Eden, had gone as far as was prudent in making concessions. Let the Chinese Communists continue claiming the right to Taiwan, but let them also make clear that they would not seek a verdict by force. At the moment Washington could not press Chiang to surrender Quemoy and Matsu. Communist control would increase the capacity to attack Taiwan, weaken the morale of the Republic of China, and maybe even lead the communists to probe American resolution to defend Taiwan by putting it to the test.

Eden agreed that Taiwan should not fall into communist hands. British public opinion would probably support the United States in defending the main island, but not Quemoy and Matsu. A week later Eden in Commons urged that Chiang withdraw from Quemoy and that Mao Tse-tung abstain from attacking Taiwan and the Pescadores. Two weeks later the Canadian External Affairs Secretary, Lester Pearson, announced that Canada would not fight over the offshore islands.[16]

Fear increased that the United States might involve

itself in a nuclear war. Quemoy and Matsu, islands hitherto unknown to most Americans, became topics of conversation. Returning from a two-week trip in Southeast Asia, Dulles brought ominous news, telling Eisenhower on March 8: "The situation out there in the Formosa Strait is far more serious than I thought before my trip. The Chinese Communists are determined to capture Formosa. Surrendering Quemoy and Matsu won't end that determination. If we defend Quemoy and Matsu we'll have to use atomic weapons." One question he could not answer: "How loyal would Chiang's troops be if attacked?" Eisenhower agreed that small atomic weapons would probably have to be used against communist airfields and marshalling areas, but asked how the United States could save the Nationalists "if they don't want to be saved." Some advisers thought morale high in Taiwan, but that it depended on hope of returning to the mainland, a hope nourished by possession of Quemoy and Matsu. From press conferences and cabinet discussions Eisenhower gathered "a very definite feeling" that within a month the United States would be fighting in the straits. He saw "two unpleasant alternatives": assist Chiang in defense of Quemoy and Matsu, thus risking a world war in which the United States would fight alone; or press Chiang "to change the offshore islands, by partial evacuation and intensive fortification . . . into fortress outposts."[17]

The President wrote a long and remarkable memorandum to Dulles on the subject of Taiwan and the related question of Quemoy and Matsu. This statement of April 5, 1955, set the lines of American policy and was to serve as an instruction for Admiral Radford and Assistant Secretary Robertson who two weeks later went as emissaries to Chiang Kai-shek. The United States, Eisenhower declared, had committed itself by treaty with the Republic of China to defend only Taiwan and the Pescadores. During the years, particularly since the Korean War, the Indochina crisis, and various diplomatic negotiations, public statements and military understandings of one kind or another had given Chiang some right to assume that the United States would participate in defense of Quemoy and Matsu. This idea needed correction, for otherwise it would commit American military prestige to a campaign favorable to the attacker. Public opinion would not favor American defense of these offshore islands which many people regarded as part of the Chinese mainland. Even if the United States were successful in defending the islands, there would not be stability in the Formosan Straits but an attack elsewhere. Finally, it was not good military policy to tie down large American forces in that area.

The President knew that refusal to defend the offshore islands would have disadvantages: morale of the Chinese Nationalists would deteriorate, weakening their defense of Taiwan, in itself essential to the United States and the Western world; retreat from Taiwan would disintegrate all Asian opposition to communism. The answer was to encourage peaceful change rather than remain inert.

The military reasons for holding Quemoy and Matsu were the estimated effect of their loss on morale in Taiwan and the possible psychological effect on other Asian countries. All risks and disadvantages existed because of such assumptions. At the same time it had become clear that the United States and the Republic of China would be much better off without a commitment to defense of the islands. If there were some way to extricate each nation by a course which would increase rather than diminish their strategic positions!

The questions, Eisenhower wrote Dulles, were what could the United States do to establish a situation most advantageous to defense of Taiwan and the Pescadores, solidifying American and world opinion behind the Administration, sustaining Chinese Nationalist forces, securing support of friends in Southeast Asia and neighboring islands? And what could the United States do to persuade Chiang Kai-shek to cooperate? The President suggested making clear "that neither Chiang nor ourselves is committed to *full-out* defense of Quemoy and Matsu, so that no matter what the outcome of an attack upon them, there would be no danger of a collapse of the free world position in that region." Eisenhower doubted Chiang's contention that loss of the offshore islands would destroy the Nationalist government in Taiwan; if this were Chiang's opinion he should have moved his headquarters to Quemoy or Matsu. The Generalissimo should learn "the great advantages, political and military, that would result from certain alterations in his present military plans." The Republic of

China, Eisenhower reasoned, should regard the offshore islands as outposts "and consequently to be garrisoned in accordance with the requirements of outpost positions" which would be well supported by Chiang's main forces from Taiwan.[18]

Radford and Robertson did their best to persuade Chiang. The Generalissimo was obdurate. But almost at the same moment the crisis ended. The expected attack on Quemoy and Matsu did not begin. What caused Peking to give up? American determination and strength probably was decisive. Related was another factor. While Radford and Robertson negotiated with a recalcitrant Chiang, Chou En-lai at the Afro-Asian Conference at Bandung (April 18-24, 1955) gave some evidence that Communist China would like to find a peaceful way out of the crisis in the straits. His reasonable and even humble behavior at Bandung increased his stature among the unaligned nations—but it also brought the straits crisis to a close. He perhaps needed a way out, a respite, a more propitious time to liquidate Chiang.[19]

The China question was a difficult one, and Dulles did not resolve it. The Quemoy-Matsu crisis resumed in 1958 when Peking again shelled the islands. American reaction was swift. The Seventh Fleet on orders from Eisenhower convoyed Chinese Nationalist supply ships to the offshore islands. The Chinese Communists, convinced that American forces would fight alongside those of the Republic of China, eased off their bombardment. Secretary Dulles now decided to make another effort to take the straits off the list of the world's trouble spots, and late in October, 1958, he flew to Taiwan to tell Chiang of the need of new policy. Dulles respected the Nationalist leader, but on this occasion as on others was not able to get close to him. Madame Chiang, acting as interpreter, was always present, and Dulles was never sure the opinions expressed were hers or those of her husband, who did not speak or understand English.

Dulles talked bluntly during this visit of 1958. The greatest danger facing the Republic of China, he began, was not military but political. The whole world was longing for the peace which relations between the two Chinas were preventing. Many people believed that Chiang wanted to endanger peace. Unlike Korea and Indochina, China had no armistice. Everywhere was concern that the United States as an ally of the Republic of China would find itself in a war which, because of America's position, might extend around the world. No wonder the world desired to eliminate this trouble spot. The prevalence of this desire was a serious threat to Chiang's regime. The United States, his only vigorous ally, had done its utmost to prevent allies and friends from recognizing Communist China. Dulles doubted that Washington could continue the effort; subsequent administrations might not pay the price. He called Chiang's attention to the wide belief that life expectancy of his Republic was limited for three reasons: (1) an expansionist Communist China was a military and political threat; (2) the Republic of China increasingly depended on native Taiwanese; and (3) "free world opinion" wanted to end the civil war which threatened a general war.

Dulles suggested a way out. Chiang should try to dramatize the "larger and enduring role" of the Republic of China. He should act as if an armistice existed along lines of the present division, and even be willing to conclude such an armistice. He should make no attempt to return to the mainland by force; avoid commando raids and other provocations; and accept any solution which would neutralize Quemoy and Matsu. Dulles also recommended a dramatic "shift of effort to assure the survival of Chinese civilization." The Republic of China should become the custodian of China's greatness, emphasizing education, arts, and other aspects of culture. The Republic of China would become a symbol which mainland Chinese could observe and envy, attract more lasting support on Taiwan, hold the loyalty of overseas Chinese, and win "free peoples everywhere."

Chiang listened quietly. Did he understand? The Secretary was not sure. The Generalissimo reaffirmed his determination to return to the mainland, but only if there were a desire by people there as evidenced by revolution against the communists. He asked for more trust and confidence. Undoubtedly Chiang understood the Secretary; he responded as if he did not.[20]

Through the rest of his tenure Dulles opposed *de jure* recognition and the seating of Communist China in the United Nations, not because of emotional dislike of communism or sentimental loyalty to Chiang but for national and international reasons. He likened the communists to the old Japanese warlords. Both had wanted control of all Asia and to expel Western nations. As long as the Communist Chinese wished to expand by force, Dulles opposed them. While waiting for Communist China to mellow, if that were possible, he continued to support the Republic of China and encouraged Chiang to make it the repository of Chinese culture, the symbol of "the China they knew" to millions of overseas Chinese.

CHAPTER THIRTEEN

THE ROAD TO THE SUMMIT: THE GENEVA CONFERENCE OF 1955

THE GENEVA CONFERENCE of 1955—the famous summit conference in which Eisenhower, Eden, Edgar Faure, and Nikolai Bulganin sat out on the lawn in front of the old League of Nations building near the Lake of Geneva—had its origin in the mind of Prime Minister Churchill. The leader of Great Britain had begun in 1953 to agitate for a summit meeting. His correspondence with Eisenhower on that subject had begun with a telegram of May 4, 1953. There was a speech of May 11. Until retirement in April, 1955, the Prime Minister did not waver from conviction that direct contact with Stalin's successors would improve East-West relations. A successful meeting sponsored by the octogenarian statesman would have crowned his days in office with a diplomatic achievement of magnitude. This was not to be. A conference of the heads of government was indeed held in 1955, but ill health had forced Churchill to retire in advance of it.[1]

1

Sometime in the spring of 1954 Churchill had sounded Molotov privately, and without authorization of the cabinet or consultation with Eisenhower, about a friendly and informal two-power meeting between himself and Soviet leaders, with no set agenda. Molotov's reply was encouraging. It strengthened the Prime Minister's belief that the arms race was a serious concern of the Russian Government, which wanted a thaw in the cold war. Churchill expected his excursion to create conditions leading to a three- and perhaps, with the French, four-power conference. He had agreed with Eisenhower and Dulles that Russian deeds must match words, and had prepared to ask some gesture—an act of faith. After all, was it not Stalin's aggressive policies in Poland, Czechoslovakia, Greece, Turkey and Korea that had shattered Anglo-American cooperation with the Soviet Union and led to NATO, SEATO, ANZUS, and METO (the Middle East Treaty Organization, for which see below, pp. 257-259)? Churchill wanted an Austrian treaty to end military occupation of that country. He hoped for, but not as *sine qua non*, acceptance of Eisenhower's atoms for peace plan. He was not unduly optimistic. The cause, he felt, was worth personal failure—even in the evening of his life. Before embarking on his journey to some neutral city to meet the Russians he sought Eisenhower's advice.

Eisenhower did not attempt to stop Churchill, and wished him godspeed. The need for peace and understanding in the world, he said, transcended pride. Should his friend go on this mission and succeed, Eisenhower would be the first to admit, and gladly, that he was wrong in believing that one could not trust Soviet leaders no matter how great their apparent sincerity. The President warned Churchill that he could not deliver the American public, but promised to do his best to lessen unfavorable reaction. The majority of the American people, he believed, would consider Churchill's venture like Prohibition in the 1920s—"a noble experiment."[2]

Dulles was against a meeting. During Churchill's visit to Washington in late June, 1954, he tried to dissuade the Prime Minister from a two-nation confabulation because it might lead to a three-power summit conference. The Secretary feared lest Eisenhower succumb to Churchill's pressure to endorse publicly such a conference, then agree to a brief appearance, and leave him or Vice President Nixon in charge of an American delegation there. Dulles told Churchill it would be dangerous to hold a summit conference unless the West could have assurance of a favorable outcome. Illusory success or obvious failure might create an impression that the alternative was war. Dulles did not think Churchill's exploratory mission could succeed; the American people would not favor it, requiring Washington to say that Churchill did not speak for the United States. Churchill understood Dulles' position and again reminded the Secretary that he was not going as an intermediary between the United States and the Soviet Union, but as a representative of the spirit and purpose of the West. Dulles urged him to reconsider carefully. The Prime Minister remained unconvinced.

But Churchill did not embark on a personal mission after all. On August 30, 1954, France rejected the European Defense Community by vote of 319 to 264, with 43 abstentions, and the Prime Minister, who never forgave the French for "inventing" EDC, concluded that its collapse adversely affected his proposed meeting. Much to the relief of Dulles he decided that a meeting of heads of government should not occur until discovery of a substitute for EDC. Rejection was a shattering blow to Dulles and Adenauer. Both men felt EDC's failure was a personal defeat; both had committed their governments to passage. To Dulles this was a crisis. He had warned France that defeat would lead to an agonizing reappraisal of American policy toward Europe.

It was Eden who solved Dulles' problem, for within several days of the collapse of EDC the Foreign Secretary hit on the idea of converting the Brussels Treaty of 1948 into a Western European Union (WEU) as a substitute for the defunct EDC. This treaty, which had been against Germany, had bound Britain, France, Belgium, the Netherlands, and Luxembourg to come to each other's defense. Eden hoped to transform and expand it to include Germany and Italy in a regional defensive alliance against Russia. He saw many advantages: abandonment of supranational features of EDC would make possible for the United Kingdom to become a full member, "sharing from within instead of buttressing from without"; the pact would be for fifty years, as against twenty for NATO; the new form "could provide a focus for those in all countries, including Western Germany, who cherished the vision of a united Europe"; Germany would become a member of NATO. After a month of frantic diplomatic activity, a nine-power conference of representatives of the United States, Britain, France, West Germany, Italy, Belgium, the Netherlands, Luxembourg, and Canada met in London on September 28, 1954, to revise and elaborate the Brussels Treaty. Final agreement came on October 31. A grateful Dulles congratulated Eden for magnificent statesmanship. To Eisenhower it was one of the diplomatic achievements of modern times.[3]

The London Agreement looked to the end of military occupation of West Germany. The Federal Republic as a fully recognized sovereign state, and also Italy, would join the Brussels Treaty. West Germany was thus to become a member of NATO. The United States repeated its pledge to maintain forces in Europe. For the first time in modern history Great Britain committed specific forces for defense of the Continent in peacetime. The agreement emphasized the peaceful, defensive character of NATO and the Brussels Treaty; Germany undertook never "to have recourse to force to achieve the reunification of Germany or the modification of the present boundaries" of the Federal Republic. Protocols elaborating these agreements were signed in Paris on October 23, 1954, and two months later, on December 28-30, France ratified them. The complex WEU and related treaties became operative on May 5, 1955. Western Europe was now in a stronger position to meet the Russians at the summit.[4]

Dulles would have preferred WEU to have supranational characteristics with parliamentary controls like the abortive EDC. The British commitment to continental Europe offset this disadvantage. He accepted it hoping that it might become a foundation for European federation—political, economic, military. During the hectic negotiations he took a secondary role, believing that final agreement should be essentially European. Unlike his activities in behalf of EDC, he avoided even the appearance of American pressure. The Secretary liked Eden's frankness which had not, so he believed, always been so obvious. He thought that Churchill's and Eden's lukewarm attitude toward EDC had accounted for its failure. But he was most annoyed with Mendes-France; the French Premier, he was sure, had killed EDC and desired to prevent German admission to NATO. The American and British pledges to commit specific forces on the Continent, particularly the British, had caught the Frenchman by surprise; it produced a situation impossible for France to reject or delay.

Incidentally, perhaps it is worth mentioning that at approximately the same time as the negotiation over revising the Brussels Treaty so as to get Germany into NATO, a long argument—a seemingly interminable argument—over Trieste came to a happy ending on October 5, 1954: Italy and Yugoslavia signed an agreement leaving the city of Trieste in Italian hands, and allotting the hinterlands in a way that the Yugoslavs received slightly more square miles and four thousand more people. Each government was to protect the rights of minorities on its side of the boundary line. This dispute over the onetime port of Austria-Hungary had agitated successive Italian governments since 1945. It had threatened to keep Italy out of the EDC, and might even have taken Italy out of NATO. As for President Tito, he probably would not have changed his coolness to Moscow just for the sake of Trieste (the Russians, perhaps fortunately, were not in a position to help him), but he had been willing to push the issue very far. The diplomacy of settling this imbroglio had been fantastically complicated. Now it was over, and British and American troops could leave the city in peace.

Following the Paris protocols of October, 1954, pressure increased for a summit conference. The Soviets clamored for it, and Eden echoed the call, as did Nehru who maintained that the Soviet Union desired peace. He believed that the Russians wished to concentrate on internal economic development.

Dulles sensed that Soviet pressure for a summit meeting came from anxiety to obtain a relaxation with the Western world, not because of any new purpose but because of the need for new policies to meet the changing world configuration of power. The aggressive policies of the Soviet Union during the first decade of the cold war, including the hot war in Korea, had produced diminishing results. Latest proof of failure was the Soviet inability to prevent the accords on Western European Union. The vast Soviet military establishment was proving costly. Sensational Soviet efforts to expand their industrial base—one third that of the United States—and repeated troubles in agriculture, which could not keep up with population, had been diverting economic effort from consumer goods. The Soviet people wanted a breathing spell. It was no accident, Dulles thought, that after Soviet failure to block Western European Union the Kremlin took a series of well-prepared steps. First was the disarmament proposal of May 10, 1955. Then the Austrian State Treaty on May 15, which provided for withdrawal of foreign troops from Austrian soil and the neutralization of that little country—a cause for great rejoicing in this nation of Central Europe where occupying troops had been coming and going for years. It was in this general period, preparatory for the summit meeting, that the Russians sought a *rapprochement* with Yugoslavia, invited Adenauer to come to Moscow, and offered to talk with the Japanese. All these moves seemed to meet Western demands for deeds as requisite to the summit meeting which Churchill had been suggesting and which now caught public imagination and support.

Since the death of Stalin, Dulles had viewed with foreboding the relaxation among the allies, and this increase of pressure for a summit meeting. The moment of relaxation was the moment of peril. "I'm concerned," he mused, "lest a summit meeting be nothing but a spectacle and promote a false euphoria. Under those circumstances we and our allies might not take the necessary steps to keep the free world together. If there's no evident menace from the Soviet bloc our will to maintain unity and strength may weaken." He thought it unfortunate "that in promoting our programs in Congress we have to make evident the international communist menace. Otherwise such programs as the mutual security one would be decimated."[5] He believed the same problem faced the allies. A summit conference gave the Soviets an advantage, for they could prepare their position without concern about allies or public opinion.

Soviet policy, Dulles said at the opening session of the fifteenth meeting of the North Atlantic Council on December 17, 1954, was like a "powerful stream, the surface of which is sometimes ruffled . . . sometimes calm." The force of the current cannot be judged merely by looking at the surface. The surface of the Soviet stream could lull the West, and then a change in the current might frighten the allies into paralysis or ill-considered action. He called attention to communist activity outside the Soviet-Chinese orbit, particularly subversion in the developing nations. He reminded his audience of the well-known sentence of Stalin's lecture on Leninism of April, 1924: "The road to victory of the Revolution in the West lies through the revolutionary alliance with the liberation movement of the colonies and the dependent countries against imperialism."

Did not the Kremlin vilify all the moves of the free world: Marshall Plan, NATO, Japanese Peace Treaty, Yugoslavia's improved relations with the West, SEATO, EDC, Western European Union, attempts to unite Germany? The West must be careful not to endanger NATO. In the recent crisis over the Formosan Straits the United States had met severe provocation planned to trigger Washington into action which its European allies would regard as ill-advised. Events of recent years demonstrated that even in the face of provocation the Western nations should not act in a way which any of them could not justify as other than peaceful, defensive, and consistent with international honor. The communists were "pushing history," Dulles said. One of the most dangerous characteristics of the communist movement was that it thought itself timeless, that achievement of results required "an entire historical era." Unlike Hitler, the Soviets did not operate in terms of individual lives. Hitler told the German people that they must win, if at all, under him because there would never be anyone else like him. The communists, Dulles concluded, do not operate in terms of victory merely to please some particular ruler like Stalin.[6]

2

By the spring of 1955 Dulles reluctantly had accepted the idea of a summit conference. He succeeded in toning down the invitation for a Big Four conference and in limiting it, but he thought that preparation still would be an affair of magnitude. There was need of preliminary agreement with the British and French, as well as with Adenauer although Germany would not be present. He wanted to raise such matters as free elections in Poland, greater freedom for all the satellites, activities of international communism, disarmament—these and other topics demanded an exchange of views among the allies. He was concerned about the length of the conference. Should it occur while Congress was in session? Should Congressmen attend?

By the middle of June, 1955, he had developed some ideas about a summit meeting and sent them in rough form to the President. The Secretary expected the Soviets to bring up world disarmament, atomic and conventional. He preferred to keep this subject within the narrow and theoretically confidential confines of the United Nations Disarmament Committee. He felt that the Russians would urge a world disarmament conference for two reasons: desire to reduce the economic burdens of the arms race, and belief that it would so arouse world public opinion that Washington might accept disarmament under imprudent conditions. German unification was certain to come up. Adenauer had urged Dulles to make it the principal item. (The Soviets had invited Adenauer to visit Moscow before the conference, but he declined.) Dulles anticipated that the Russians would resubmit their plan for a European regional security system which they had introduced at the Berlin Conference of 1954.[7]

The Secretary informed the President that the allies consented to raise the issue of liberation of the satellite states. Eden now had become Prime Minister, upon the retirement of Churchill, and his new Foreign Secretary, Harold Macmillan, and the new French Premier, Antoine Pinay, supported the United

States. Pinay told Dulles privately on June 17, 1955, that the allies should talk with the Russians about the satellites and international communism, causes of tension. Dulles expected strong opposition from the Russians. He wanted to discuss the matter but not insist that it be a subject of future negotiation. The Soviet chiefs should hear that if they wished to reduce tensions with the United States they should deal with this problem which Americans, especially those of East European origin, long had felt a violation of wartime agreements and a hindrance to American-Soviet relations. The Secretary suggested that Eisenhower reason privately with the Russian leaders; he could accomplish more informally. The same procedure, Dulles advised, should go for international communism. He thought that the Roosevelt-Litvinov Agreement of 1933, in which the Russians gave assurance that they would refrain from propaganda in the United States, should be the basis for discussion. During a recent conversation between Pinay and Molotov the Frenchman had raised the question of the French Communist Party. Molotov shrugged it off: "Why don't you use your police?" And shortly thereafter the Soviet Foreign Minister met with French communist leaders in Cherbourg. The best card the United States could play, Dulles thought in mid-June, 1955, was trade. The Soviet block was a deficit area. He was certain the Russians would want Western surpluses; he would not acquiesce unless the Soviets reciprocated on German unification, the satellites, and international communism.[8]

During the last week of June, Dulles met privately

with Molotov in Hillsborough, California. The Russian had come to San Francisco for the tenth anniversary of the United Nations. As they strolled in the garden he asked Molotov what topics the Soviets would bring up at the forthcoming conference. Molotov listed three: disarmament, European security, economic cooperation. He asked Dulles what the Americans would bring up. The Secretary answered: disarmament and German unification. Dulles alerted the Soviet leader to his intent to bring up the East European nations. He was aware that the Russian Government would not favor this topic at an international conference, but the summit meeting was to discuss international tension. Many Americans of East European origin insisted on this issue. Molotov replied that the Soviet position had been clear in the past, and he had no wish to add comments.

The Secretary touched on international communism, and told Molotov that activities of the Party throughout the world and in the Western Hemisphere were highly objectionable and that he would want to talk about them at Geneva. Molotov replied that communism was a matter of a state's internal affairs. Dulles disagreed, saying there was nothing "internal" about the activities of the Party. The vast quantity of anti-American propaganda fabricated, printed, and shipped from Prague and Budapest to Latin America gravely concerned the United States. Molotov doubted that propaganda in Spanish was printed in European capitals, but promised to look into the matter.

Dulles informed Molotov that he did not oppose

economic cooperation in principle—hinting that economic problems related to political issues—but was skeptical of the summit conference as the best forum for such discussion.

In their private talk Dulles had hoped to obtain from Molotov some indication that the Soviet Union might favor German unification. During discussion of a treaty with Austria in February, 1954, Molotov had indicated that the Kremlin would support a united but neutral Germany. Dulles suggested that bringing Germany into a European security system would assuage Soviet fears of Germany; it would be the best way to prevent Germany from threatening the Soviet Union. Molotov thought a European army which included the Germans would set one part of Europe against the other. The Secretary pointed out that since the end of the First World War discrimination against Germany and attempts to control the Germans had not prevented German militarism. An integrated European army in which Germany was an equal partner would be a restraining influence. Molotov was unconvinced and would only discuss a unified Germany with a limited army and a government directed against none of the Big Four. The German problem, he hinted, could go the same way as the Austrian: neutralization. Dulles rejected such a notion immediately; Germany was not Austria. To neutralize Germany would mean control from without, which experience had proved unreliable. The United States could not support the kind of government Moscow suggested for Germany. The very idea of giving the

United States, the Soviet Union, and other nations the right to choose a government for Germany, control German elections and, by implication, their outcome, was repugnant. Molotov commented that his country was not the only nation concerned about Germany, and he doubted that German military leaders would agree to subordinate or even equal roles in the European army. There was no assurance that other members of the European army would have the power or resolution to curb German militarism which in the end might dominate not only Germany but the Continent. Dulles reemphasized that the chief purpose was not to direct Germany against the Soviet Union, but to prevent revival of German militarism: a reunified Germany under the umbrella of a European security system was the greatest safeguard Russia could have. Molotov was skeptical, and on that note the talks ended.

At the end of June, after Eisenhower apprised Dulles of the position he wished to take at the Geneva summit conference, the Secretary drafted a set of position papers for the American delegation. Here Dulles set forth objectives, outlined probable attitudes of Great Britain and France, anticipated Soviet purposes, and estimated the possible achievement. The first American goal was unification of Germany under conditions which would not demilitarize or deny membership in NATO. Dulles thought that Britain and France would support this objective. Related was the European security system which envisioned a common reduction and control of Soviet forces in Eastern Europe and NATO forces in Western Europe, but not at a price of allowing the Soviet Union to consolidate Eastern Europe. Dulles expected support from the allies for this too. The third American goal was control of armaments based on supervision and inspection to prevent evasion and surprise. The Secretary was sure of British support and uncertain of French. The next concerned the satellite states. Washington hoped to increase opportunities for East European nations to gain greater independence and eventually cease to be an extension of the Soviet empire. Dulles believed that Great Britain would support him, but that France would be indifferent. The fifth American objective looked toward an agreement with the Soviet Union to end international communist subversion. The French were expected to favor this position; the British to remain indifferent. The last goal was East-West cultural exchange. Britain and France, Dulles felt, would give only mild support. The Secretary included a marginal goal: Soviet participation in Eisenhower's atoms for peace plan; from the two allies he expected a lukewarm response.

The Soviet goal at Geneva, Dulles suggested, was to gain a psychological world-wide victory through acceptance of Soviet leadership as morally and socially equal to that of the West. He feared it would help the Russians to maintain their hold on the satellites and facilitate neutralism by spreading the impression that only power rivalries and not principles created tensions. Russia would push for relaxation of military and nonmilitary activities of the Western powers, particularly the United States, and thus obtain a respite to improve the internal economic position under the new leaders. Dulles wished to deny them such a moratorium, and expected the British to aid him but not the French. He was certain the Russians would press for disarmament by such slogans as "ban the bomb," and by a world disarmament conference, which would subject Western negotiators to organized emotional pressures calculated to prevent painstaking preparations to assure safeguards. He feared a discussion of war propaganda as likely to give the impression that the United States harbored a preventive-war psychology. He was concerned lest world public opinion might force the West to agree on a disarmament treaty favored by Moscow. Dulles foresaw a Soviet effort to reach accord on a statement of principles, a Geneva Charter, calculated to give Moscow a trademark in its world propaganda, symbolizing Soviet communism as a moral force which noncommunists should accept. The Russians would urge a European security system based on elimination of American bases and troops. The three allies would reject this. There was also an expectation that the Russians would advance Communist China as a great power by calling for a Far Eastern conference. Dulles looked for the British but not the French to join him against such a session.

Dulles thought that Russia would gain more at Geneva than the West, and foresaw the emergence of the Soviet Union as a moral and social equal of the United States. He would caution the President to avoid socializing with Bulganin and Khrushchev when photographers were present. Recognizing that camera men were difficult to exclude, he hoped that Eisenhower would maintain an austere countenance whenever photographed with the Russians. Public knowledge that the United States called for liberation of satellites and liquidation of international communism, Dulles thought, would lessen Soviet gains. He did not want to turn the conference into a propaganda forum, but felt the need to indicate American opposition. Unless it ended on discord the summit conference, he believed, would relax the West, weaken NATO, and delay German rearmament. He knew the difficulty, perhaps impossibility, of preventing some slight increase of neutralism within Germany, and in France a return to a nostalgia for special relations with Russia to contain Germany. Dulles was not at all sanguine about liberation of the satellites. The Soviets were sure to reject this as improper for discussion. Nevertheless he determined to impress on them privately the importance Washington attached to it. Dulles was more optimistic on international communism. Earlier conversation with Molotov encouraged his belief that Moscow might agree to some psychological move such as eliminating the Cominform. The Secretary expected reciprocal agreements ending propaganda by radio and balloon flights, and some token Soviet acceptance of the atoms for peace plan. Forced to go to the summit, Dulles wanted it to succeed.

CHAPTER FOURTEEN

THE SUMMIT: GLOW AND AFTERGLOW

In midsummer of 1955 leaders of the Big Four gathered in Geneva, and for six days—from July 18 to 23—President Eisenhower, Prime Minister Eden, Premier Faure, and Premier Bulganin (accompanied by Nikita Khrushchev), with their foreign ministers and top-ranking advisers, met and talked. Here was great drama, a diplomatic climax to the cold war. The world watched, and read the news accounts and polemics of journalists, commentators, columnists. Everything said was promising and exhilarating. In the production, so well prepared, now "premiered" in the Swiss city, there were no villains, only heroes. The play's theme was relaxation. For the first time in years Russian leaders smiled in public, were polite, and gave some indication of a desire to end the arms race.

Preconference statements of heads of government were so encouraging. Before departing for Geneva, Eisenhower told the American people that, "for the first time, a President goes to engage in a conference with the heads of other governments in order to prevent wars, in order to see whether in this time of stress and strain we cannot devise measures that will keep from us this terrible scourge that afflicts mankind." He asked all of his countrymen to attend church to ask Divine help. (Dulles had questioned this appeal to attend church, fearing what might seem an artificially stimulated demonstration.) In Moscow, Bulganin told the press his delegation would "discuss frankly with the other great powers the most important international problems, to find a common language and by joint efforts to achieve a relaxation of international tension and the strengthening of confidence in the relations between states. . . . We will undoubtedly be able to find common ground." Eden and Faure spoke in similar vein.[1]

Eisenhower as chairman of the first session delivered the opening statement, and reminded world leaders that the conference was a response to a universal urge for peace. He indicated issues for discussion. First was German unity through free elections and safeguards to calm the fear of a rearmed Hitler-type regime. Other desiderata were self-determination for Eastern Europe, free communication among nations and peoples, abridgment or an end to the activities of international communism, reduction of armaments with dependable inspection, and peaceful use of atomic energy. Faure and Eden endorsed Eisenhower's remarks, with minor additions.

Bulganin spoke softly, but, as Eisenhower later recalled, "his tone could not conceal hard realities."[2] The Russian called for a pan-European security system to replace WEU, NATO, and the Warsaw Alliance. This plan looked to withdrawal of American influence. Only then, apparently, could German unification occur. Bulganin refused to discuss the satellite question on the ground of interference in the internal affairs of other states. The Soviet Premier wanted the Taiwan problem settled in favor of Communist China. He endorsed more economic and cultural contacts between nations.

In ensuing days the heads of government discussed, at length and with little progress, the four main points of the agenda: German unification, European security, disarmament, and development of contacts between East and West. As the summit threatened to become a colossal bore, Eisenhower dramatically brought it to life: taking the center of the stage he turned toward the Russian delegation and vowed, "The United States will never take part in an aggressive war." He was so convincing that Bulganin spontaneously replied, "We believe the statement." The President suggested that the Soviet Union and the United States indicate their good faith by supplying each other with blueprints of their military establishments and allowing photo-reconnaissance planes over their territories. This open-skies plan was widely accepted as evidence of his sincerity, but not by the Russians and their adherents.

The final meeting was a tedious affair; participants argued on the wording of a directive for the foreign ministers who were to meet in Geneva that October. There were to be no secret agreements or treaties. The directive took the place of a communique and enjoined the foreign ministers to consider a European security pact, disarmament with safeguards, unification of Germany by free elections, and contacts between the two blocks. The October meeting was to test the generalities uttered at the summit.[3]

The optimism of many observers now turned into pessimism. Joseph Newman, writing for the *Herald Tribune*, thought the only change was in the way the Russians said "*Nyet.*" Gone was the familiar belligerent growl; now they said it with a smile. Roscoe Drummond in a dispatch to the same paper was not impressed by Soviet good manners; the "massive cordiality," he wrote, was a facade hiding "massive hostility." James Reston of the *Times* felt the Russians were playing a game of watchful waiting, hoping to wear out Western patience. "The prosperity in the West and the blandishments from the East, they are convinced, will work to their advantage. Meanwhile they will smile and smile, negotiate and negotiate, divide and divide."[4]

Despite such warnings the world liked what it saw.

On return to Washington, Dulles took a careful look at the summit conference. The meeting had created problems for the West, and solved none. For more than a decade Western unity had continued, so Dulles believed, out of fear of the Soviet Union and a sense of moral superiority. Fear had diminished and moral lines had blurred. The West, its people and leaders, seemed bewildered, but were optimistic about the "spirit" of Geneva. In this grand but private analysis the Secretary did not think that the Geneva Conference justified relaxation of the Western program for self-defense. The recent change in Soviet policy was a classic maneuver: a temporary retreat. The new and welcome Soviet methods—peaceful accommodation, social amenities—made him ready to pursue a policy which would reciprocate the Russian good attitudes, but he was not willing to alter programs and give over American objectives to achieve a problematical international order and justice. Under no circumstances would he accept the Soviet power position in Europe, tolerating covert aggression and sanctifying wrongs in Eastern Europe and elsewhere. The West should correct the gross international injustices committed by the Soviets: unnatural partition of Germany, subjugation of satellite nations, and subversive activities of communist parties under orders from Moscow.

Dulles disliked Bulganin's maneuvering to sit next to the President when pictures were taken of the four heads of government. The Russians had enlarged one picture out of all proportion, cutting off Eden and Faure, and duplicated it endlessly. He was peeved when the cropped photograph of a smiling Eisenhower and an amiable Bulganin appeared at the Leipzig Fair and throughout Italy, to help the local communist parties gain respectability.

In coming months and especially during the October conference of foreign ministers the Secretary determined to test Soviet willingness to solve the German problem, eliminate trade barriers, agree to inspection as a basis for foolproof disarmament, cooperate with Eisenhower's aerial inspection (which

Dulles felt highly imaginative and realistic), give more responsibilities to satellite countries, and lessen activities of international communism. He thought that the Kremlin did not want to hurt the spirit of Geneva, and would pay to avoid doing so. He looked forward to a conference.

The foreign ministers—Dulles, Macmillan, Molotov, and Pinay—met in Geneva from October 27 to November 16, 1955. The Russians, under cover of reasonableness, were fishing in the troubled waters of the Middle East and about to sign an arms deal with Egypt. Eisenhower, immobilized by a heart attack, was unable to guide, and his illness weakened Dulles' position. Soon after the Secretary arrived, Macmillan suggested that they condemn Soviet moves in the Middle East which he thought were the gravest threat to the West. The Foreign Secretary felt that the West should not toy with the Russians at Geneva while they were consolidating in the Middle East and capitalizing the spirit of Geneva in France and Italy where communist parites were advertised as respectable allies of socialist parties. Dulles declined drastic action against the Russians; it might seem he was taking advantage of an incapacitated President. Apprehensive about the President's health and its effect on the work at hand, Dulles asked Macmillan to be ready to take leadership. He wanted no accusation that he was moving without guidance, abandoning Eisenhower's pacific purposes.

Dulles kept the President fully informed, and Eisenhower emphasized to the Secretary through his special assistant, Sherman Adams, that under no circumstances should the United States be party to a false peace, or prolongation of the conference if the Soviets were acting in bad faith.

The first round on German unification and European security took place on October 29, 1955, and after the three Western ministers presented their case, Molotov asked for a European security system to which both West and East Germany would be parties, with Germany divided indefinitely. Dulles had expected this; if the Russians were ready to change they would not do so until the last moment. During the ensuing days Dulles thought he saw evidence that Russia would accept the Western security proposal, but as debate shifted from European security to unification of Germany by free elections, his hopes disappeared. Molotov went only so far as to suggest that the two German states establish a council for cooperation. He refused to endorse or discuss the directive of the summit conference on unification. Dulles and his Western colleagues were quick to note Soviet deviation from the directive, but Molotov was immovable. The Secretary now thought Molotov was attempting to convince the Germans that the Western powers could do nothing for them, that they must deal with Moscow.

The Russian position hardened on November 8, after Molotov returned from a brief visit to his capital. That afternoon he delivered an uncompromising speech. He rejected all Western proposals for European security and German unification. The Soviet

Union, he said, would never allow East Germany to unite with West Germany except under conditions which implied communization of both. Not one phrase was conciliatory; not one word endorsed the summit agreement. The British and French ministers decided not to reply, and Dulles, presiding, said Molotov's speech was so serious he did not want to respond to it without deliberation. Next day he castigated Molotov for undoing even the small amount of good achieved at the summit. The foreign ministers conference came to an end, and with it the spirit of Geneva, its glow and afterglow.

Following the Geneva meetings Khrushchev and Bulganin exuded a confidence which went beyond the characteristic Soviet exaggeration of strength and victories. These successors to Stalin had gone through the transition of power smoothly. They accepted Eden's invitation to visit Great Britain, the first such journey for the top Soviet leadership. They believed in the present and future of their regime. It seemed as if for the first time in Soviet history the leaders were sure of their communist society. The summit conference had convinced them that neither the United States nor the West planned to attack. British and French weakness, differences among the allies in non-European areas, developments in the Middle East, all increased Soviet confidence. Assured by military power and fortified by their creed, the Soviets began to exploit areas hitherto untouched. In many parts of the world they were ready, for they had a surplus of arms and industrial equipment.

The Russian leaders turned toward underdeveloped areas—Africa, the Middle East, Latin America. Anti-colonialism had been a communist theme, oft-repeated on ceremonial occasions. After Geneva, Soviet leaders were sure that they had the power to make it part of Soviet diplomacy. All states wishing to be neutral would have support of the Kremlin. From the end of the Geneva meetings of 1955 until death in 1959, Dulles would attempt to answer this new challenge.

CHAPTER FIFTEEN

SECURITY FOR THE MIDDLE EAST

1

NOW WE approach the infinitely complicated, and eternal, Near Eastern Question. John Foster Dulles had anticipated Russian moves into the Middle East, and from the first days of assuming office as Secretary of State he was certain the Soviet Union had begun a covert effort to turn that vast area into a communist sphere of influence, and that the United States was the only nation capable of preventing it. Alarmed by documents of the previous Administration and disquieting reports from American ambassadors and other officials, the new Secretary decided to increase American influence there at the earliest possible moment. He was less concerned with Soviet reaction to an expanded American involvement in the predominantly Moslem world than with effects of his action on Israeli-American and British-American relations. He thought it imperative to find solutions to the Arab-Israeli conflict and intra-Arab hostilities, and to ease the British position in the Middle East. This, of course, meant raising fundamental problems with the government of the United Kingdom, which showed resentment whenever the United States tried to be impartial. Dulles was sympathetic with the

British view that any action of the United States in this region hastened the loss of British prestige; he viewed that loss as a result of a natural political evolution within the area.

Dulles was not the first Secretary of State to seek independent action in the Middle East. Dean Acheson at a meeting of Churchill and Truman on the U.S.S. *Williamsburg* on the Potomac, January 5, 1952, had called attention to the area—a situation, he told Churchill and Eden, which fitted Marxist hopes: masses of impoverished people, no middle class, an incompetent and corrupt small governing and owning class, foreign influences against which communist agitators could arouse the masses, precisely the right ingredients for communist takeover. Western Europe, Acheson had said, was not in danger of Soviet attack; what he feared was creeping actions, covert or through proxies, in such scattered parts of the world as Indochina and the Middle East, with a view toward exhausting the Western powers. The United States and Great Britain should devise new Middle East policies. He was ready to suggest some, Acheson remarked in the presence of Truman, but unwilling to support British policy which he felt did not reflect realities. Washington could work with London, but not in their present positions which he likened to two people locked in loving embrace in a rowboat about to go over Niagara Falls. A break in the embrace was necessary to reach safety.

The metaphor amused Churchill. But the Prime Minister equated American commitment in the Far

East with that of the British in the Middle East. The United States, he told Truman, carried a burden in the Far East and he was anxious to ease it; he offered no specific assistance but suggested a need for study. Churchill then wanted the President to lighten his task in the Middle East by sending a contingent of troops to the Suez Canal. The presence of even a small number of American soldiers would relieve an entire British division, and stop what he considered Egyptian unlawful conduct in sponsoring guerrilla raids on the British base along the canal. Churchill also wanted the United States to halt financial aid to Iran, to stand against its emotional leader Mossadegh and force the Iranians to come to terms with the British. But Truman and Acheson were unwilling to commit America's prestige and power to back British policies in the Middle East.[1]

Early in January, 1953—almost precisely a year later—Churchill came to the United States to see Eisenhower, and again urged support for the British position. He did not ask military aid. The British had built a gigantic base on the west side of the canal, perhaps the largest base in the world: three miles wide and sixty-five long, with one and a half billion dollars worth of workshops and supplies. Eighty thousand men were garrisoned there, at an annual cost of over fifty million dollars. General Mohammed Naguib, after overthrowing King Farouk in July, 1952, had sought to force out the British. Churchill and Eden had been ready to agree to a phased withdrawal, but wanted to maintain the base. They hoped Egypt would become a member of a Middle East defense organization. All this in return for American-British aid.

Two months later Eden talked in Washington with the President and Dulles, and gained the impression that Eisenhower thought it essential for the British to maintain the base, and that to "evacuate the canal zone before making a Middle Eastern defence arrangement" would expose London to Egyptian blackmail. "In contrast to Dulles," Eden recalled, Eisenhower "was clear and firm on this point."[2] The Foreign Secretary told the President that Egypt was "the key to Middle East defence." He suggested three alternatives for negotiation with Egypt. Britain could hand over the canal zone, along with the zone base area during peacetime, keeping certain installations which would require some seven thousand troops. Should the Egyptians refuse, the British were ready to give full responsibility for all installations; but since the Egyptians had little experience and training, they would require allied supervisory and technical personnel. Should this arrangement too be unacceptable, the British would evacuate the whole base, retaining only occasional inspection privileges. All these plans anticipated that the base would be available for wartime allied use, particularly British, and that Egypt would be a member in a Middle East defense arrangement.

Eisenhower thought the British proposals reasonable, and agreed to support them if Cairo asked the United States to join the discussions. Otherwise the

Egyptian Government might think the British and the Americans came to the conference to announce an ultimatum. "An uninvited guest," he wrote Churchill, "cannot possibly come into your house, be asked to leave, and then expect cordial and courteous treatment if he insists upon staying." The President did try to influence General Naguib to invite the United States, but urged that the British meanwhile begin negotiations, hoping that when "discussions reached the point where Egypt's need of military assistance came to the fore, the United States might then be invited to join the group."[3] The British and Egyptians opened talks on April 27, 1953, which broke down hopelessly on May 5. Soon Naguib rejected American participation on the ground that the British must first agree to evacuate their troops; only then would Egypt consider a Middle East defense setup.

Churchill and Eden were disappointed. "If we had been able to bring about joint Anglo-American negotiations with Egypt at this stage," Eden speculated in his memoirs, ". . . the future position in the Middle East would have worked out differently. It was unfortunate that the United States Government . . . [was] not prepared to put any pressure upon the Egyptians to bring this about." The Foreign Secretary did not understand how the United States could ever have been accused of "gate-crashing" when, as a willing supplier of large financial and other aid to Egypt, it was in fact a welcome guest in Naguib's house.[4]

2

Early in the spring of 1953 Dulles embarked on a three-week tour, May 9 to 29, of the Middle East and adjoining areas, coinciding with Naguib's turndown of American entry into the Anglo-Egyptian talks. Before departing, Dulles was briefed by Eisenhower, orally and through several memoranda. The President shared Dulles' concern about vulnerability of the region. His suggestions he based on long talks with Paul G. Hoffman, the former administrator of the Marshall Plan who had become head of the Ford Foundation, and Eric Johnston, head of the advisory board of the Point IV program, and with other individuals having knowledge of the Middle East. Evidently these people "jammed full of ideas" impressed Eisenhower; so much that he suggested that the Department consider establishing an office of "miscellaneous contacts" through which to channel the ideas of American businessmen, educators, and even casual travelers. The President believed Egypt could be the key to the Middle East. American initiative in the establishment of Israel and the resulting Arab refugee problem had embittered American-Arab relations. Eisenhower wondered whether aid that the United States had been supplying Israel delayed settlement of the Israeli-Arab conflict; did it not enable Israel to avoid facing the issue that unless the Israelis traded with Arab countries their nation could not be a viable state? The question of Israel—

a rallying point for Arab leaders—was distracting Egypt. No Egyptian government, Eisenhower thought, could carry on foreign policy without a domestic base. The living standard of the Egyptian people had to go up, and he was willing to increase economic aid. The President called Dulles' attention to a project the Egyptians had in mind, a higher dam on the Nile above Aswan. Preliminary studies had shown that raising the height of the waters in Nubia would increase Egypt's tillable area by as much as a third, and also provide electric power and supply fertilizers. Would it be possible for the United States, perhaps jointly with Britain, to support an Egyptian loan from the International Bank, perhaps supplementing it with American grants? Would such an offer persuade the Egyptians to settle issues peacefully?[5]

Dulles' first stop was Cairo where the Egyptian-British talks were reaching a dead end and Naguib announcing that independence could come "only by sacrifice and blood." He came at an inopportune time, bringing from Eisenhower a gift later much remarked—a Colt .38. This gesture from one chief of state to another was unfortunate; it aroused comment in London, Jerusalem, Cairo, indeed throughout the Middle East. Eisenhower had not expected an untoward reaction for he thought the revolver "a fine gift, particularly in view of the distinctive American flavor of this weapon, which would be as exotic and interesting to the general as an old Egyptian sword would have been" to him.[6] Commentators had a holiday theorizing on conscious, subconscious, and symbolic meanings of the token. Pictures of Naguib with an American revolver were on the front pages of London tabloids along with critical comments about Dulles' partiality for Egypt. Some Israeli journalists thought the pistol pointed at Israel. Egyptians were not sure of the Colt's meaning; one magazine asked: was the Secretary suggesting that Naguib shoot the British in Suez? did the gun imply American desire that Naguib preserve public order by gunfire in Egypt, "which, after all, is a democracy"? that Naguib needed "a revolver to protect himself"?[7] Eisenhower had to assure Churchill that the gift did not presage a flow of arms to Egypt.

Dulles had learned from resident American and foreign officials of the tense Egyptian situation which promised to erupt into open hostilities, and Naguib did not quiet the Secretary's apprehension. The Revolutionary Council, dominated by a lieutenant colonel named Gamal Abdel Nasser, was riding a crest of popular support. It had determined to push the British out of Egypt and operate the Suez base without help of foreign soldiers, technicians, or occasional inspectors. The Egyptian leaders would rather die as martyrs and plunge the nation into chaos than agree to anything their people might interpret as an infringement of sovereignty. Dulles understood their position, but wondered whether the Egyptians could maintain the Suez installation in working condition. And he doubted that Egypt would consent to British or Western occupation of the canal in event of war or emergency. Naguib told Dulles he could not openly commit his government to any defense arrangement with the West because of public opinion, but promised on his "word of honor" to cooperate with the United States and even with Britain once anti-British feelings disappeared. He indicated that some agreement with Israel could come without difficulty once he solved the British problem. Dulles was skeptical; these promises seemed like window dressing to win American support. The Secretary left Cairo convinced that Naguib had determined to make Egypt the leader of the Arab world.

The Israelis, apprehensive about the new leadership in Washington, had not worried about Dulles when they welcomed him in Tel Aviv. They recalled that as a member of the American delegation at the United Nations during the Truman Administration he had supported Israel against the Bernadotte Plan, which had approval of Secretary of State George C. Marshall and Assistant Secretary Rusk. (Count Bernadotte, the recently-assassinated United Nations mediator, had asked Israel to surrender about half its territory—the Negev—and suggested that Jerusalem become an international enclave.) After defeat of the Plan, Dulles as head of the delegation had introduced a resolution which did not mention frontiers; it recommended that, following an armistice, Israel and the Arab states negotiate boundary lines, and that Arab refugees have the right to return provided they lived in peace with their neighbors. Israel was grateful to Dulles, the architect of the 1948 resolution which broke the United Nations deadlock.

In subsequent years whenever Dulles discussed the

Arab-Israel conflict he would emphasize this episode as the starting point of his interest in the problem. One might add that Israel's Ambassador to the United States, Abba Eban, had been pleased when Dulles sought his advice on the Middle East plank for the Republican platform of 1952, in which the future Secretary of State committed his party to assist Israel. Eban would have liked a stronger statement, but was satisfied that the Republicans continued the tradition of support.

Dulles' meeting with Prime Minister David Ben-Gurion was pleasant. He was delighted when Ben-Gurion publicly favored his mission "to win friends with the Arabs" and saw nothing in it inconsistent with the interests of Israel. He found the Prime Minister inclined to relax his previous position of "total peace or nothing," and willing to reduce tensions step by step to create the right atmosphere for a peace settlement. He gathered that Israel was concerned about the Republican Administration, jittery that Washington might attempt to impose an unjust peace in order to humor the Arabs, and might proceed on a water development plan which would conflict with the Israeli scheme to irrigate the Negev with water from the Jordan. Dulles assured Ben-Gurion of the good wishes of the Administration, and suggested that Israel was perhaps "taking on too much" in trying to solve all the problems of Jewish history in a decade. This had led to an admirable dynamism, but did it not also lead to an overburdening program? The Secretary told Israeli leaders he realized the serious effects on the Israeli economy of the Arab boycott and closure of the Suez Canal.[8]

3

Leaving Israel, Dulles made a tour of Jordan, Syria, Lebanon, Iraq, and Saudi Arabia. He found hatred of Israel, apprehension over Zionist influences on American policy, great poverty in the midst of vast oil reserves, concern over Arab refugees, weak military establishments, anti-British feeling, social and political turmoil, and absence of worry over the Soviet Union. Iraq, and to a lesser extent Syria, showed some awareness of Soviet danger. Lebanon, half-Christian and half-Arab, considered itself a possible bridge between the United States and the Arab nations. The Lebanese Government also was conscious of communist subversion. Iraq was the only Arab state where the question of Israel was not acute, relations with Great Britain relatively good, economy progressing, and where Dulles saw a willingness to consider defensive arrangements with the West, particularly the United States. The Secretary credited all of these feelings to the Iraqi Prime Minister, General Nuri as Said.

Dulles ended his tour with short visits to India, Pakistan, Turkey, Greece, and Libya. Nehru's determination to develop India and dedication to democracy impressed him, but the revered leader's lack of knowledge of world affairs dismayed him. Dulles thought Nehru naive and misinformed. Pakistan was a pleasant surprise, for although predominantly Moslem it was "extremely friendly" to the United States, much aware of Soviet danger, and desirous of American military assistance and economic aid.

Dulles was delighted with Turkey's strength, such a contrast to the rest of the Middle East, and the only difficulty was that the Turks wanted to expand their military establishment beyond their economic capacity. Turkish leaders thought that only they could prevent a Soviet advance in the area, and doubted the will of Arab states to cooperate in regional defense. They were eager to discuss United States bases on their soil, suggested Yugoslavia for NATO membership, and that the NATO Council take responsibility for the Suez Canal and French North Africa. The Secretary found the Greek Government stable, the monarchy shaky; as expected, Athens wanted more economic aid and association in a Middle East defense scheme. Libya, a new member of the Arab League, seemed anxious to take a moderate course. Dulles doubted Libya's viability; he expected this erstwhile Italian colony to disintegrate into the three former provinces, which would please the French and perhaps the British. Here the only problem for the United States was negotiation for American bases.[9]

These were first impressions, and there was a need to reflect on them. There was no question but that the whole area lacked political stability. The fanatical revolutionary spirit demanding rapid industrial, agricultural, and military progress increased immediate problems and ignored the Soviet threat. The Egyptian-British dispute, Arab-Israeli conflict, Arab-British boundary problems, Iranian-British controversy, and French difficulties in North Africa—all produced xenophobia. The quarrel between India and Pakistan over Kashmir made for a delicate balance in the southern half of the Asian continent.

In all these nations the hitherto apathetic masses wanted to rid themselves of age-long poverty and class distinction, and were now making demands which their governments were unable to fulfill. Rising expectations came when the aftermath of the Second World War had broken the ties with Western nations. Exhausted, the Western European powers were unable to offer leadership. The British position, Dulles concluded, was deteriorating, probably to the point of no repair; everywhere, with the possible exception of India and Jordan, he found distrust of the British; those days when the Middle East could relax under British protection were gone; and remnants of British troops here and there were now contributing to instability. The same was true of French influence. Nor was the American position good. Dulles was saddened by the loss of respect for the United States, which he felt varied "almost directly with the nearness of the respective Arab states to Israel." The establishment of Israel, and "association of the United States in the minds of the people of the area with French and British colonial and imperialistic policies," the Secretary reflected, "are millstones around our neck."

The Middle East was wavering between neutralism and desire, mixed with fear, for Western protection. States near the Soviet empire were more willing to cooperate in some defense arrangement. All nations in this vast region were waiting American action; all thought Britain and France no longer major powers. The United States, Dulles concluded, had to increase its influence in the Middle East as quickly as possible. The United States had to take some action to influence British and Israeli policies, which tended to converge into aggression against Arabs. British pride demanded delicate policies so as not to damage the Atlantic alliance. Public disagreement would accomplish one of the aims of the Soviet Union. The first problem was the Israeli-Arab conflict. Dulles resolved to seek every means to allay Arab fear by assuring that American policy would be impartial. He wanted the Arabs to know that the United States accepted Israel, with no thought of "turning back the pages." The way forward was "step-by-step" reduction of tension, such as the resettlement of refugees, lessening of friction along boundaries, modification of the status of Jerusalem, and cooperative approaches to the water problem. He hoped to convince the Arabs that policy toward the Middle East would be based on aspirations of the Moslem peoples in accord with American traditions, not those of the Western allies. The Secretary determined to press the British and French to acquiesce in some Arab demands and at the same time persuade Moslem leaders of the importance of orderly evolution. He was anxious to alert the Arab states to Soviet strategy which sought to encourage extreme nationalism.[10]

The Secretary was ready to recommend an immediate increase in economic aid, to assist with the water problem, and to resettle the Arab refugees. He foresaw limited military aid to selected states for internal security. Except for the Turkish flank the Middle East was virtually defenseless, a gap in the "northern tier" of allies. He was not ready to recommend that Arab nations join the Western powers; the political situation, he thought, was not ready. He was fascinated by the idea of a Middle Eastern equivalent of NATO, but concluded that it lacked reality. He wanted to improve conditions without making *quid pro quo* demands. Where guarantees for American investments were necessary they should be simple, and devoid of legalism. The object was to win friendship.[11]

4

Within a few days after returning to Washington, Dulles reviewed his impressions in a televised address of June 1, 1953. His public disclosures came remarkably near to his confidential report to the President.[12] Neither Israel nor Britain was happy about it.

Meanwhile Anglo-Egyptian relations began to improve. In the winter of 1953-54 Egypt indicated willingness to let the British reenter the canal if Turkey were threatened. London resumed negotiations. In midsummer 1954, Churchill and Eden visited Washington to persuade Eisenhower to employ American economic aid to the new regime, now headed by Colonel Nasser, "to induce the Egyptians to make and keep an agreement on acceptable terms," and give public support to the principle of freedom of transit through the Suez Canal.[13] Eisenhower and Dulles promised to do so. An understanding was reached by the United Kingdom and Egypt in July, 1954; a settlement was signed two months later on October 19.

This complex Anglo-Egyptian agreement of 1954 terminated the Anglo-Egyptian treaty of 1936. Britain was to withdraw all forces from Egyptian territory by June 18, 1956. Egypt was to maintain the principal military installations in the area of the canal, with maintenance carried out by British and Egyptian commercial firms using both British and Egyptian civil personnel, the number of British employees to be kept to an agreed limit. After consultation with Egypt, British forces could return to the base in event of "an armed attack by an outside power" on one of the Arab states or Turkey. There were no provisions for the eventuality of an outside attack on Iran, or against any state other than those mentioned. Both powers recognized that the Suez Maritime Canal, though part of Egypt, was a "waterway economically, commercially and strategically of international importance," and expressed determination "to uphold the convention guaranteeing the freedom of navigation of the Canal signed at Constantinople on the 29th of October, 1888." This article was to become an issue during the crisis of 1956.

American diplomacy worked quietly and effectively during the secret negotiations that led to this accord. Nasser appreciatively acknowledged United States help. So did Eden. The Foreign Secretary stated publicly that the agreement preserved Britain's "essential requirements." He would change his mind; the agreement of 1954, he wrote in his memoirs, was a "declaration of convenience for Britain and Egypt." There was nothing in the clauses to restrain Egyptian ambition. The agreement's strength, he recalled, depended on Anglo-American cooperation—the only means to curb Nasser and improve relations between Israel and Egypt and other Arab states.[14]

The Suez base agreement of 1954 encouraged Dulles to follow it up with a general collective security system in the Middle East. Since 1951 the Western powers, pleased with the Truman Doctrine and inclusion of Greece and Turkey in NATO, had hoped for a Middle East Defense Organization (MEDO) with Turkey, Iraq, and Iran as charter members. MEDO was to be a bulwark against the Soviet Union, whose interest in the area was dormant but by no means dead. In the address of June 1, 1953, after his Middle East tour, Dulles had rejected this undertaking. "A Middle East Defense Organization," he said, "is a future rather than an immediate possibility. . . . No such system can be imposed from without. It should be designed and grow from within out of a sense of common destiny and common danger."

It was clear that any such pact would not include the Egyptians. Nasser was not interested in joining the West in a Middle East security pact. General Naguib's successor did not think there was any danger from the Soviet Union, only from Israel. What he wanted, he said, was the higher Aswan dam. There were other reasons for Nasser's rejection, for he wanted to unite the Arabs under his leadership and was jealous of the Prime Minister of Iraq, old Nuri as Said, who had come out for an alliance with the Western powers and approved a "northern tier" defense arrangement. Nor was he happy with the Turkish-Pakistani Alliance of April 2, 1954, which he opposed on the ground that Pakistan had nothing in common with any Arab state. And when on February 24, 1955, Iraq and Turkey signed the Pact of Mutual Cooperation (Baghdad Pact), which promised to become a larger Middle East defense security arrangement, he determined to oppose it at all costs.

Nasser notwithstanding, Dulles greeted the Turkish-Pakistani Alliance and the Baghdad Pact. Great Britain joined the Baghdad Pact on April 5, 1955, as did Pakistan and Iran later that same year. All members of the pact wanted the United States to join. Dulles sent observers to council meetings and gave military aid, but refused to make the United States a full member. He was caught by surprise when the British entered the pact; he may not have wanted London as a member. Evidently he did not wish to antagonize Nasser, alienate Israel, and increase anti-colonial protests. As events turned out, American refusal to join the pact did not appease the Egyptians; Washington's support was enough to augment Nasser's animosity. In retrospect Eden thought Dulles' diplomacy devious and, in the end, disastrous. "Having played a leading part," he wrote several years later, ". . . the United States Government held back while Britain alone of the Western powers joined it. Worse still, they tried to take credit for this attitude in capitals like Cairo. . . . An ounce of membership would have been worth all the havering and saved a ton of trouble."[15]

The Baghdad Pact also was a challenge to the Soviet Union, and the Russians immediately sought ways to leapfrog over the northern tier and recognize Nasser as the dominant figure in the Arab world. They would supply him with arms, give him economic aid, and tie him to Moscow. Soviet determination to expand into the Middle East began to appear almost at once after the signing of the Baghdad Pact and after the Geneva summit conference of 1955. This activity gave a new turn to the Near Eastern Question in which the United States was now deeply involved.

CHAPTER SIXTEEN

SOVIET ARMS FOR THE MIDDLE EAST

IN EGYPT during the summer of 1955, Gamal Abdel Nasser, that tall man with an enigmatic smile, was dreaming of a grand future. He was pleased with himself: he was courted by the Russians, wooed by the Americans, accepted by the Indians, adored by the Egyptians. Tito had invited him to his island paradise on Brioni, and Khrushchev in Moscow was preparing for him a state visit and spontaneous demonstrations of support. Nasser's vision of a pan-Arab federation led by himself seemed near reality.

Across the Red Sea the Russian-born David Ben-Gurion, the prophet-like patriarch of Israel, paced impatiently in his pioneer cabin in Sdeh Boker in the Sinai desert. To him Nasser was Hitler incarnate, a modern-day Haman who plotted to annihilate the Jewish state. Would a preventive war be the only way to stop him? The *fedayeen* bases, the sanctuaries from which Egyptian guerrillas raided into Israeli territory, must be destroyed. The Arabs must know that Israel was strong, that it had allies in the West. Ben-Gurion was comforted by unmistakable French support, hopeful of American aid, and of course consoled by Arab divisions, but suspicious of Britain. The Arabs hated Israel, but fear of Nasser's purposes might well outweigh their animosity. So he thought as he surveyed conditions in the Middle East, now complicated by the Soviet designs.

1

When Secretary Dulles returned from the Geneva Conference of July, 1955, he had determined to find new programs for the Middle East, for the time seemed right: the new satrap of Egypt, emotionally volatile and very ambitious, appeared friendly toward the United States. It was true that Eric Johnston's projected regional Arab-Israeli irrigation scheme had run into difficulty. The Arabs, at first sympathetic, now were suspicious because of Johnston's connections with the pro-Israeli American Christian Palestine Committee. There was the possibility of an Arab-Soviet *rapprochement*, forcing stronger American backing of Israel and the abandonment of impartiality. These problems seemed no large barrier to what Dulles hoped would be a successful diplomacy in that area.

In mid-August he drafted a proposal (code name "Alpha") for the President's consideration, a public statement to be translated into Hebrew and Arabic and transmitted to American missions abroad. He anticipated reactions from both sides, for the Arabs did not want peace with Israel and the Jewish state would not consider any boundary adjustments at its expense. Nevertheless a statement on the problems of the Middle East should command a serious hearing, and it was imperative before the forthcoming presidential campaign. Dulles had shown a draft to Vice President Nixon and Attorney General Herbert Brownell, Jr., some Democratic Congressional leaders, and the British Government—all had approved. The Secretary wished Eisenhower's permission to present this statement publicly and with "the authority of the President."

Receiving Eisenhower's approval Dulles spoke before the Council on Foreign Relations on August 26, 1955, and the address mirrored his "Alpha" memorandum. He called attention to his tour in 1953. Since then the Suez base issue had been "successfully resolved"; Arab-Israeli differences over water gave some evidence of moving toward a settlement. Dulles singled out three problems: the 900,000 Arab refugees, the "pall of fear that hangs over the Arab and Israeli people alike," and the lack of permanent boundaries between Israel and its neighbors. For the refugees the Secretary suggested resettlement and repatriation through creation of arable land by water development projects. This would benefit all people of the Middle East and assist Israel's border security. The United States would pay part of the cost. Dulles thought that Israel should help. He also recommended an international loan backed by the United States. Washington would enter into "formal treaty engagements to prevent or thwart any effort by either side to alter by force the boundaries between Israel and its Arab neighbors." He called on other nations to join in this security guarantee which he hoped the

United Nations would sponsor. Recalling his United Nations resolution of 1948, the Secretary advised the Arabs and Israelis to reach an accord. Would not converting "armistice lines of danger into boundary lines of safety" outweigh any loss of territory?[1]

Within a week he was able to report to Eisenhower that the first reactions of Arab states to "Alpha" were not as violent as feared. He was pleased with the more favorable sentiments of the Israelis and Jewish-American leaders. Abba Eban thought the speech statesmanlike, and appreciated the offer to assist in water development and refugee resettlement. He welcomed a treaty with the United States, but criticized Dulles' condition of agreement on frontiers. Israel, he told Dulles, needed a guarantee of the *status quo.*[2]

The Secretary's optimism was ever so brief, for on return from a two-week vacation he learned that Czechoslovakia was contemplating delivery of large supplies of arms to Egypt.

Prime Minister Eden wrote to Bulganin and sent a copy of the letter to Eisenhower. The President appealed directly to the Soviet Premier not to endanger the spirit of Geneva. Bulganin's replies were discouraging. Was it not a fact that Egypt had an army and had received arms from the United States and Great Britain? Bulganin did not think the Egyptian-Czechoslovakian arrangement meant an arms race or violation of peace. The communists, he pointed out, did not tie arms deliveries to political conditions, forcing recipients into military alliances against other states, which led to an armaments race! Was it not natural for Nasser, who did not want a Western-sponsored Middle East alliance, to seek arms to safeguard Egypt's independence? Bulganin implied that the Soviet Union would join the United States and Britain to settle problems in the Middle East.

Now trouble loomed everywhere. Nasser took not merely a few arms from Czechoslovakia but weapons valued at between $90,000,000 and $200,000,000. To pay for them he bartered Egyptian cotton. In open challenge the Egyptian leader was testing the Tripartite Declaration of 1950 which had pledged the British, French, and Americans to regulate the supply of Middle East arms on the basis of parity between Israelis and Arabs. The Israelis now sought arms. The United Nations Truce Supervisory Organization in the Middle East alerted the Security Council.

Challenging the Baghdad Pact, Nasser was negotiating a defense treaty with Syria and Saudi Arabia. The Saudis were angry at British occupation of a cluster of villages on the Arabian peninsula, the Buraimi oasis, blaming the West for an "audacious and arrogant" British move in the "old imperialist tradition."[3]

In Cyprus the British, Turks, and Greeks were in a nasty quarrel, for Britain after withdrawal from the Suez Canal base was building a military base on this only territory remaining under British sovereignty in the Middle East. Caught between Greek Cypriots and a Turkish minority, the London government refused self-determination.

In the midst of these troubles President Eisenhower suffered a heart attack on September 23, 1955.

As mentioned in a previous chapter, Dulles worried about the President's illness and its effect on his influence, and could only move with caution. He did not wish to oppose the Egyptian-Syrian pact lest he consolidate Arab support of it. Nor would he expose and condemn Soviet infiltration in the Middle East at the forthcoming meeting of the foreign ministers at Geneva, as urged by Foreign Secretary Macmillan; rather he would raise the issue privately with Molotov. Meanwhile he supported the Baghdad Pact and secretly urged Lebanon and Jordan to stay away from the Egyptian-Syrian alliance, or to make a similar one between themselves. He was ready to offer arms, and propose that the Arab states and Israel meet separately with the United States to discuss a solution to frontiers.

Then the conference of foreign ministers of the Big Four opened in Geneva on October 27, 1955. Sunday, October 30, began for Dulles with enjoyable services by a young minister at the American Church. The rest of the day was not so pleasant: the Secretary had a difficult conference with Molotov on the Egyptian arms deal, followed by a longer talk on the same subject with the Prime Minister of Israel, Moshe Sharett, who had replaced Ben-Gurion. Dulles told Molotov that arms to Egypt had increased the risk of war between Israel and the Arabs and created anti-Soviet feeling in the United States. Molotov saw no danger but worried about anti-Russian sentiment among the Americans. Until recently only the United States, Great Britain, and France were sending arms to the Middle East. Why, Molotov asked, should not communists? Dulles replied that he had no desire to argue the right of Russians or Czechs to sell arms, or the right of Egyptians to purchase. If the arms negotiation were an isolated and limited venture—publicly acknowledged as such by the Russians—the problem could be handled with greater ease. Not so if it presaged a vast clandestine transaction. Molotov asked if the United States sought information on sale and delivery of arms. Dulles reiterated the need for a Soviet public statement, and denied he was suggesting an exchange of information.

Two days later the Western foreign ministers discussed their talks with Molotov. All evidently had taken the same line and received the same answers. Should they try to force the Soviets to a specific consideration of the Egyptian-Israeli problem? Would that not bring the Russians into a wider range of Middle Eastern affairs? Had not Molotov hinted for such an invitation?

In the meantime the Secretary sent instructions through the Department to American ambassadors in the Middle East to meet with officials of the Arab governments. They were to emphasize that recent developments indicated Soviet intent to subvert the area. Washington did not question the right of the Russian block to sell arms, or of Arabs to buy; it wanted to show that communists, mortal enemies of the Moslem religion, never considered arms sales as commercial ventures and had never made them without political strings. The United States would continue to provide moderate supplies of arms to Arabs and Israelis alike, but would do its best to prevent an all-out race in accord with the Tripartite Declaration of 1950.

2

Dulles saw Sharett at Geneva, and the Israeli Prime Minister who within a few days would give his office back to Ben-Gurion (Sharett would remain several weeks as Foreign Minister) asked the Secretary for guarantees. Dulles appreciated the Israeli position but did not think the time right for such engagements. He did not want to lose Arab good will. Neither he nor Congress was ready for a treaty with Israel. Dulles was aware of the American-Jewish vote in the next year's election, but felt that the future in the Middle East was too big to get involved in American domestic politics. The Secretary did promise support of Israel's request for more arms—reassurance by weapons instead of treaty. On November 7, 1955, the United States agreed to sell arms to Israel; this agreement he suspended after several weeks when Israelis killed 73 Arabs in retaliation for an attack on a fishing vessel which had resulted in only small damage and no casualties.[4]

Sharett also talked with Molotov, and a few days later Molotov asked Dulles what he thought of Sharett. Was he strong? Emotional? Did he have a large following? Dulles replied that Sharett was a moderate, had influence, and was against preventive war. The Soviet Foreign Minister saw no advantage in the latter. Dulles pointed out that the Israelis were under tremendous pressure. Molotov did not think the Arabs wanted to destroy Israel. And even if they should attack, the United Nations would stop them. That might be true, Dulles answered, but was it not also true that many Arabs believed the Soviets would veto any resolution against them? Not so, Molotov said—the Soviet Union would honor the United Nations.

The first reactions to Dulles' directive to the American chiefs of mission in the Middle East were mixed. From Cairo came news of profitable discussion between Ambassador Henry A. Byroade and Nasser. The Egyptian leader showed concern about communist infiltration, wanted to improve relations with the United States, denied that arrangements with the Soviet block had gone as far as the West thought, and indicated that Egypt was not sending arms to Syria and Saudi Arabia. Nasser did not ask arms from the United States; he did not want, so he claimed, to embarrass the United States. He urged that the United States stay away from the Baghdad Pact, and asked economic aid to build the higher dam at Aswan. From other sources came reports that Egypt was unhappy with the arms from the Soviet block; their inferior quality was arousing suspicion. There was also the revelation that the Egyptians through the West German Foreign Office had requested additional German officers to train the Egyptian army, while warning that if West Germany did not supply the officers they would get them from the communists. The Bonn regime did not wish to comply unless the United States and Great Britain urged it.

King Hussein of Jordan advised against selling arms to Israel. Jordan would not join the Baghdad Pact, although it wished the pact well. Nor was Jordan ready to agree with Israel on a boundary. From Syria came reports that France desired to strengthen its traditional influence, and had promised military aid against possible Iraqi domination.

Representatives of the Soviet block at the United Nations and in Jerusalem evidently warned the Israeli Government not to align with the West, nor to conclude a security pact with the United States and permit American bases on its soil. Should Israel heed the communist request the Soviet Union and its East European allies might allow emigration of Jews to Israel. In Washington, Eban stressed to Under Secretary of State Herbert Hoover, Jr.—who had replaced Bedell Smith—the need of weapons, recalled Israel's quest for a security guarantee, and recommended American participation in the Baghdad Pact to precede or be accompanied by a treaty. The Ambassador said Israel would not make territorial concessions to the Arabs, and was willing to open discussions in accord with Dulles' proposal of August 26 on financing compensation to Arab refugees.[5]

Dulles on November 4, 1955, met in Geneva with

the foreign ministers of Great Britain and France, who agreed to coordinate policies and arms to the Middle East. The French proposed a modest supply of arms to Syria and Lebanon, to keep those little nations in line. Pinay did not think Israel would object because of Syria's desire to remain independent. Dulles wanted to know if France had consented to ship arms to Israel. Pinay said there was a request, and France would probably send equipment. The French were willing to send arms to Egypt if Nasser would agree to stop meddling in North Africa.

During a lull in the conference Dulles, accompanied by his wife, called on President Tito in Yugoslavia. (Five days earlier he had gone to Spain to see Generalissimo Francisco Franco, to offset the trip to Yugoslavia.) It was a pleasant and rewarding visit, one of the most interesting he had ever had. Tito lived in capitalistic splendor on the island of Brioni, where he kept busy with masonry, cultivating plants, raising exotic animals, and boating. The talks were leisurely, friendly, candid. They confirmed Dulles' opinion that the Marshal wanted to live in the best of both worlds; he had no desire either to be part of the Soviet Union or tied to the West. Khrushchev and Bulganin, he informed Dulles, wanted to uproot Stalin's policies, but Stalinists were still active in the Soviet Union. Dulles and Tito were sure that peace had loosened ties among the noncommunist nations and also within the Soviet block. Tito thought the Soviets did not want war. The Russian grip had now relaxed, and Soviet authority—diluted and diversified—encouraged more freedom in the satellites.

Full freedom in these nations would not come quickly.

The Yugoslav also had something to say about Communist China: it was not a Soviet satellite nor a Russian spearhead for Asian penetration. The Russians were worried about the Chinese Communists. Stalin had had great difficulty with Mao Tse-tung, and did not trust national communism. At times the Soviet Union exercised a restraining influence on the Chinese. Mainland China was in the bloom of youth, intoxicated by revolutionary fever, wild but growing wiser—the exact thoughts Molotov recently had expressed to Dulles. Tito's evaluation of Soviet-Chinese relations coincided with recent American intelligence reports that Soviet moves in the Middle East had irked the Communist Chinese for reasons which still seemed obscure.

Tito and Dulles also discussed the Middle East. The Marshal told the Secretary that during a recent visit to Cairo he had advised Nasser to open contact with Israel, but the Egyptian refused.

On returning to Geneva, Dulles learned that Sharett, now Foreign Minister, was about to embark on a visit to the United States to support a bond drive for Israel, sponsored by the United Jewish Appeal. This was a serious problem. Dulles was in an awkward political and, even, moral position. Many people would not understand why at the time when the Soviets were supplying quantities of war material to the Arabs he refused to give Israel a treaty and arms. The time had not yet arrived for backing Israel in an arms race with Egypt.

At this juncture Dulles received some interesting

opinions from Under Secretary Hoover and from the President. Hoover had lost confidence in Byroade. The new Under Secretary thought Nasser might go back on the track, and that peace could revive on the basis of "Alpha." Neither Egypt nor Israel could win by arms. As for the President, Eisenhower wanted to get tough in the Middle East. The Russians, he said, were not trustworthy when they talked nicely or when they talked roughly. He wanted a new effort to buy Egypt away from the Russians by support of the Aswan dam.

3

The British took the same cautious policy. Eden asked the Arabs and Israelis to get together. Alluding to the arms deal arranged with Egypt by the Czechoslovak Government, and to the Kremlin's duplicity, he advised treating "the root cause of the trouble." He in effect suggested that Israel compromise on the boundary question in favor of the Arabs—a calculated indiscretion, he later would explain. The Israelis reacted with criticism, while Nasser called Eden's proposals "constructive" and "fair." Eden informed Eisenhower that the Arabs seemed to accept Israel; its leaders would be wise to adopt a peace guaranteed by the West, which would be more worthwhile than the armistice. Eden thought Israel in a better military position than the Arabs. It could win the battles, but could it win the war? Here was a question Eden would hear with a different dramatis personae at the time of the Suez crisis of 1956.

The Middle East threatened once again to get out of hand. In January, 1956, Eden informed Eisenhower that the situation was deteriorating. The Saudis for varying reasons had bribed Arab leaders, bought ministers and deputies, subsidized leftist, communist, near-communist, and nationalist newspapers in Syria, Jordan, and Lebanon. The Russians were plotting to subvert Jordan, and offered inducements to obtain a revocation of the Anglo-Jordanian treaty. Egyptians, Saudis, Syrians, Russians, all were working together. A distraught Eden wanted the United States and Britain to back the friends of the West: Jordan and Iraq, but not Israel. Something had to be done before the bear's claws reached out for control of the oil so necessary to the defense and economy of the West.[6]

At the end of January, Eden and his new Foreign Secretary, Selwyn Lloyd, arrived in Washington. The recent visit of Bulganin and Khrushchev to India and Burma, climaxed by an anticolonial manifesto endorsed by Nehru, had concerned the Prime Minister. Everywhere, he thought, the West was on the defensive. Before leaving London he had sent Eisenhower a cable: "I am not suggesting anything as grandiloquent as the Atlantic Charter, but something which shows that, both materially and in true values, the West has its own message to give." He wanted "to put teeth into the Tripartite Declaration." Eisenhower and Dulles, he would recall, emphasized constitutional difficulties. Most annoying was Washington's criticism of British actions over the Buraimi oasis; Eden thought Eisenhower and Dulles misinformed.

Discussions on Egypt were more pleasant and "closely in accord." A door had to open to Nasser. Present talks between Egyptians and the president of the International Bank for Reconstruction and Development, Eugene R. Black, might show Nasser's state of mind.[7]

Early in March, 1956, panic gripped Eden, for the Russians, he now wrote Eisenhower, had determined to liquidate the Baghdad Pact. To everyone it was visible that Cairo and Moscow were moving closer. King Hussein had dismissed his long-time British adviser, Lieutenant General John Bagot Glubb, commander of the Arab Legion, on whom Britain had counted to stabilize that country. Cairo had increased its propaganda against pro-Western Arab states through the "Voice of the Arabs." The time had come to shore up the Baghdad Pact and strengthen Iraq. All attempts to compromise, appease, and cajole had failed. Nasser had to be stopped, and the only way to do it would be for the United States to join the Baghdad Pact. Ambassador Winthrop W. Aldrich agreed; Eden had received much criticism for joining without the United States.

Eden's plea came when Dulles was attending a SEATO conference at Karachi, and after reading the correspondence and Department reports the Secretary wrote out a speculative, interim memorandum. He was ready to recommend that the United States join the Baghdad Pact. He hoped Britain first would settle its controversy with Saudi Arabia. He thought it wise if Congress, preferably in response to a United Nations request, authorized the President to cooperate with other member nations to ensure compliance with an Israeli-Arab armistice which would not demand boundary revision except by mutual agreement. Should the latter come about, the United States would provide military support to Saudi Arabia and Iraq, increase aid to Iran and Pakistan, and sell arms to Israel.

Hoover discussed Dulles' memorandum with Eisenhower, who informed Eden that there was no question of Soviet intent in the Middle East and of Nasser's duplicity, but the time to close the door on Nasser had not come, although it could appear at any moment. Such a decision would cancel prospects of an Arab-Israeli settlement. Nor was Eisenhower ready to bring the United States into the Baghdad Pact. American participation would either frighten the Arabs who were not members or increase their desire for arms; and Israel would demand a security treaty. A more effective course would be to aid Iran and Pakistan.

Eisenhower increasingly noticed the ominous reports from the Middle East and elsewhere: the Arab-Israeli frontier ablaze with forays and reprisals, American Zionists unhappy, Algerian rebels armed by Nasser, Cyprus aflame, the French government of Faure replaced by that of Guy Mollet, increasing differences among the allies, the British Commonwealth divided, the Soviets—ebullient, self-righteous—everywhere but most of all in Egypt. He looked forward to Dulles' return from the Far East.[8]

American efforts to persuade Nasser to a conciliatory policy had failed. Nasser, the Secretary now decided, had to learn that he could not expect good treatment from the United States while working with the Soviet Union. Dulles did not want a break, which might force Nasser into the arms of the bear. The United States and Britain should deny arms, delay arrangements for the high dam, postpone grain and oil, suspend the 1956 CARE program which anticipated an expenditure of more than $100,000,000, and offer radio facilities to Iraq. The United States and Britain, Dulles suggested, should negotiate with the Sudan to limit Egyptian influence there. He was ready to give Britain aid, covert and overt, to stabilize the Jordanian Government. Contrary to his tentative views while in Karachi, he now would not have the United States join the Baghdad Pact, or even show an intent to do so. He recommended more American participation in its military and economic committees. He saw the need of shoring up pro-Western elements in Lebanon, persuading Saudi Arabia to rival Egypt, helping Ethiopia and the Saudis counter Egyptian and Soviet influence in Yemen and other Arabian principalities. At the same time the United States would press for a United Nations move to reduce tension.

And what of Israel? Dulles determined to dissuade the Israelis from hostilities. He would deny export licenses for any major military items for Israel or the Arab states excepting Saudi Arabia and Iraq, but encourage other Western powers to sell Israel arms.

Here was an operation to balance Soviet aid to the Arabs. Israel had asked for F-86 aircraft to meet the MIG-15s. Dulles thought Israel should have them, but pressed Canada and France to supply F-86s and Mystères, the French equivalent. Neither ally liked the arrangement: why should they incur Arab wrath? Both wanted Washington to admit an American request for planes. Dulles was willing to say only that sales by the allies were with American acquiescence. The Israelis liked this Dullesian stratagem, although some Israeli leaders would say afterward that had it happened earlier, had Dulles been more decisive in replying to arms requests, the invasion of Sinai might not have occurred. For by spring, 1956, the Israelis were headlong in preparation with the impatient French for a Sinai-Suez campaign.[9]

CHAPTER SEVENTEEN

DEBACLE AT SUEZ

In the autumn of 1956, on the very eve of presidential elections in the United States, two complex events—one in Hungary, the other in Egypt—began and ended with dramatic suddenness. Both arose in midsummer, and disappeared with the onset of winter. Both showed a confusion, long in the making, within the Eastern and Western camps.

In the communist world, trouble started with Polish requests for more independence from the Soviet Union. The unexpected success of the Polish people, moderate as it was, emboldened the Hungarians to an open revolt which brought several days of mad and joyous freedom.

In the West difficulties began with Nasser's nationalization of the Suez Canal Company, and ended with an American-Soviet alignment against France and Great Britain at the same time the Red Army was crushing the Hungarian revolution. Eden and Mollet, condemned before the United Nations, retreated from Suez. Khrushchev and Bulganin, criticized before the same forum, ignored the protests and kept their troops in Hungary. Was ever the cold war more baffling?

1

By the end of June, 1956, Dulles' patience with Nasser had run out. For months the Secretary had tried to pacify the ambitious Egyptian, to the increasing displeasure of Britain, France, Israel, Congress, and Jewish-American leaders. Despite this pressure and his own dislike of Nasser, Dulles had kept the door ajar. Nasser's threats had seemed laughable, his needs tremendous. Dulles hoped the American offer to help with the Aswan dam would bring the Egyptian to reason. The dam was a gigantic undertaking certain to appeal to a man like Nasser: a pyramid to his greatness. It would be a solution to the economic needs of his countrymen. To build the dam would require twelve to fifteen years, and more than one and a half billion dollars, most of the cost to be loaned by the United States, Great Britain, and the World Bank. The joint offer of funds from the West was announced in December, 1955, and shortly thereafter Cairo expressed its intention to accept. Six months passed. Despite urging from Washington, Nasser refused to discuss the details necessary for making the loan. The Egyptian Government indeed seemed to be doing everything to destroy the Middle Eastern tranquility which Dulles thought essential to the great hydraulic undertaking—which involved not only the interests of Egypt but also of the Sudan, Ethiopia, and Uganda. Nasser was in no hurry, as the Secretary had expected; he enjoyed blackmailing the West by making overtures to the East. Evidently the Egyptian and the American played the same delaying game: Dulles to influence Nasser to come to terms, and Nasser to strengthen his position with the East to force Western acquiescence. Nasser dallied, extended the cold war rivalry into the Middle East, made arrangements for a second big arms deal with the Communist block, entertained the Russian Foreign Minister, Dimitri Shepilov, prepared to journey to Moscow, flirted with Communist China, and became an active member of the nonaligned nations.[1]

At this critical point Cairo suddenly decided to ask immediate American aid. After consulting with Nasser, the Egyptian Ambassador to the United States, Ahmed Hussein, announced he was leaving for Washington to sign the Aswan dam agreement. Arriving in Washington, Hussein on July 19 demanded an immediate American commitment and brushed aside the need for negotiation. If the United States, he told Dulles, "would not guarantee to foot . . . the Aswan bill, the Soviet Union would do so." Here was an ultimatum to underwrite practically all of the expenses for the dam. Dulles answered in "precise terms" that the United States "did not submit to blackmail." The Western powers had long concluded that Egyptian silence and unacceptable counterproposals meant that Nasser was not interested in their offer, and considered it withdrawn. Conditions to embark on such a vast project, he told Hussein, were no longer auspicious.

Was Dulles abrupt? Many observers thought so.

Few if any persons in the West doubted the wisdom of cancellation, but in light of the consequences many have criticized the way he acted. "Those of us who worked with Dulles," Robert Murphy recalled, "were never told explicitly why he acted so abruptly."[2] But there is, in truth, evidence that the Secretary had been anything but abrupt—and that the accusation of haste was something later pinned on him by his domestic critics and by the angered Egyptians. For one thing, the British had agreed, in advance of the famous Dulles-Hussein conference, to the withdrawal or at least the nonrenewal of the offer to Egypt. For another, interested officers in the State Department had been consulted the day before Hussein's arrival and had agreed that the offer had to be withdrawn. For a third, Dulles' treatment of Hussein during the interview was courteous and friendly, and the joint communique issued afterward showed the door left open to further United States aid to Egypt. A short time after the Secretary withdrew the offer to help with the Aswan dam, Eisenhower asked whether his action "could properly be deemed 'abrupt.'" Dulles thought not, certainly as far as Egypt was concerned. "For several months," he wrote Eisenhower on September 15, 1956, "we had left unanswered an Egyptian memorandum on this subject, and the Egyptians knew full well the reasons why. Telephone conversations of which we learned indicated that the Egyptian Government knew that when they came, as they did, to get a definitive reply it would be negative." Congress, he continued, had opposed aid to Egypt; the Senate Appropriations Committee had passed a resolution of disapproval. "If I had not announced our withdrawal when I did, the Congress would certainly have imposed it on us, almost unanimously. As it was, we retained some flexibility." It was Egypt in its "flirtations with the Soviet Union" that "consciously jeopardized our sharing in this project, and they had tried to bluff us by pretending to Soviet 'offers.'" The decision, he concluded, could not have been a shock or surprise to the Egyptians.[3]

Nasser put on a convincing act five days after cancellation. At the opening of an oil refinery near Cairo on July 24 he accused the United States and Britain of perfidy, attacked the World Bank as pro-Zionist, and praised the Soviet Union for helping the Arabs against Israel and its Western allies. Two days later during a rousing address in Alexandria he announced the nationalization of the Suez Canal with its properties and assets, to finance the Aswan dam. This was no sudden decision. His international lawyers had worked for months on a brief justifying seizure, and his technicians, secretly trained, were ready to run the canal. The Secretary's act gave Nasser a grand excuse, even a *cause célèbre*. If Dulles had not withdrawn the offer, the Egyptian leader would have had no difficulty finding another pretext in the turbulent Middle East with which to further his design.

The first government to react was Paris, and from the day of Nasser's nationalization until the military attack on Suez, France would remain the principal protagonist, relentlessly pressing the allies for military moves. Here was an opportunity to end Nasser's meddling in Algeria and Syria. Foreign Minister Christian Pineau wanted Britain to freeze Egyptian assets, and urged that employees of the Suez Canal Company leave their posts. He saw an easy victory over Egypt, and predicted that the Soviet Union would be unable to take countermeasures. Before leaving for London to talk with the British he asked Dulles to join him and Eden in a tripartite conference.

Dulles was in Peru attending the inaugural ceremonies of President Manuel Prado when Acting Secretary Hoover telephoned of Nasser's deed. He was surprised but, unlike his Western colleagues, composed. He did not think it necessary to return to Washington or go to London, and suggested that Hoover try to hold down developments and discourage the French and British from armed action.

Meanwhile on Saturday, July 28, 1956, an important meeting convened at the White House; it was there, with Dulles absent, that President Eisenhower set American policy. After reading the dispatches from ambassadors and the telegrams from Eden, the President called in Hoover and Deputy Under Secretary Murphy. "The President," the latter wrote in his memoirs, "was not greatly concerned, and there was no talk of recalling Dulles from Peru."[4] Eisenhower thought Nasser should be condemned for his unilateral action. The Egyptian needed deflating. But the President doubted that the Suez Canal was the right issue for military action.

Eisenhower, of course, was no stranger to the Middle East. He had commanded an invasion of North Africa where he learned firsthand about Arab politics and temperament. He was aware of the strong anticolonial feelings. He appreciated the British desire for support. He thought it difficult to aid the French and British and at the same time remain uncommitted to force. The Israeli problem, Eisenhower said, should be separate from the Suez Canal. The objectives of the British, French, and Israelis went far beyond the canal. Britain was concerned with Jordan, Iraq, the oil sheikdom of Kuwait, and Iran. France worried over North Africa, most of all Algeria. Both countries were anxious about oil. Israel feared a Nasser-led Arab coalition. Nasser's seizure of the canal had been deliberate, and the world expected some reaction from the West. If no intervention took place, canal operations might deteriorate without yielding an occasion for action. But Eisenhower did not think a military operation could succeed. Britain and France might occupy the canal and topple Nasser. What then? Were they going to occupy Egypt indefinitely? Would the Arabs accept a return to colonialism? How about the United Nations? Eisenhower did not believe the Soviet Union could be militarily effective, even if it wished, but nobody could be sure such a conflict would not escalate into a major war or produce military diversion elsewhere.

Eisenhower told Hoover and Murphy that the United States must stand clear of precipitate action. Should some action occur, it must include all maritime powers, NATO members, and friendly nations east of Suez. Perhaps France and Britain should issue a statement expressing willingness to put the matter before the International Court. The United States and the other NATO nations might sign. The situation demanded deliberation, and world public opinion had to be won. At the conclusion of the talk Eisenhower asked Murphy to go to London to "hold the fort."

2

The appearance of Murphy in London marked the beginning, if ever so delicate on the part of the United States, of Western reaction to the Egyptian unilateral occupation of the canal, contrary to the Convention of 1888. Murphy arrived in London that Saturday night, carrying "no formal instructions whatever."[5] At the first meeting with the British and French on Sunday evening, July 29, he restated faithfully the American position as outlined by Eisenhower. The consensus of the British cabinet was that as long as nationalization did not impair the navigation of the canal there was no violation of the Convention. Eden said that Nasser had to be punished, otherwise no political and economic measures would be effective. "The British seemed to feel that if a firm stand were taken at the outset," Murphy would recall, "all maritime powers would support it, but there was no suggestion of imminent military activity." Eden and his advisers thought that American policy did not reflect a sufficient interest in the affair. Eden was confident that Washington "would go along with anything Britain and France did." He did not wish to ask the United States for anything, but hoped that Eisenhower would "take care of the Bear." The British agreed with Eisenhower that the Arab-Israeli problem was separate. They accepted his suggestion, with important modifications, that all maritime nations concerned should meet to devise a strategy. Unlike the President, they wanted a conference in London in a few days, preceded by a joint warning to Nasser to keep the international waterway open. This meant that the United States as well as the other interested nations had to decide within twenty-four hours.

There was evidently a lack of unity within the British cabinet. So at least it seemed to Murphy and other Americans present. Some Britishers apparently thought that France was pressing Eden and wanted the United States to restrain Paris. They feared the French might jeopardize a British-American position. Others worried about Eden's physical condition—his health had not been robust. Murphy thought Eden "laboring under the impression that a common identity of interest existed among the allies," which "was not the American view." Eden had not "adjusted his thoughts to the altered world status of Great Britain, and he never did."[6]

The aggressive attitude of the French persisted. Pineau publicly attacked the Americans as naive. Murphy annoyed him, and he criticized Dulles for refusal to attend the London meeting. "He acted as if he had received a blank check from the United States Government," Murphy recalled, "but he did not take me into his confidence." Pineau claimed the canal seizure was a political problem, not legal. He said Nasser took over the canal because of withdrawal of the Aswan offer and Dulles should be responsible for the consequences. He likened Nasser to Hitler. Should Nasser succeed, the French position in North Africa would collapse and so, too, would the whole Western position in the Middle East. Pineau was willing to hold a conference of users of the canal, but only if a strong note to Nasser preceded it. Under no circumstances would he allow talks to delay military preparation.

While Pineau remonstrated in London, Mollet vented his bitterness to Ambassador Dillon. The Premier blamed allied disunity on the Americans and British. He saw Nasser's arms deal with the Soviets as similar to the Hitler-Stalin nonaggression pact. Mollet could not understand why the United States did not appreciate the situation. Why was Dulles absent? Why did he send Murphy who had the wrong attitudes and lacked the power of decision? Did Washington not know that Moscow was behind the affair? What a calamity for the West that the United States was unable to act because of the presidential election! What irony that this democratic process should bring the whole of the Middle East and North Africa under Soviet control! French opinion, Mollet claimed, was wholly behind the government. Frenchmen could not see why Washington refused support, particularly because the crisis started with Dulles' withdrawal of the Aswan offer. The seizure was not a local problem; Nasser must not get away with it. Military action against Egypt, the Premier insisted, was inevitable. He wanted the United States to join the allies and turned aside talk of Congressional authorization. Preliminary French military studies indicated that Egypt was surprisingly strong. Its bomber force, piloted by Czechs and Poles, was far superior to that of France. Mollet again blamed the United States: France as a loyal NATO ally had carried out NATO directives to build only fighter aircraft, leaving heavy bombers to the United States and Britain.

Mollet did not hesitate to indulge in a bit of blackmail. The Russians, he wanted Washington to know, had been telling French leaders they were prepared, jointly with Nasser, to bring peace in Algeria on French terms provided France cooperated with the Soviet Union in Europe. Moscow did not ask that Paris leave NATO, but only that France be less faithful to the United States and Britain—becoming semineutralist. Here was the same strategy the Russians had tried on France during the Indochina crisis of 1954. Mollet claimed he had rejected these overtures, but that other French leaders would find them tempting. That he had refused the Russians won him, he felt, the right to speak to the United States. The Premier feared that the United States was leaning toward the idea of Fortress America, losing interest in the Middle East and Europe. If so, France must adjust.

President Eisenhower read the dispatches from

Murphy and the ambassadors in Paris and London and foresaw a French-English military action. Under no circumstances would he allow the United States to become a cat's paw. He asked Dulles, still in Lima, to go to London. Dulles arrived in London on August 1 during a driving cold rain, with apparel for a hot climate.[7]

The new conversations began badly. Aided by Herman Phleger, his able Legal Adviser, Dulles determined to carry out instructions of the President. Murphy afterward noted the teamwork between Eisenhower and the Secretary: "The President behaved like the chairman of the board, leaving it to his Secretary to handle details, and the latter acted as a buffer so far as the public was concerned." Dulles was aware that an American commitment to support military action could have a disastrous effect in the coming election.[8] The Secretary talked with Eden, Selwyn Lloyd, Macmillan, and Pineau. His meeting with Eden was strained, each uncomfortable with the other. Dulles evidently disliked Eden's attitude. Nor did Dulles get along with Pineau whose behavior was arrogant.

The purpose during these talks was to stave off military intervention. Prolonged negotiation might take the steam out of the situation. Nasser should not have an ultimatum to reverse nationalization. As long as there was no clear evidence that Nasser's deed had impeded international traffic the President would not reconvene Congress. The Secretary proposed a meeting of maritime powers, including the

Soviet Union and Egypt, on August 15, in Geneva. Should Nasser refuse to attend or to accept reasonable proposals, there would be a broader base for other actions, free of imputation that the United States was backing France and Britain for purposes not directly connected with the canal. He agreed with the allies that the United Nations should not be involved because of likelihood that the Security Council or General Assembly would be slow to act. Dulles had another reason: he was concerned about the Panama Canal and did not want to be a party to a precedent which might give the United Nations authority to interfere with America's position there.

For the next few days Dulles and Phleger conducted a tedious diplomatic marathon, seeking to calm down Eden and Pineau who were annoyed with lawyers' devices. To them this was Munich all over again. Only Macmillan and Selwyn Lloyd took a more moderate position. It was agreed to invite twenty-four nations from three distinctive groups: the first eight were original or surviving parties to the Convention of 1888; the next eight were those who owned the largest tonnage passing through the canal; the last eight were those whose international trade indicated dependence on the canal. The purposes of the conference—to be held in London on August 16—were to reaffirm the Convention which Nasser had pledged to honor in his 1954 agreement with London just before British withdrawal from the canal base, and to consider the operation of the canal. Dulles left London having convinced himself that he had introduced a valuable stopgap.

Two weeks later twenty-two delegations met in London, from August 16 to 23. Two powers refused to attend: Egypt and Greece, the latter because of the dispute with Britain over Cyprus. Nasser sent his top political aide to keep abreast of the proceeding and in touch with the heads of two of the delegations, Shepilov of Russia and Krishna Menon of India—both of whom supported Egypt.

Dulles this time was surprised to find the allied leaders more relaxed. Had they moved toward the American position? Had France and Great Britain given up military action? Perhaps they had discovered that their forces were inadequate? The atmosphere was more pleasant, and Dulles also noted opposition within Britain to military action, particularly from the Labor Party.

The conference ended with a majority proposal for an "international system," a Suez Canal Board, which would operate the waterway, safeguard Egyptian interests, and adhere to the Convention.[9] It was to be presented to Nasser as a basis of negotiation. Eden hoped Dulles would go to Cairo as head of the delegation, but the Secretary feared it would take too much of his time. It also would be preferable for the United States, he told Eisenhower, to take a less conspicuous part, because he had a dominant position during the conference. Dulles may have suspected Eden's request as a design to get him so involved he would be unable to extricate himself.

Prime Minister Robert G. Menzies of Australia became the envoy, heading a delegation representing five nations, one of which was the United States. The committee stayed in Cairo for a week, September 3-10, 1956, and never had a chance of success. Menzies later blamed Eisenhower. While he was negotiating, he wrote, the Egyptian newspapers headlined a presidential press conference statement: "There must be no use of force and . . . if the proposals of the London conference were rejected, others must be considered." It is doubtful that this statement influenced Nasser who now had the support of the Russians. A few days before Menzies arrived, Khrushchev had promised that if war broke out the Arabs would not stand alone, there would be volunteers.[10]

When news of the failure of Menzies' mission reached Washington, Eisenhower and Dulles after a White House meeting on the evening of September 8 offered another plan prepared solely by Dulles: the Suez Canal Users Association (SCUA).

Here was a device to prevent breakdown of canal traffic once the 150-odd foreign canal pilots left their posts. The Association would employ pilots, coordinate traffic, collect transit dues, and enlist Egyptian cooperation. Should Egypt refuse, and interrupt traffic, the Association would invoke the requirements of the Convention. Dulles announced the plan on September 12; next day the British and French showed interest. But on September 24 Nasser did not hinder the departing foreign pilots, and on the following day surprised everyone by maintaining navigation without difficulty, and thereafter with even greater efficiency. The assumption upon which SCUA was based—that the Egyptians could not run the canal—was no longer believable.

The Users Association was dead but not buried, for the British and French accepted it, and twice, on September 19-21 and during the first week of October, a conference of eighteen nations—which by October had dwindled to fifteen—met in London and agreed to form the Association. All this was another delaying marathon which alienated the Arabs from the West, prolonged the drama on which Nasser thrived, extended the rift between the two European allies and the United States and other NATO powers, confused public opinion, and perhaps amused the Russians.[11]

In this developing muddle, or era of pseudo diplomacy, Dulles did his best to keep the talk going. Then he learned that Britain and France, without informing him, had decided to take the Suez issue to the United Nations. He called in the British, French, and Israeli Ambassadors, but they could not explain their countries' policies; they too were in the dark, evidently. Something malign and evil, it now seemed, had entered the Suez negotiation.

3

The debate in the United Nations in mid-October, 1956, was the last intermission before the crisis in the Suez drama—a quiet interlude during which, unknown to the speakers, leaders of Britain, France, and Israel met surreptitiously in Paris to prepare the final act. Security Council deliberations ended on October 13 with a resolution for free and open transit of the canal, promptly vetoed by the Soviet Union, which left Nasser with a more clear international position as to the legality of seizure. No reactions followed immediately. Washington relaxed, Dulles' confidence in the delaying tactics increased (military plans, he said, were "withering on the vine"), Eisenhower was grateful that "a very great crisis is behind us." Europe seemed less anxious; British public indignation against Nasser was subsiding, and some prominent Frenchmen were urging moderation.[12]

But there was a blackout of news, disturbing to official Washington. "It's very strange," Dulles said in staff conference, "that we have heard nothing whatever from the British for ten days. We must try to find out what they and the French are up to."

Then the bolt struck, the storm began. While Hungarians fought Russians in Budapest, Israel mobilized; Jordan, Egypt, and Syria on October 25 signed the Pact of Amman, a joint military alliance against Israel; British and French warships moved toward Egypt. On the evening of October 29, 1956, Israel in a brilliant demonstration of military power knifed through Sinai toward Egypt. And when Israeli troops were within striking distance of the canal, Britain and France as if by arrangement called on Egypt and Israel to withdraw troops from the canal area. What a package of crises! On October 31, Britain and France launched their own military operation. After several days of air strikes at Egyptian airfields the Anglo-French invaded Egypt with one hundred warships and troop transports. There was heavy fighting at Port Said. The Egyptians sank a total of thirty-two ships in the canal, and blocked it. Meanwhile Syrian saboteurs blew up the British oil pipelines running through their country from Iraq to the Mediterranean.

Then, after a few more days, everything began to reduce itself—in Suez, and in Hungary—toward normality. The Russians did well enough in Hungary, by their own standards: they overturned the regime of Imre Nagy and brought the Hungarians back to communism. But that is another story. In Egypt the maladroit Anglo-French invasion, with its foolish prelude of aerial bombardment, proved a saddening contrast to the quick Israeli operation. Britain and France could have defeated Egypt.

The first days of the war did not paralyze the Egyptians, Nasser did not run away. Unforeseen delay brought other effects: world public opinion turned against the British and French; the Labor Party attacked Eden; India and other members of the Commonwealth publicly criticized Her Majesty's Government; influential Conservatives were unhappy with their Prime Minister; the British pound dropped; Moscow, bloodied and compromised by the Hungarian revolution, issued threats of missiles and atomic bombs. Most of all Eden had displeased the one man whose support he needed, Eisenhower. Eden did not take his advice, had not consulted him, and launched a colonial expedition on the eve of the presidential election. What an unfortunate climax to the career of a trusted lieutenant of Churchill, the prophetic opponent of appeasement in the interwar period. Eden's ill health, worsened by the crisis, would lead him to announce his retirement.[13]

The denouement was all anticlimax. A worried Eisenhower decided to bring the allies and Israel before the United Nations. The President on October 31 asked Dulles to obtain a cease-fire through the UN. He wanted a resolution placing the blame where it belonged, and a future course devised. He hoped to avoid a harsh resolution against the allies, but it might be necessary to prevent the Soviets from seizing world leadership by proposing a more severe punishment which all the African, Arab, and most of the Asian states were certain to endorse.

To Dulles this was an abhorrent task. "It was in many ways the hardest decision . . . that the President and I ever had to take." On the night of November 1, 1956, Dulles came to the rostrum of the United Nations "with a very heavy heart" to urge all parties to agree to a cease-fire, stop military movements, and withdraw behind armistice lines pending the reopening of the canal.[14]

For the American Secretary there was a further complication of momentous, calamitous personal implication. The night following his United Nations appearance, namely, November 2 at 11:30, Dulles awoke in his Washington house feeling ill and chilled. Three hours later he awoke again, this time with a sharp pain in the abdomen. Noting his high fever, Mrs. Dulles called a doctor who immediately advised that the Secretary go to Walter Reed Hospital. Dulles, that strong, energetic, iron-willed man, had felt the first symptoms of cancer. Operated upon the next day, he was away from the Department for a whole recuperative month, November 3 to December 3.

It fell to Henry Cabot Lodge to put through a General Assembly resolution condemning Israel, Britain, and France, which Lodge did without a "heavy heart."

Ben-Gurion, censured by the United Nations, gave up some of the spoils of conquest; Nasser, defeated in battle by Israel, emerged as the victor over Britain and France; Eisenhower and Dulles, blamed by the two allies, praised by enemies, applauded by nonaligned nations, disquieted by the rush of events, but heartened by overwhelming approval in the national election of 1956, set about clearing the debris to save the Western alliance and secure the Middle East from Nasser's irresponsibility and Soviet ambition.

4

There was yet another chapter in relations between the United States and the Middle East, a chapter to follow the Suez affair, and of course, closely related to it: the sending of troops into Lebanon during the civil war in that country in July, 1958.

Prior to that time Congress in March, 1957, passed the so-called Eisenhower Doctrine for the Middle East, which authorized the President to offer economic and military assistance to any nation in the region requesting it, so long as that nation were threatened by international communism. This common-sense doctrine produced a trip through the area by a special presidential representative, with funds for disbursement up to $200,000,000. The Middle Eastern nations were embarrassed, for they wanted the money but did not like the imputation by their enemies, domestic and foreign, of taking money from the United States and thereby coming into the "American camp." In the event the Eisenhower Doctrine turned out to be more of an American declaration than donation.

One of the nations which did take the money was Lebanon, the tiny country along the Mediterranean east coast which for years has been a sort of broker, or international banker, for the Middle East. The Lebanese not merely by location but by population were likely to look both to the East and the West, as about half of the populace was Moslem and half Christian. Taking funds from the United States tended to disturb, ever so little, the equilibrium of the country. Then the influx of Palestinian refugees, incident upon the independence of Israel some years before, had also affected the population balance.

As it turned out, the factor of most disturbance was perhaps the President of Lebanon, Camille Chamoun, who decided to opt for a second term as president, even if that move meant amending the Lebanese Constitution. A rebellion broke out. The Lebanese Army, half Christian and half Moslem, was not enthusiastic about restoring order. It looked as if Nasser's agents were active in Lebanon, as the ruler of Egypt in February, 1958, had joined Syria with Egypt in a new political entity, the United Arab Republic, and there was some evidence that Lebanon might be next. When a truly murderous revolution broke out in Iraq on July 14, 1958, which brought the deaths of Iraq's Premier, Nuri as Said, and the young King Faisal, there seemed more evidence of Egyptian subversion. Meanwhile the regime of King Faisal's second cousin, young King Hussein of Jordan, threatened to go into convulsions, apparently under the inspiration of Nasser. There appeared to be a crisis in governments all over the Middle East, those fragile regimes perhaps all suddenly disappearing before the attractions of a United Arab Republic of the Middle East.

President Chamoun beseeched President Eisenhower for troops, under the Eisenhower Doctrine, and the President consulted Secretary Dulles who said that the Russians would not make any serious moves unless they considered the entire world situation favorable to them. The American Government dispatched troops to the scene, sending in three Marine battalions and following them with more Marines and with Army troops, to a total of 14,357. The British flew troops into Jordan. After a considerable verbal contretemps, both in Lebanon with Chamoun's critics and with the other nations of the Middle East whose governments were not always as unsympathetic with American anti-Nasser moves as they sounded, an arrangement for a suitable change of government in Lebanon was made, with President Chamoun retiring in favor of the commander of the

Lebanese Army, General Fuad Chehab. The troops of the British and Americans then departed, the Americans leaving in entirety by October 25, 1958. The crisis, if such it was, was over.

After this taste of American intervention the Middle East returned to a relative tranquillity, and neither for the short remainder of Secretary Dulles' era at the State Department nor for the secretaryships of his immediate successors was much more of a serious nature heard from the area.

CHAPTER EIGHTEEN

LAST ACTIVITY

1

JOHN FOSTER DULLES, so James Reston commented toward the end of the Secretary's tenure at the Department of State, was "still the hardest working man in town, and still stands above the foreign secretaries of Britain, France, Germany, Japan or the Soviet Union."[1] In the 1950s Dulles was not merely the architect of American foreign policy, but he was its principal negotiator. He had full support of the President. No Secretary of modern times, not even Acheson, had wielded more power. Unfortunately he held office at a time when the United States was the strongest of all nations, yet insecure. Dulles had the misfortune, some would say fortune, to represent the United States when the world was undergoing unprecedented political, social, economic, and scientific revolutions. His tenure had commenced when the Stalin era ended and Republican responsibility began. It continued through a period of increased confusion within the Western alliance, a heightened challenge from Moscow, and the appearance of both intercontinental missiles and a nuclear stalemate.

There had been plenty of criticism, much of it unfair, of his actions as Secretary. In his attempts to ensure a peaceful world he became the scapegoat for all the unresolved ills. Frequently the critics raged. He had come under fire, foreign and domestic, when he seemed to have coined a new word, "brinkmanship." An article in *Life* magazine of January 16, 1956, had detailed the story of three "brinks of war." A cover-page note related in lurid fashion: "Three Times at Brink of War: How Dulles Gambled and Won." The smart word "brinkmanship," of course, was not his. The critics invented it, in imitation of words employed by the popular English humorist, Stephen Potter, who wrote engagingly about such matters as "oneupmanship," that is, how to impress people. And in the context in which Dulles had used part of the word "brinkmanship," namely the word "brink," there was nothing really wrong with what he said. All the Secretary had been trying to explain was that on the questions of enlarging the Korean War, getting into the Indochina fighting, and involvement in the Formosan Straits, the United States had taken a strong stand:

> You have to take chances for peace, just as you must take chances in war. Some say that we were brought to the verge of war. Of course we were brought to the verge of war. The ability to get to the verge without getting into the war is the necessary art. If you cannot master it, you inevitably get into war. If you try to run away from it, if you are scared to go to the brink, you are lost. We've had to look it square in the face—on the question of enlarging the Korean war, on the question of

getting into the Indochina war, on the question of Formosa. We walked to the brink and we looked it in the face. We took strong action.

To show the iron-like nature of the Secretary it is worth noting, even emphasizing, that he often worked against this background of criticism. Some of it he ignored, but some of it got under his skin. Judgments of religious leaders bothered him. "The church people," he wrote in 1958 to his brother-in-law, the Reverend Deane Edwards, "have been clamoring for a long time for the application of moral principles to public affairs and to foreign relations. Now when we try to do that, and explain what we are doing—and foreign policy has to be explained—we are accused of hypocrisy."[2]

The work had to go on, such as the continuing task of ensuring Western European unity, mentioned above. Dulles was not anti-British, anti-French, pro-German; he was pro-European. The Secretary was close to Britain by inheritance. He loved France, savored its culture, relished its food, delighted in speaking its tongue, but despaired over its unstable government. He admired Adenauer, but was not so sure of the Germans. He wanted to group Germany within a federated Western European community. Long before he became Secretary he had argued for Western European unity. After Suez he labored to make NATO into the West's sword and shield. Despite some strengthening of organization in the last months of 1957—the power of the NATO Council increased and there was a unified NATO position on disarmament—he was not satisfied. The allies seemed willing to follow the Italian line, to turn NATO into an economic body supported with American dollars, but balked at plans to develop Western European unity or common policies toward the Soviet Union.[3] Britain was more interested in the sword than the shield; France, fearful of Germany, wanted more freedom to deal with the Russians; West Germany, suspicious of France and apprehensive about Russia, demanded ever greater support from the United States; all the continental European countries were in doubt as to their precise part in NATO strategy. The Secretary was well aware of the difficulty of alliances in time of peace. American experience told him that international contracts did not last beyond the emergency which brought them, and he tried to introduce in NATO features to counter divisive tendencies, and hoped to improve political consultation. He trusted that there would be time for Western Europe to become a political, economic, and military third force.[4]

During his last years Dulles groped to provide more understanding among the allies for the disagreements between regional and world-wide approaches to collective defense. European nations had a broad idea of alliances: members should support each other on all political issues. Dulles took a less inclusive view, for otherwise the United States would associate itself with colonialism. Moreover, did not NATO powers feel free to object to American defense of

Taiwan, and containment of Communist China? Perhaps a single organization could resolve these dilemmas, but might compete with the United Nations and alienate neutrals. Some sort of interlocking system? If so, what and how? The best place to coordinate policies was Washington, the capital of the free world. Latin American nations had so concluded when they set up the Organization of American States (OAS) in Washington. Would SEATO and NATO members agree? How could grand designs become realities when political instability plagued even democratic countries? The postwar record of American diplomacy showed that the United States with full support of both political parties had carried out long-range policies. It was possible to find ways to increase confidence in Washington, but trust, Dulles maintained, was a mutual matter, with tasks allocated and responsibility shared.

As for the perennial Soviet problem, there was some reason to believe that the monolithic power of the Soviet Union was deteriorating. Since Khrushchev's famous speech to the Twentieth Party Congress on February 25, 1956, in which he had exposed the criminality of Stalin, the communist parties were in confusion, the satellites moving wildly through the political skies. The Soviet people were demanding intellectual freedom and economic enjoyment; a trend had established itself which, Dulles thought, might prove irresistible, although Khrushchev and Bulganin if confronted with unsatisfactory choices might take risks in foreign relations. After Khrushchev assumed sole power on March 27, 1958, Dulles told the Western European chiefs of mission in Paris on May 9 that the new Soviet leader was a great advantage to the United States, although more dangerous than Stalin, excitable, irresponsible, short-tempered, subtle, devious, impulsive. His long speech denouncing Stalin had indicated his explosive nature. The Soviet leader had gone into details of Stalin's barbarities, and harmed the Soviet-dominated world communist movement. Nothing should happen to discourage Khrushchev from the course which reminded Dulles of La Rochefoucauld's maxim: "Hypocrisy is the homage that vice pays to virtue." The Soviet Union, he said, might well become what it pretends to be. If the West could force the Soviet Union even to appear to behave decently, that was to the good. "I have seen lots of tough guys," Dulles recalled, "who have made their pile . . . come to New York and . . . get into society and . . . behave differently. They became slightly different people." Dulles did not want to make it too easy for the Soviets to become social equals. "You can't let them into the house if they are going to steal the silver or the furniture."

Even so, Khrushchev's new actions increased the possibility of error by the West. If the second decade of the cold war was one of promise, it was an era of danger. A new period in American-Soviet relations had followed the failure of the Geneva Conference of 1955. Gone was the Stalin era with its constant threats and propaganda. After 1955 the new Soviet leadership decided to challenge the United States with economic weapons and "political warfare." Eisenhower and Dulles feared this tactic, although it was in the area of America's strength. The President believed that in economic warfare, as in military, the nation on the offensive had the most flexibility. The defending power had to secure an area, while the aggressor concentrated on any point. Democracies had to be on the defensive, anticipate struggles, debate every issue, and publicize actions.

Khrushchev's continued intransigence over the problem of Germany had revived the idea of disengagement, a notion that dated back to the first Soviet-American confrontations immediately after the Second World War. Elaborated in varying forms by the Foreign Minister of Poland, Adam Rapacki, by Germans of differing political persuasions, and even by the former American diplomat, now turned historian, George Kennan (who gave several lectures on the subject over the network of the British Broadcasting Corporation), the idea looked to the departure of Western and Eastern forces—NATO and Russian—from the center of Europe, a center construed sometimes as Hungary-Czechoslovakia-Austria-Germany, or with addition of Poland, or just Germany alone, or maybe all of Europe between the Russian borders and the Channel. It was a dangerous idea. Dulles agreed with Paul-Henri Spaak of Belgium that disengagement was a naughty word which could not even be translated into a good language like French. It seemed reasonable, but in reality meant demilitarization of Germany. "If I had to choose between a neutralized Germany and Germany in the Soviet bloc," Dulles said, "it might be almost better to have it in that bloc. That, clearly, is not acceptable. But disengagement is absolutely not acceptable either."[5]

During his last years the increasing numbers of nuclear weapons and their carriers also weighed heavily upon his thoughts. The first sputnik went up on October 4, 1957, seeming evidence that the United States was behind in the armaments race. Some people urged agreements for limitation of arms. The Secretary was skeptical. "Reduction of armaments," he had written back in 1952, "is more apt to be an evidence of restored confidence than be itself a means of restoring confidence."[6] It was of course true that no longer was the continental United States safe from Soviet nuclear attack. For the first time the nation lay exposed. Soviet advances in nuclear weaponry and delivery systems forced the United States to continue its post-1945 policy of seeking to deter all-out war through its capacity for nuclear retaliation. At the same time the new Soviet nuclear power tended to discredit American nuclear power as a deterrent to local aggression. Washington had to maintain military forces for both massive and limited retaliation to prevent enemy attacks on the United States, allies, and nonaligned friends. Dulles anticipated increased communist pressure for local gains through overt or covert military action, in belief that their nuclear power would cancel the likelihood of a general war, except in case of large-scale attack against the United States and allied positions. The allies doubted that the United States would risk destruction in their behalf. The Secretary saw the need for flexible military strength which would convince an aggressor that the United States and its allies had ability to counter local aggression, and convince the allies that local actions would not invite all-out nuclear war.[7]

As for an end to nuclear testing with its poisonous effects, he feared the moral isolation of the United States. In the spring of 1958 he advocated a suspension of testing, despite objections from the Defense Department and the Atomic Energy Commission. He held back from a public statement because Britain and France wanted to become proficient in the nuclear field. It was ironic that the United States had to take a propaganda beating, so to speak, when in fact the two allies had forestalled negotiation with the Soviet Union. Privately they urged Washington to continue exploding hydrogen bombs, publicly they seemed to condemn the action. One way to overcome this problem would have been to amend the Atomic Energy Act to permit the allies to share information from testing. Dulles doubted that Congress would do so; it would allow Britain to share this information but not France or any other country. At his urging Congress did admit Britain to atomic findings, and thereby wounded Gallic sensibilities.

2

The present volume has said little about Latin American policy. Unfortunately, absorbed as was the

Secretary in larger problems of the cold war, he neglected Latin America. President Eisenhower showed a greater interest and often complained that the Department of State did not give sensitive Latin Americans the feeling that they were important. It pleased Dulles to have the President's brother Milton take on many assignments there.[8] (A fuller analysis of the Latin American policy of the Eisenhower Administration will appear in the succeeding Volume XVIII of this Series, on Secretary Christian A. Herter.)

The President at the outset of the first term, in 1953, had appointed Milton as his personal representative and special ambassador on matters affecting Latin America, and the President's scholarly brother, who became president of Johns Hopkins University, eventually produced a touching memoir of this experience entitled *The Wine Is Bitter.* President Eisenhower made a personal visit to Latin America in 1960, in which he made stopovers in Brazil, Argentina, Uruguay, and Chile. Dulles did go to Latin America on occasion, and attended the Tenth Inter-American Conference at Caracas in 1954. As we have seen, he was in the southern part of the Western Hemisphere witnessing the inauguration of a new president in Lima, Peru, when word came that President Nasser had nationalized the Suez Canal. All in all, though, it is fair to say that the Secretary did not find affairs in Latin America as threatening, and therefore as interesting, as those in Europe or the Middle East or Asia.

There was plenty of potential crisis in Latin America, and the government of the United States during the Eisenhower-Dulles years made some efforts to anticipate trouble. In his memoirs the President has related how American public and private capital went in increasing amounts to the countries south of the Rio Grande.[9] Aggregate American assets and investments in Latin America totaled about $7,000,000,000 in 1952, and had nearly doubled by 1960. Of this sum, only $2,000,000,000 came from public funds. In 1958 the Export-Import Bank, which did about half of its business with Latin America, received from Congress an increase in its lending authority, from $5,000,000,000 to $7,000,000,000. In an era replete with challenges to the United States from almost all corners of the world the Administration hoped that somehow the lid would stay on in Latin America, and for the most part it did, perhaps because of this economic aid.

Meanwhile at Caracas in March, 1954, Secretary Dulles had obtained a resolution against communist subversion. The vote was 17-1, the objector being Guatemala. Two states abstained—Argentina and Mexico. Costa Rica was absent. The hope was that the states of the New World, other than the United States and Canada which already had taken their stand in the North Atlantic Treaty, would feel strong enough to stand up to communism even if it entered their countries in the guise of democratic nationalism. The ruling groups in most of the Latin American countries feared communism, knowing full well what it meant not merely for their nations but for their own social classes. It was difficult, though, for them to take a position openly against communist-inspired proposals, and Dulles trusted that the Caracas resolve would help.

There nonetheless were three outstanding crises regarding Latin America during his secretaryship, each one communist-inspired or assisted. None of these, it is fair to say, received his entire personal attention, for one reason or another, and it is difficult to say therefore that he had a "policy" toward them. As a prominent member of the Eisenhower Administration, and that Administration's mouthpiece on foreign policy, he necessarily shared in the praise or blame for his government's moves.

The first of the troubles was the Guatemala regime which had voted against the resolution on communist subversion at the Caracas Conference.[10] This regime had been some years in the making, and its communism was never perfectly clear, but there was an almost overwhelming presumption of aid from sources outside of Guatemala and the Western world. Difficulties for the tiny country had begun when during the presidency of Dr. Juan José Arevalo there was a struggle for the succession (Arevalo could not succeed himself) between Francisco Javier Arana, chief of the armed forces, and Jacobo Arbenz Guzmán who had support of a "popular front." Supporters of Arbenz assassinated Arana in 1949. Upon Arbenz' election in January, 1953, the communists came out in the open. The country seemed to be turning toward communism. About then trouble began in Honduras where it looked as if Arbenz was causing strikes by labor organizations. Then a Swedish freighter, the *Alfhem,* sailing from Stettin, brought 15,424 cases of Czechoslovak-made military equipment, totaling 2,000 tons of arms, into Puerto Barrios where they were unloaded in the presence of the minister of defense. "The extension of Communist colonialism to this hemisphere would, in the words of the Caracas resolution," Dulles said on May 25, 1954, "endanger the peace of this hemisphere." Nothing, though, seemed to stop the Guatemalan communists.

The crisis came to white heat when early in June, 1954, Arbenz proclaimed a dictatorship, in the immediate course of which there was cold-blooded killing of opponents, a practice then frowned upon in Latin America. In mid-June a small revolutionary force of a few hundred men led by Colonel Carlos Enrique Castillo Armas invaded from Honduras. It quickly gained adherents, and within two weeks was victorious. Arbenz decamped to Czechoslovakia. Guatemala—a land which would have been a convenient base for the United States's enemies, too close for comfort to the Panama Canal and the southern part of the United States—returned to peaceful ways.

An interesting debate within the government of the United States had occurred in regard to Guatemala, which is worth recording in some detail to show the reluctance with which important members of the Administration faced the Guatemalan troubles, and the steely manner in which President Eisenhower viewed them. In the midst of the crisis the Assistant Secretary of State for Inter-American Affairs, Henry F. Holland, armed with three large law books, one day joined a small group in the President's office. The Castillo Armas rebels had lost two of their three old bombing planes, and the question was whether the United States Government should replace them. Holland was against any American action.

"What do you think Castillo's chances would be without the aircraft?" Eisenhower asked Allen Dulles, the CIA head (afterward reputedly the mastermind of the Guatemalan Revolution).

The answer was unequivocal: "About zero."

"Suppose we supply the aircraft. What would the chances be then?"

Again the CIA chief did not hesitate: "About 20 per cent."

Eisenhower considered the matter carefully. He knew about the blame that always descended upon the United States in any cases or supposed cases of intervention in the affairs of Latin America. But he "knew from experience the important psychological impact of even a small amount of air support. In any event, our proper course of action—indeed my duty—was clear to me. We would replace the airplanes."[11]

The second crisis over Latin America occurred during a good-will trip of Vice President Nixon in 1958. The Vice President on May 8 had received a lively welcome when he visited San Marcos University in Lima, where he was shoved, stoned, and booed. He put up bravely with this discourtesy and continued his trip to Caracas, Venezuela, where on May 13 a mob smashed the automobile in which he was riding and threatened its overturn. Nixon and party could have been dragged into the street. It was serious business, and a gross affront to a high representative of a friendly nation. President Eisenhower was furious, and willing to send troops into Venezuela to preserve the Nixon party's safety. "Maybe I should be digging out my uniforms," he told Mrs. Eisenhower that evening, "to see whether they still fit."[12] Nothing more untoward occurred. The uniforms remained in mothballs. It was just a close call.

The third crisis was only in part the Administration's problem, as it passed over—with its highly dangerous possibilities—into the Kennedy Administration. This of course was the Cuban Revolution, which came into power at the beginning of the new year in 1959 when President Fulgencio Batista sought refuge in the Dominican Republic and the tall young man with the jeep and khaki fatigues and beard, Fidel Castro, took over. Everyone was in a quandary as to what this change meant. With some asperity Eisenhower has noted in his memoirs that shortly before it occurred the CIA through its director, Allen Dulles, decided that some communist elements were involved, although previously it had beheld no communist elements. He has recalled that former President Truman and Senator Kennedy both had seen some good in Castro at the outset of the Cuban leader's takeover. To be sure, disenchantment came rapidly. Eisenhower was angered that after the extraordinary executions of Castro's opponents, conducted as if the trials were circuses, the American Society of Newspaper Editors invited the Cuban leader to Washington to give a speech at the National Press Club on April 17, 1959. The President would have liked to have refused Castro a visa, and did refuse to invite him to the White House.[13] Shortly thereafter Cuban-United States relations began to sink like a stone, and before the end of its tenure the Eisenhower Administration was training revolutionaries for the ill-fated invasion. The movement of Castro to the front of the Cuban stage came just at the time when Secretary Dulles was leaving the Department. Castro's conversion of that stage into a place of near tragedy for the world came after the Secretary's death. Dulles hardly had opportunity to consider Castroism, so close to the nation's shores, before he passed on his tasks to other hands.

3

The Lebanese and Straits of Formosa crises, which so levied upon Dulles' energies during his second term at the Department of State, have been discussed in other chapters of the present volume. So far as concerned specific problems in foreign affairs, these brought him the most worries. For the rest of it he could ruminate upon, and within his power try to solve, the continuing problems in NATO, the challenges of the new Soviet leadership, and the increasing difficulties of weaponry. It was enough to keep any man busy. But Dulles' last years of service were also a time of personal worry, for ever since his operation for cancer in November, 1956, he must have kept in the back of his mind, in some secret place where he would not reveal his concern to people whom he met, the possibility of a resurgence of the dread disease. And by the turn of the new year, 1959, the disease again was upon him.

The incessant combinations of policy, the calculus of power and opinion and international misbehavior, had to go on. During the first week of February, 1959, when he flew to Paris and Bonn, his last overseas journey, he worried about Berlin policy. Khrushchev had declared on November 10, 1958, that the Soviet Union would sign at an early date a "peace treaty" with East Germany, which agreement—so the Russian leader contended—would end allied rights in West Berlin. This *démarche* reopened the Berlin question, which had been relatively quiet since the end of the Berlin blockade in 1949. Dulles would not have time to deal with this problem, which not merely passed into the era of the secretaryship of Christian Herter but into that of Herter's successor Dean Rusk. Fortunately Khrushchev's peace treaty never materialized.

In his last journey Dulles also was concerned about Charles de Gaulle, inaugurated for a seven-year term as President of the Fifth French Republic. He had met De Gaulle twice in 1958; their talks had been unsatisfactory. The charismatic Frenchman, then Premier, had embarked on a mission to make France feel it was a world power. His France, he said, must have a leading part in NATO. It must also become a nuclear power. And De Gaulle blamed Washington for the deteriorating French position in North Africa, a charge which Dulles thought ridiculous. The United States, the Secretary had told De Gaulle, wanted France to keep its influence in Algeria, but was against its policies there. Fighting would extend into Tunisia and Morocco, encourage nationalist elements to look to the Soviet Union, and might lead to a defeat like Dienbienphu. He recalled that the French government which surrendered Indochina had killed EDC. The government which surrendered Algeria could kill NATO. At the December, 1958, NATO meeting in Paris, De Gaulle had suggested a three-power directorate for the alliance—France, Britain, United States. He told Dulles that as long as the United States ran the whole show he would not cooperate, or participate in discussions on atomic stockpiles and intercontinental missiles. The Secretary's talk with De Gaulle on February 6, 1959, was surprisingly good, but inconclusive.[14]

Chancellor Adenauer was the last statesman Dulles saw in Europe before his death. When the Secretary arrived at the Schaumburg Palace he looked ill. The German leader feared the worst. Their friendship, if not admiration, had begun with their first meeting in 1953 and had deepened after the Suez crisis. Each was religious, each thought the other the better statesman. Like Dulles, Adenauer believed in European unity. The Chancellor did not think Britain or France capable of a European policy. Churchill while in power was old and ill, and the French Government weak and ever-changing. British military ineptness at Suez depressed Adenauer, and he wondered whether London would fight for West Germany. Europe, Adenauer said to Dulles, was the prisoner of its past. Only the United States could bring Europe into the mid-twentieth century. Adenauer knew he could rely on Dulles as an "angel from heaven." Still, the Chancellor continually demanded assurance of American support. This the Secretary had found annoying but understandable.

Their last meeting was pleasant, and reassuring to Adenauer. The Chancellor was a solicitous, perfect host. En route to the airport Dulles suddenly turned to him and said: "I know you know I've been feeling pretty badly on this trip . . . some people think this is a recurrence of the cancer . . . I want to say to you that I myself don't think so . . . I must have an operation for hernia when I return to Washington . . . I mention it to you so that you won't be shocked when you hear about the operation and so you won't think it was because of a return of cancer."[15] Adenauer prayed that Dulles was right.

The operation disclosed the spread of cancer. As soon as Dulles learned the ominous news he sent a message to Adenauer, for he did not want the Chancellor to think he had deceived him. "I recall our conversation going to the airport and the statement I made to you concerning my condition. I am sorry to have to inform you that what I have told you turned out to be wrong. But I am confident I can overcome this." A few days later he sent two photographs showing them together, one autographed and the other for Adenauer to inscribe for him. To Adenauer this gesture seemed a way of saying a final good-by.[16]

For Dulles the following two months were a struggle. Within a day after his operation the Secretary on February 9, 1959, asked the President to turn over to Under Secretary Herter (who had displaced Herbert Hoover, Jr.) the duties of Secretary of State "for a short period." He wrote Eisenhower that during the weeks of recuperation he would "concentrate on the complicated and grave problems raised by the Soviet threats regarding Berlin and the Allies' response thereto," and be available for consultation.[17] During this time he stayed in the South, hoping to overcome the onslaught of his disease. But on a warm day, April 11, 1959, Allen Dulles, accompanied by the Secretary's Special Assistant, Joseph N. Greene, Jr., called on the President who was then at a summer cottage in Augusta, Georgia. He brought bad news: his brother was getting weaker, pain spreading through his body and into his neck. The Secretary wanted to return to Walter Reed Hospital, and resign. Eisenhower did not wish to hear about a resignation; he did not want to hurry matters, to do anything that might disturb the Secretary. "I don't want to take any action that would tend to discourage him. Please tell him this personally." But Dulles had made the decision; his brother produced a letter of resignation written in longhand on the familiar lawyer's yellow, lined paper. Dulles knew he was dying and his last official letter was his epitaph:

> I was brought up in the belief that this nation of ours was not merely a self-serving society but was founded with a mission to help build a world where liberty and justice would prevail. Today that concept faces a formidable and ruthless challenge from International Communism. This has made it manifestly difficult to adhere steadfastly to our national idealism and national mission and at the same time avoid the awful catastrophe of war.[18]

The President read the letter, and kept it. Four days later he accepted the resignation of his Secretary of State, and appointed him Special Consultant on Foreign Affairs.

The next month, on May 24, 1959, John Foster Dulles died.

Many people mourned the death. Allied leaders looked back and saw how strong a defender of liberty he had been. No one questioned his courage. On learning of Dulles' illness, Prime Minister Macmillan had spoken for the House of Commons: "Mr. Dulles is a figure whose very bigness is hardly realised until we are threatened with its absence. He is one of those men whose devotion to duty and strength of purpose have made him a great, important and vital figure in the life of the world."[19] Even adversaries respected his character and ability. "I feel very sorry for Dulles," Khrushchev told Dag Hammarskjold after Dulles had resigned. "I admire his intelligence, his wide knowledge, his integrity and his courage. Dulles invented brinkmanship, but he would never step over the brink."[20]

At home many people who had been critical expressed their respect, weeks before he died. "There are so few men in our day and country with the capacity to follow a sustained train of thought," said the *Reporter,* "to be themselves to the farthest reaches of loneliness and of risk. Mr. Dulles has proved to be one of the very, very few. When we learned of his resignation, we knew that our lives had become the poorer."[21]

Richard H. Rovere, writing for the *New Yorker,* saw no one in Washington "who has not been greatly stirred by John Foster Dulles's courage and by his display of grace under pressure of a kind that few men are ever called upon to bear." He wanted the fatally stricken Secretary to know during his last "awful moments" that there was "a far wider appreciation of Mr. Dulles's services than there has been at any other time, and that this appreciation is in no sense the product of sympathy or pity or piety." This well-known political writer observed that many statesmen who a year or two earlier would have welcomed a resignation now were fervently wishing he could stay on. They missed his power, skill, experience, what seemed a great promise to lead the West out of the cold war.[22]

The Democratic Party could not question Dulles' strength of character and love of country. The young Senator John F. Kennedy, a Democratic presidential hopeful presumably with a long political future, author of *Profiles in Courage,* added the Republican Secretary of State to his gallery: "The name of John Foster Dulles will not quickly fade from honor." Dulles, he wrote, was a controversial man who chose policies which, "in his conscience and judgment, would allow the American people to make their greatest contribution to peace and freedom. In that faith he toiled heroically against grievous odds."[23] Dulles, by this time gone, would have been proud to see himself in such a gallant profile.

NOTES

JOHN FOSTER DULLES

CHAPTER ONE

1. Dept. of State press release 50, Jan. 28, 1953. New York *Herald Tribune*, Jan. 29.

2. Eleanor Lansing Dulles, *John Foster Dulles: The Last Year* (New York, 1963), p. 160.

3. Allen Welsh Dulles, *The Boer War: A History* (Washington, 1902). At the time of publication Allen Dulles was eight years old. As his grandfather remarked in the preface, Allen was "an ardent admirer and partisan of the Boers, and this in spite of the fact that all his immediate family favor the British cause." Foster Dulles wrote his younger brother: "Dear Allie: I have just finished reading your book and I want to congratulate you. It is fine, and you must have worked very hard on it. Mother has sold five copies already. With love from John Foster Dulles." Allen W. Dulles MSS, in personal possession of Mr. Dulles, Washington, D.C.

4. *Diplomatic Memoirs* (2 vols., Boston, 1909). See also *A Century of American Diplomacy* (Boston, 1901); *American Diplomacy in the Orient* (Boston, 1903); *Arbitration and the Hague Court* (Boston, 1904); *The Practice of Diplomacy* (Boston, 1906).

5. *Diplomatic Memoirs*, II, 156-157.

6. John Foster Dulles MSS deposited in Princeton University Library. Hereafter cited as Dulles MSS.

7. Eleanor Lansing Dulles, *John Foster Dulles*, p. 126.

8. Address at Watertown, Apr. 30, 1952, Dulles MSS.

9. Eleanor Lansing Dulles, *John Foster Dulles*, p. 126; Arthur H. Dean, *John Foster Dulles: 1888-1959* (pamphlet, privately printed), pp. 4-5.

10. *Diplomatic Memoirs*, II, 212.

11. Eleanor Lansing Dulles, *John Foster Dulles*, pp. 61-62.

12. John Robinson Beal, *John Foster Dulles: 1888-1959* (New York, 1959), p. 55.

13. Arthur H. Dean, *John Foster Dulles*, pp. 13-15, 34. Also correspondence with Mr. Dean.

CHAPTER TWO

1. (New York, 1939).

2. Address at Princeton, Mar. 19, 1936. Copy in Dulles MSS. See also John Foster Dulles, *War or Peace* (New York, 1950).

3. "The Church's Contribution Toward a Warless World," *Religion in Life* (winter, 1939). Copy in Dulles MSS.

4. *Loc. cit.*

5. "American Foreign Policy," Mar. 18, 1939.

6. "America's Role in World Affairs," Oct. 28, 1939.

7. "The Christian Forces and a Stable Peace," address to YMCA National Board, New York, Jan. 25, 1941.

8. John Robinson Beal, *John Foster Dulles*, pp. 90-91; "Toward World Order," Merrick-McDowell Lecture at Ohio Wesleyan University, Mar. 5, 1942.

9. Notes of trip to England, July, 1942, Dulles MSS.

10. File 213, Franklin D. Roosevelt MSS deposited in Franklin D. Roosevelt Library, Hyde Park.

11. *War or Peace*, pp. 34-36.

12. Dulles MSS.

13. Dulles to Elsie Sloan Farley, Feb. 13, 1950, Dulles MSS.

14. Dept. of State press release 1062, Nov. 29, 1951.

CHAPTER THREE

1. Cordell Hull, *Memoirs* (2 vols., New York, 1948), II, 1656.

2. *Ibid.*, p. 1686.

3. Arthur H. Vandenberg, Jr., and Joe Alex Morris, eds., *The Private Papers of Senator Vandenberg* (Boston, 1952), pp. 86-88.

4. Cordell Hull, *Memoirs*, II, 1657.

5. *Ibid.*, pp. 1690-1693; John Foster Dulles, *War or Peace*, p. 123.

6. Arthur H. Vandenberg, Jr., and Joe Alex Morris, eds., *The Private Papers of Senator Vandenberg*, pp. 112-113. See also Cordell Hull, *Memoirs*, II, 1686-1694.

7. *Ibid.*, p. 124.

8. Address of Jan. 16, 1945, Dulles MSS.

9. *Ibid.*

10. "An Appraisal of United States Foreign Policy," address of Feb. 5, 1945, Dulles MSS.

11. Dulles had supported Roosevelt's policy of recognition of the Soviet Union in 1933. "It is my opinion," he had written in March of that year, "that the USSR should be recognized by us as a government. Their tenure of power seems to me clearly to justify this and to show that we should no longer maintain the legal fiction that they are not the government of Russia." He did not believe any condition should attach to recognition. He did suggest that diplomatic relations with the USSR, not determined by recognition, could depend on the attitude of the Soviet Government toward organized propaganda against the United States, and on willingness to recognize, at least in principle, a duty to compensate for losses inflicted on Americans. Letter to Esther Everett Lape, Mar. 16, 1933, Dulles MSS.

12. "From Yalta to San Francisco," address of Mar. 17, 1945, Dulles MSS.

13. "The General Assembly," XXIV, 1-11.

14. John Foster Dulles, *War or Peace*, pp. 24-30.

15. *Ibid.*, pp. 30-31.

16. Letter to Roswell T. Barnes *et al.*, May 8, 1946, Dulles MSS.

17. Immediately after publication the *Reporter* (June 15, 1946) carried an article on American-Soviet relations which attacked Dulles' prewar position. Dulles prepared a refutation for private distribution, denying that he had been a lawyer for the Franco regime. He denied that he represented Pierre Laval's son-in-law, Count René de Chambrun. As to the charge that he had defended a diplomatic agent of the Nazi Government in the United States in 1941 he said he not only had not defended him but refused to see him despite prior acquaintance. He dismissed allegations that he had untoward relations with German banking circles which helped Hitler, that he had supported the attempt of the Polish Government-in-Exile to recover sixty million dollars resting in the banks of France to the detriment of France (Dulles contended he had tried to prevent France from handing over this sum to Germany), and finally that his *War, Peace and Change* was a defense of "the dynamism of the fascist states." "The truth," he wrote, "is that my book analyzed the dynamism as an *evil*." The French edition of the book "was the only book by an American author on the first Nazi purge list. Of that I am proud." To Robert White Johnson *et al.*, Oct. 8, 1946, Dulles MSS.

18. "Thoughts on Soviet Foreign Policy and What To Do About It," *Life*, June 3, 10, 1946, condensed in *Reader's Digest*, Aug., 1946; letters to Dean Acheson, May 9, 1946, Walter Lippmann, June 4, Dulles MSS.

19. Vandenberg to Dulles, Apr. 7, May 13, 1946, Dulles MSS.

20. Allen to Foster Dulles, May 14, 1946, Dulles MSS.

21. Address of Feb. 5, 1945, Dulles MSS.

22. Letter to Dewey, Nov. 3, 1948, Dulles MSS.

23. "Our International Responsibilities," address at Vanderbilt University, June 4, 1950. See also John Foster Dulles, *War or Peace*, pp. 178-184.

24. *Ibid.*, p. 136.

CHAPTER FOUR

1. The following material draws on interviews with Acheson in 1962-64, and occasionally material in the so-called Acheson seminar held at Princeton in 1953 (for the seminar see below, p. 362 in the Bibliographical Essay).

2. Interview with Acheson.

3. Late in September, 1949, in response to Dewey's plea that if Dulles met defeat in the forthcoming senatorial election he should go back to the Department, Acheson informed the Governor he would be glad to have him. Acheson told Dewey that he had previously asked Dulles to work with Philip C. Jessup on Far Eastern problems, but that senatorial duties had prevented this assignment. But until March, 1950, when a prominent Republican, John Sherman Cooper of Kentucky, was appointed consultant to Acheson, there was no significant bipartisan cooperation. Dulles greeted the appointment of Cooper as a "step toward restoring bipartisanship in foreign policy," reasserting the "cooperation, good spirit and vigorous policies needed to win the Cold War and win the peace." *War or Peace*, p. 137. Letters to Acheson, Mar. 29, 1950, and to Truman, Nov. 8, 1948, May 10, 1949, Dulles MSS.

4. John Robinson Beal, *John Foster Dulles*, p. 114.

5. Dulles later would analyze Lehman's effort to portray him as "a bigot and an associate of anti-Semitics" as a calculated attempt "to get virtually one hundred per cent of the Jewish vote in New York City." Lehman, he believed, needed it. "I would get," he wrote Richard Stone, "approximately sixty per cent upstate. He would lose much of the New York City Catholic vote because of his getting into the Cardinal

Spellman controversy with Mrs. Roosevelt. That made him wholly dependent on the Jewish vote." Dulles agreed with some politicians that he "could have overcome the bigotry charge and gotten an appreciable percentage of the Jewish vote, but time ran out." To Richard Stone, Feb. 13, 1952, Dulles MSS.

6. Vandenberg to Acheson, Mar. 31, 1950, Dulles MSS.

7. Interview with Acheson.

8. *Ibid.* See also Frederick S. Dunn, *Peace-Making and the Settlement with Japan* (Princeton, 1963), pp. 95ff.

9. Vandenberg to Homer Ferguson, May 31, 1950, Dulles MSS; Dulles to Truman, July 20, 1950, Truman MSS. "At the moment," Dulles wrote Jean Monnet, "while I am following affairs generally, I am also trying to educate myself about the Eastern situation where there has not, as yet, been any bipartisan cooperation, and where there is a great need for more solid national position. I shall probably go to Japan in a few days." Letter of May 23, 1950, Dulles MSS.

10. Eleanor Lansing Dulles, *John Foster Dulles*, p. 33.

11. Acheson seminar. Truman to Dulles, June 29, July 5, 1950, Dulles to Truman, June 28, 29, Truman MSS; Dulles and John M. Allison to Acheson and Rusk, June 25. See also Harry S. Truman, *Memoirs: Years of Trial and Hope* (Garden City, N. Y., 1956), p. 336.

12. Truman to Dulles, Jan. 10, 1951, Truman MSS.

13. Fifty-two nations attended the Japanese Peace Conference at San Francisco; only three refused to sign the Peace Treaty: the Soviet Union, Poland, and Czechoslovakia.

14. *Conference for the Conclusion and Signature of the Treaty of Peace with Japan: Record of Proceedings* (Washington, 1951), pp. 33, 300-303, 307-309. In the Dulles MSS there is a huge folder entitled "Draft-Treaty of Peace with Japan, September 5, 1951," containing all sorts of material on the treaty.

15. Address at Watertown, Apr. 30, 1952, Dulles MSS.

16. Dulles to Truman, Mar. 21, 1952, Truman to Dulles,

Mar. 24, Truman MSS. During a press conference in October, 1951, Truman said he had just offered Dulles the post of ambassador to Japan, but the latter had refused because "he didn't think he should take the job . . . he ought to try to save the Republican Party from going isolationist." When asked if he thought that a worthy objective, the President answered, "I certainly do." Press and radio conference 281, Oct. 4, 1951, Truman MSS.

CHAPTER FIVE

1. Interview with Eisenhower.

2. John Robinson Beal, *John Foster Dulles*, p. 129. Dulles was not only widely known but highly considered by the American people. *Saturday Review* in a poll of its readers obtained the following results from the question, "Regardless of availability, what living American would you most like to see elected President of the United States in 1952?": Eisenhower, 54.6%; Taft, 22.9%; Kefauver, 18.7%; *Dulles*, 16.9%; Warren, 15.9%; Stassen, 13.1%; Eleanor Roosevelt, 11.8%; Henry Cabot Lodge, Jr., 9.6%; Paul Douglas, 6.6%; Dean Acheson, 6.4%. Issue of Feb. 16, 1952. The percentage figures total more than 100 because each respondent could name more than one candidate.

3. See "Where Are We?," address to the American Association for the United Nations, Dec. 29, 1950, in which Dulles talked about the "deterrent of retaliatory power." Also "Foreign Policy and the National Welfare," address to the National Farm Institute, Feb. 16, 1952, and address to the Princeton National Alumni Luncheon, Feb. 22. Years later Dulles revealed to Andrew H. Berding that "his greatest success as Secretary of State was in what he called 'peace through deterrence.'" *Dulles on Diplomacy* (Princeton, 1965), pp. 6-7.

4. See also "A Policy of Boldness," *Life*, May 19, 1952, a

reprint with minor alterations of the memorandum given to Eisenhower in March.

5. Dwight D. Eisenhower, *Mandate for Change: 1953-1956* (Garden City, N. Y., 1963), p. 23. See also Eisenhower to Dulles, Apr. 15, 1952, Dulles MSS.

6. Dulles believed it possible to deter Chinese Communist action but not "to stop it at whatever time and place they select." Letter to Chester Bowles, Mar. 25, 1952, Dulles MSS. In the same letter Dulles expressed his views on how to separate Communist China from the Soviet Union: press Communist China and make its way difficult "so long as it is in partnership with Soviet Russia." Tito, he explained, did not break with Stalin because the United States was nice to him; on the contrary.

7. New York *Herald Tribune*, May 7, 9, 11, 1952; *Herald Tribune* Paris edition, May 5, 6.

8. New York *Times*, May 14, 17; *Herald Tribune*, May 7.

9. Statement of Mar. 25, 1952, Dulles MSS.

CHAPTER SIX

1. New York *Herald Tribune*, May 9, 1952. See also Dulles to Eisenhower, May 20, 1952, Dulles MSS.

2. See "Foreign Policy Needs," address reprinted in *Congressional Record*, vol. 98, No. 82, May 14, 1952, and "A Policy of Boldness," *Life*, May 19.

3. Dulles to Eisenhower, May 20, Dulles MSS.

4. New York *Sunday News*, June 22. See also New York *Times* and *Herald Tribune*, June 22.

5. New York *Herald Tribune*, June 20.

6. See Louis L. Gerson, *The Hyphenate in Recent American Politics and Diplomacy* (Lawrence, Kansas, 1964), pp. 178-199. Also New York *Times*, Oct. 5, 1952.

7. Dwight D. Eisenhower, *Mandate for Change*, p. 41.

8. Kirk H. Porter and Donald Bruce Johnson, comps., *National Party Platforms: 1840-1956* (Urbana, Ill., 1956).

9. Interview with Eisenhower. Not until October 11, 1952, did Eisenhower consent to give a public promise to repudiate Yalta. See New York *Times*, Oct. 12, 19.

10. Louis L. Gerson, *The Hyphenate in Recent American Politics and Diplomacy*, p. 201.

11. "Freedom and Its Purpose," address to the General Assembly of the National Council of Churches, Dec. 11, 1952.

12. Dulles replied to Acheson's criticism; see New York *Herald Tribune*, Sept. 13.

13. Louis L. Gerson, *The Hyphenate in Recent American Politics and Diplomacy*, p. 195.

14. Dulles to Douglas, Aug. 13, Dean Acheson MSS, Washington, D.C. Also New York *Times*, Aug. 17.

15. New York *Times* and San Francisco *Chronicle*, Sept. 17. Dulles suggested these main points: "Neither party should use confidential information against the other." "The opposition should not be bound by the action of a bipartisan delegation to the United Nations." "Credits and debits should be shared when there has been genuine sharing of responsibility." "Opposition members who have co-operated with the Administration in some matters should be free to criticize in others, or where their advice was not taken."

16. New York *Times*, Oct. 2.

17. New York *Herald Tribune*, Nov. 26; New York *Times*, Aug. 29.

18. "Foreign Report," Feb. 14, 1952.

19. Interviews with Eisenhower and Eden. Also *Mandate for Change*, p. 142.

20. Interviews with Acheson and Eden; Acheson seminar; Dulles correspondence of Jan. 16, 1952, in Acheson MSS. Both in his memoirs (*Full Circle* [Boston, 1960], p. 21) and in discussion with the author, Eden claimed he had not seen beforehand the text of the Yoshida letter, and related his surprise when the United States and Japan simultaneously published it.

21. Interview with Acheson. Harry S. Truman, *Years of Trial and Hope*, pp. 505-521. Dwight D. Eisenhower, *Mandate for Change*, p. 85.

22. Interview with Eisenhower.

CHAPTER SEVEN

1. Interview with Eisenhower.
2. *Ibid.*
3. "A Survey of Foreign Policy Problems," Jan. 27, 1953, Dept. of State publication 4911.
4. In the Dulles MSS there is a folder entitled "Travel—European Trip—Jan. 31-Feb. 9, 1953."
5. See Dwight D. Eisenhower, *Mandate for Change*, p. 123.
6. *Ibid.*, pp. 142-143.
7. House of Commons *Debates*, Feb. 3, 1953, pp. 1674-1680. See also Richard P. Stebbins, *United States in World Affairs: 1953* (New York, 1955), pp. 26-28.
8. *Loc. cit.*
9. Dept. of State *Bulletin*, XXVIII (Feb. 23, 1953), 289.
10. Dulles MSS.
11. Dept. of State press release 40, Jan. 22, 1953. Italics added.
12. John Robinson Beal, *John Foster Dulles*, p. 141. See also Dulles to Walter H. Judd, Feb. 2, 1948, Dulles MSS. There is a folder in the Dulles MSS marked "Carnegie (Hiss) Files."
13. *US in World Affairs: 1953*, pp. 40-43; and John Robinson Beal, *John Foster Dulles*, pp. 138-152. In the spring of 1953, Eisenhower wrote the Department that while it was vital to get rid of subversive individuals, this should not be done unless every man were sure he would be considered innocent until proved guilty, and that superiors should back their men to the limit until proved guilty.
14. Interview with Kennan.

15. 83d Cong., 1st Sess., *Nomination of John Foster Dulles: Hearing before the Senate Committe on Foreign Relations* (Washington, 1953).

16. Dept. of State *Bulletin*, XXVIII (Feb. 9, 1953), 207-211; 83d Cong., 1st Sess., *Congressional Record*, vol. 99, pt. 9, pp. 756, 1344; Dept. of State, *American Foreign Policy, 1950-1955: Basic Documents* (2 vols., Washington, 1957), II, 1957-1959. See also 83d Cong., 1st Sess., *Congressional Record*, vol. 99, pt. 9, pp. A820-821; and *ibid.*, pt. 10, p. A1801. In review of the first session Senator Lyndon B. Johnson, Democratic minority leader, stated, "President Eisenhower's request that Congress join him in a condemnation of Soviet bad faith was buried in committee because the Republican members could not accept the language that he proposed." 83d Cong., 1st Sess., *Legislative Review*, Senate Doc. 76. Senator Knowland, Republican majority leader, did not allude to the request in his review of the first session. 83d Cong., 1st Sess., *Republican Congress: Seven Months' Progress*, Senate Doc. 75; and Louis L. Gerson, *The Hyphenate in Recent American Politics and Diplomacy*, pp. 200-209.

17. 83d Cong., 1st Sess., *Nomination of Charles E. Bohlen: Hearings before the Senate Foreign Relations Committee* (Washington, 1953).

18. Dept. of State, *American Foreign Policy, 1950-1955: Basic Documents,* II, 1745-1746, 1957-1959; and Louis L. Gerson, *The Hyphenate in Recent American Politics and Diplomacy*, p. 212.

19. *Ibid.*, pp. 26-27; and Dept. of State *Bulletin*, XXVIII (Mar. 2, 1953), 330.

20. *US in World Affairs: 1953*, pp. 47-49.

21. Peter V. Curl, ed., *Documents on American Foreign Relations: 1953* (New York, 1954), p. 101.

22. See Arthur Krock in New York *Times*, Apr. 7, 1953.

23. Interview with Phleger. Years later when Phleger resigned as Legal Adviser to the Department, the Washington *Post* in a lead editorial on March 19, 1959, praised him for

his quiet and effective work which "was in large measure responsible for the defeat of the ill-conceived Bricker amendment."

24. *Docs. on Amer. For. Rels.: 1953,* pp. 102-110.

25. Interview with Eisenhower. See also *Mandate for Change,* pp. 278-285, 432.

26. *US in World Affairs: 1953,* pp. 52-58. In subsequent volumes this series traces the history and demise of the amendment.

27. *Mandate for Change,* p. 285.

CHAPTER EIGHT

1. *US in World Affairs: 1953,* pp. 32-37.
2. *Docs. on Amer. For. Rels.: 1953,* pp. 247-251.
3. *US in World Affairs: 1953,* pp. 59-61, 70-73; *Docs. on Amer. For. Rels.: 1953,* pp. 110-114; New York *Times,* May 29; Dept. of State *Bulletin,* XXVIII (June 22, 1953), 863-865.
4. *Mandate for Change,* pp. 144-149.
5. *US in World Affairs: 1953,* pp. 132-136; *Docs. on Amer. For. Rels.: 1953,* pp. 240-247.
6. *Mandate for Change,* pp. 145-149; *Docs. on Amer. For. Rels.: 1953,* pp. 27-34; Dept. of State *Bulletin,* XXVIII (Apr. 27, 1953), 603-608.
7. *Docs. on Amer. For. Rels.: 1953,* pp. 240-247; *US in World Affairs: 1953,* pp. 128-136; *Current Digest of the Soviet Press,* V (May 16, 1953), 5-8.
8. *Mandate for Change,* p. 149.
9. Address of Apr. 23, 1953, Dulles MSS.
10. Dulles memorandum, Apr. [?], 1953, Dulles MSS. In the MSS there is a folder entitled "Travel–Paris–NATO Meeting, April 21-27, 1953." See *US in World Affairs: 1953,* pp. 166-168; *Docs. on Amer. For. Rels.: 1953,* pp. 192-194.
11. Quoted in *US in World Affairs: 1953,* p. 187.
12. *Ibid.,* p. 190.

13. See also Dwight D. Eisenhower, *Mandate for Change*, pp. 242-243; *Docs. on Amer. For. Rels.: 1953*, pp. 210-214.

14. *US in World Affairs: 1953*, pp. 366-372.

15. *Ibid.*, pp. 425-430; *Docs. on Amer. For. Rels.: 1953*, pp. 216-218; and Dwight D. Eisenhower, *Mandate for Change*, pp. 242-251.

16. Address in Dulles MSS. In the MSS there is a folder entitled "Travel—Paris NATO trip, Dec. 11-17, 1953." See also *US in World Affairs: 1953*, pp. 435-442.

17. Anthony Eden, *Full Circle*, pp. 62-65; House of Commons *Debates*, Dec. 17, 1953, p. 583; "1954—A Year for Decision," address to National Press Club, Washington, D.C., Dec. 22, 1953, Dept. of State *Bulletin*, XXX (Jan. 4, 1954), 3-7; *Manchester Guardian Weekly*, Dec. 18, 1953; Schonbrun to Murrow, Dec. 15, 1953, Dulles MSS.

18. Dept. of State *Bulletin*, XLVII (Dec. 17, 1962), 908.

CHAPTER NINE

1. The Director of Protocol of the Department of State noticed Dulles' unconcern about his "public image." "Perhaps there is a discreet way to tell Secretary of State Dulles," he wrote, "to keep his hands out of his pockets when he is photographed. . . . The Secretary of State should also be representative of his appearance wherever he goes." Memorandum of July 8, 1953, Dulles MSS.

2. Letter of Dec. 30, 1953, Dulles MSS.

3. "Outlines of Strategy," speech of Jan. 12, 1954, Dept. of State *Bulletin*, XXX (Jan. 25, 1954), 107-110. After reading a draft of the speech Secretary of the Treasury George M. Humphrey termed it an historic document. Dulles MSS. Perhaps at the time Humphrey was trying to be agreeable, but in retrospect he assuredly was accurate.

4. Interviews with Eisenhower. *Mandate for Change*, p. 181; Andrew H. Berding, *Dulles on Diplomacy*, p. 129.

5. Dept. of State *Bulletin*, XXX (Jan. 25, 1954), 107-110.

6. According to Admiral Arthur W. Radford, Chairman of the Joint Chiefs of Staff from August, 1953, to August, 1957, "the new look was indeed a new look." In a letter to the author of March 29, 1966, he points out that "one has to study the military posture of the United States after 1945 and through the years up until 1953 to understand what a departure it was." Until the Korean War started, "the trend in our military appropriations had been downward from 1945 through June 1950. The budget for 1951 was to take it further down and I have always been puzzled as to why the Communists decided to jump off in Korea in 1950. If they had waited one more year, the military capability of the United States in the western Pacific to effectively oppose an attack would have been much less than it was in June 1950—and even at that time our forces were small and our capability almost too little to be effective. President Eisenhower's request for what came to be called the new look was really an historical milestone in the history of our country. The new look did not place complete reliance on air power, as is so often indicated, but it did provide balanced armed forces, for the indefinite future, of a size much greater than the United States had ever had before in times of peace. It provided an army of about 1,000,000 men, a very strong navy, and a retaliatory power which was designed to be a deterrent against conventional attacks, this latter because a new development in 1952 and 1953 provided small atomic weapons. The deterrent against sudden ground attacks was to be placed on small atomic weapons primarily. Our NATO allies agreed to this policy in the fall of 1954." Admiral Radford recalls Dulles' enthusiastic backing of the Joint Chiefs of Staff when their proposal was submitted to the National Security Council in September, 1953. Dulles "felt that the power of our deterrent forces was rounded out for the first time (which they were) and that there was a real chance that the Communists would not try anything like a Korean war again

as long as we in the United States maintained such a strong military posture." See also Dwight D. Eisenhower, *Mandate for Change*, pp. 445-458.

7. Admiral Radford was out of the country when Dulles gave his speech on January 12, 1954. "I was somewhat appalled when I read of it and had quite a conversation with him when I returned. I told him I thought the use of these words was not descriptive of our new military program. It was massive deterrent power rather than massive retaliatory power. I think it was an unfortunate phrase and I think Mr. Dulles regretted it himself." Letter of Mar. 29, 1966.

8. Andrew H. Berding, *Dulles on Diplomacy*, pp. 124-125. See also Richard P. Stebbins, *United States in World Affairs: 1954* (New York, 1956), pp. 46-64; New York *Times*, Feb. 28, Mar. 6, 28, 1954; John Foster Dulles, "Policy for Security and Peace," *Foreign Affairs*, vol. 32 (April, 1954), 353-364; Peter V. Curl, ed., *Documents on American Foreign Relations: 1954* (New York, 1955), pp. 15-32; interviews with Admiral Radford, *U.S. News and World Report*, Mar. 4, 1954, Feb. 25, 1955. See also "The Foundation for a Firm Peace," address by Dulles in Chicago, Dec. 8, 1955, Dept. of State press release 683.

CHAPTER TEN

1. General de Gaulle was not present at these conferences, but Roosevelt and Churchill knew his opinions. This chapter draws heavily on interviews which the author undertook not to quote or attribute.

2. *US in World Affairs: 1954*, pp. 211ff; *Docs. on Amer. For. Rels.: 1954*, pp. 218-219.

3. Interview with Eisenhower. See also *Mandate for Change*, p. 346.

4. *Ibid.*, pp. 332-343.

5. The United States had opposed establishment of the fortress at Dienbienphu manned by more than 10,000 crack French troops. The position was not well-chosen. High hills surrounded it, and enemy artillery easily could halt reinforcements. Defenders had to depend upon airborne supplies.

6. Dept. of State *Bulletin*, XXX (Jan. 25, 1954), 107-110; "Korean Problems," broadcast address to American Legion convention, St. Louis, Sept. 2, 1953, Dept. of State publication 5190.

7. Dwight D. Eisenhower, *Mandate for Change*, p. 345; Chalmers M. Roberts, "The Day We Didn't Go to War," *Reporter*, Sept. 14, 1954; *US in World Affairs: 1954*, pp. 217-228.

8. "The Threat of a Red Asia," address to Overseas Press Club, Mar. 29, 1954, Dept. of State press release 165.

9. *US in World Affairs: 1954*, p. 221.

10. Letter of Apr. 4, 1954, in *Mandate for Change*, pp. 346-347.

11. See also James Shepley, "How Dulles Averted War," *Life*, Jan. 16, 1956, pp. 70-80.

12. *Docs. on Amer. For. Rels.: 1954*, pp. 257-258.

13. Dwight D. Eisenhower, *Mandate for Change*, pp. 347-348; *US in World Affairs: 1954*, 223ff.

14. *Docs. on Amer. For. Rels.: 1954*, pp. 258-259. Dwight D. Eisenhower, *Mandate for Change*, pp. 348-349.

15. *US in World Affairs: 1954*, p. 223.

16. See also Dwight D. Eisenhower, *Mandate for Change*, pp. 350ff.

17. Interview with Eisenhower. See also *Mandate for Change.*

18. *Full Circle*, p. 116.

19. *Ibid.*, pp. 111-119; Dwight D. Eisenhower, *Mandate for Change*, pp. 350-375; *US in World Affairs: 1954*, pp. 225-229.

CHAPTER ELEVEN

1. "Security in the Pacific," address to Los Angeles World Affairs Council, Dept. of State press release 318. See also "The Issues at Geneva," broadcast of May 7, 1954, Dept. of State press release 238. This chapter draws heavily on interviews with major participants in events.

2. Texts of the accords in *Docs. on Amer. For. Rels.: 1954*, pp. 282-318. Also *US in World Affairs: 1954*, pp. 198-254; Anthony Eden, *Full Circle*, pp. 120-163; Dwight D. Eisenhower, *Mandate for Change*, pp. 332-375.

3. Press conference, July 23, 1954, Dulles MSS. Senator Mike Mansfield of Montana annoyed Dulles in a speech to the Senate suggesting that the collapse of the French position in Indochina was because of American acquiescence to the French demand to hold a peace conference in Geneva. The French, Dulles wrote, had determined to talk peace and would have done so without American consent. American diplomacy, he continued, was not strong enough to overcome French weakness. The United States could have filled the vacuum created by the decline of French power, but this would have involved a battle with France "for the privilege of getting in to fight the Viet Minh." The United States had gone the limit. If this were not enough, and it was not enough, it was not because the American Government could not have done more, but that French weakness was too overwhelming to be bolstered even by American diplomacy. Replying to Mansfield's statement that "Geneva was a mistake; and the result was a failure in American policy," Dulles countered that it may have been a mistake, but, if so, it was not an American mistake. The Americans could not force the French after their will to fight had gone. Was Mansfield suggesting that the United States should have taken over the military operation? At Geneva the American position was "clear, strong, honorable." Dulles did not accept the view

that whenever there is trouble Washington must immediately do something. "It is a grave disservice to the United States to assume . . . that it is a 'failure' of the United States if anywhere in the world others fail. The United States is not throughout the world 'Mr. Fixit.'" Draft letter, Dulles to Mansfield, July 9, 1954, Dulles MSS. It is interesting that a recent volume by the distinguished historian Samuel Eliot Morison, *The Oxford History of the American People* (New York, 1965), has mirrored Mansfield's views (p. 1099). Were Dulles alive at the time of publication of Morison's work, he undoubtedly would have answered as on July 9, 1954.

CHAPTER TWELVE

1. *US in World Affairs: 1954*, pp. 256, 264.

2. Letter of Oct. 1, 1954, Dept. of State *Bulletin*, XXXI (Nov. 15, 1954), 735-736, quoted in *Docs. on Amer. For. Rels.: 1954*, p. 366.

3. Admiral Radford differs. "The French withdrawal from Indochina did not happen quickly. After the signing of the Geneva Accords the French were in Indochina for some time and were primarily responsible for the training of military forces in all three states. . . . I do not feel that the French had any responsibility for carrying out the political agreements of the Accords. When they did leave Indochina, they certainly had no residual responsibility there." Letter to the author, Mar. 29, 1966.

4. Admiral Radford thinks the word "monarchical" gives a wrong implication. Diem, he believes, was a very interesting and dedicated man. "He had the background to lead his people and there were very few others who had experience and competence equal to his. He was an extremely honest man, wealthy enough so that he did not have to augment his income as so many Eastern politicians do. His principal problems concerned getting adequately trained Vietnamese for

the government bureaucracy that had to be set up. I think he did an amazing job under adverse conditions. Today, 10 years later and under different circumstances, it is easy to criticize. Diem had a great deal of personal courage, traveled all over the country practically without protection. At the time and even with hindsight, I do not know of anyone else who could have done the job he did."

5. The division at the 17th parallel placed approximately two million more people under communist control than were left south of the parallel. Admiral Radford believes that Diem had good reason to refuse. "In the first place, South Viet Nam had refused to sign the Accords, and they in turn contained no provision for supervision of the elections either in the North or in the South by any impartial group. Furthermore, they contained no provision for permitting anti-Communist leaders to reach the people, particularly in North Viet Nam, to explain their position. The elections as set up in the Accords were designed to turn the country over to the Communists of North Viet Nam. Diem well understood this, as I found out in talking with him."

6. Richard P. Stebbins, *United States in World Affairs: 1956* (New York, 1957), p. 135.

7. Andrew H. Berding, *Dulles on Diplomacy*, pp. 61-63.

8. When critics said that India, Burma, and Indonesia had declined American invitations to participate in SEATO, Dulles pointed out in a memorandum to Eisenhower (Sept. 1, 1954) that Washington had not extended such invitations. It was the British who had invited the Colombo powers—India, Pakistan, Ceylon, Burma, and Indonesia. Dulles felt it had been a mistake on their part to do so, because he was sure some would decline; but he could not prevent the British from trying. Dulles MSS. See also Anthony Eden, *Full Circle*, p. 162.

9. Dulles opposed regional defense pacts made up of reluctant members. Letter to Sumner Welles, Feb. 4, 1949, Dulles MSS. To the Far East chiefs of mission he said on

March 14, 1958, that he had been against creation of SEATO in the image of NATO. Even if the United States had wanted to do so, the geographic nature of SEATO did not lend itself to such an undertaking. Dependence, he felt, was not to be on American forces, but on commitments in treaties backed by mobile power. Dulles MSS. Also *US in World Affairs: 1954*, pp. 257-258.

10. *Ibid.*, pp. 258-261. *Docs. on Amer. For. Rels.: 1954*, pp. 319-323; "The Manila Pact and the Pacific Charter," Dulles broadcast, Sept. 15, 1954, Dept. of State press release 509.

11. Dwight D. Eisenhower, *Mandate for Change*, pp. 459ff.

12. *Ibid.*, and interviews. Also *US in World Affairs: 1954*, pp. 264-266.

13. *Docs. on Amer. For. Rels.: 1954*, pp. 360-364.

14. Dwight D. Eisenhower, *Mandate for Change*, pp. 466-467.

15. *Ibid.*, pp. 466-470, 608.

16. Eisenhower to Churchill, Jan. 25, 1955, *ibid.*, pp. 609-610. Memorandum of conversation between Dulles and Eden, Feb. 24, 1955, Dulles MSS.

17. Eisenhower, *Mandate for Change*, pp. 476-480.

18. Excerpts of this memorandum of Apr. 5, 1955, in *ibid.*, pp. 611-612.

19. Hollis W. Barber, *United States in World Affairs: 1955* (New York, 1957), pp. 102-110. See also Eisenhower, *Mandate for Change*, p. 482.

20. Drafts, talking papers, and memoranda of conversations with Chiang Kai-shek, Nov., 1958, Dulles MSS.

CHAPTER THIRTEEN

1. See Dwight D. Eisenhower, *Mandate for Change*, pp. 399, 505.

2. *Ibid.*, pp. 505-506; interview with Eisenhower.

3. *Full Circle*, pp. 164-194; *Mandate for Change*, pp. 402-409. See also "Report to the President and the Cabinet," address to the nation, Oct. 25, 1954.

4. *Docs. on Amer. For. Rels.: 1954*, pp. 104-184; Paul E. Zinner, ed., *Documents on American Foreign Relations: 1955* (New York, 1956), pp. 97-107.

5. Andrew H. Berding, *Dulles on Diplomacy*, pp. 23-24.

6. Statement in Dulles MSS.

7. Memoranda, drafts, briefing papers for the Geneva Conference, Dulles MSS. See also Dwight D. Eisenhower, *Mandate for Change*, pp. 506-508.

8. *Ibid.*, pp. 504-527; Anthony Eden, *Full Circle*, pp. 319-346.

CHAPTER FOURTEEN

1. *Mandate for Change*, pp. 509-510; *US in World Affairs: 1955*, pp. 60-61.

2. *Mandate for Change*, p. 517.

3. *Ibid.*, pp. 510-531; Anthony Eden, *Full Circle*, pp. 327-346; *Docs. on Amer. For. Rels.: 1955*, pp. 171-232; Richard Goold-Adams, *The Time of Power* (London, 1962), pp. 179-199; Paul C. Davis, "The New Diplomacy: The 1955 Geneva Summit Meeting," in Roger Hilsman and Robert C. Good, eds., *Foreign Policy in the Sixties: The Issues and the Instruments* (Baltimore, 1965), pp. 159-190.

4. New York *Herald Tribune*, July 24, Aug. 1, 1955; and New York *Times*, July 24, 1955, cited in *US in World Affairs: 1955*, p. 66.

CHAPTER FIFTEEN

1. Acheson MSS, and interviews with Acheson.

2. *Full Circle*, p. 276.

3. Letter of March, 1953, *Mandate for Change*, p. 153. Also p. 155.

4. *Full Circle*, pp. 280-281, also pp. 249-290; Dwight D. Eisenhower, *Mandate for Change*, pp. 150-154.

5. Eisenhower memoranda to Dulles, April 9, 23, 27, 28, 1953; and interview with Eisenhower.

6. *Mandate for Change*, p. 155.

7. *US in World Affairs: 1953*, p. 296.

8. Memoranda, "Important points of trip," May 9-29, 1953, Dulles MSS; and interview with Abba Eban.

9. Dulles memoranda, May 9-29. Dulles MSS.

10. Memorandum, "Conclusions," May 9-29, 1953, Dulles MSS.

11. *Loc. cit.*

12. "Report on the Near East," June 1, 1953, Dept. of State publication 5088.

13. *Full Circle*, p. 288.

14. *Ibid.*, pp. 288-289.

15. *Ibid.*, p. 375.

CHAPTER SIXTEEN

1. "The Middle East," Dept. of State press release 517.

2. Interview with Abba Eban.

3. See Dwight D. Eisenhower, *Waging Peace* (Garden City, N. Y., 1965), pp. 24ff. Interview with Eisenhower. The British may have been sensitive about Saudi Arabia, fearing that American policy was trying to move the Saudis away from Egypt at expense of London's interests in Buraimi.

4. Interview with Abba Eban.

5. *Loc. cit.*

6. *Full Circle*, pp. 373-374.

7. *Ibid.*, pp. 370-379.

8. *Waging Peace*, pp. 27-28.

9. Based on interviews with Abba Eban, Jacob Herzog, and Eisenhower. See also *Waging Peace*, pp. 28-30.

CHAPTER SEVENTEEN

1. *Waging Peace*, pp. 32-33; Robert D. Murphy, *Diplomat among Warriors* (Garden City, N. Y., 1964), pp. 375ff.

2. This comment, together with quotations in the preceding paragraph, from *ibid.*, p. 377.

3. *Waging Peace*, p. 33.

4. *Diplomat among Warriors*, p. 379. Also "Report by Secretary Dulles to Latin American Ambassadors," Aug. 7, 1956, Dulles MSS.

5. *Diplomat among Warriors*, p. 379.

6. *Ibid.*, pp. 379ff.

7. "Report by Secretary Dulles to Latin American Ambassadors," Aug. 7, 1956, Dulles MSS.

8. Robert D. Murphy, *Diplomat among Warriors*, pp. 383-384.

9. "The Suez Situation," report to the nation by Eisenhower and Dulles, Aug. 3, 1956, Dulles MSS.

10. Robert D. Murphy, *Diplomat among Warriors*, p. 387.

11. See also "Extemporaneous remarks" by Dulles to Second Suez Canal Conference, Sept. 19, 1956, Dulles MSS.

12. Dwight D. Eisenhower, *Waging Peace*, pp. 55-57; and Robert D. Murphy, *Diplomat among Warriors*, p. 388.

13. *Ibid.*, p. 388. See also "The Task of Waging Peace," address to Dallas Council on World Affairs, Oct. 27, 1956, Dept. of State press release 560.

14. Andrew H. Berding, *Dulles on Diplomacy*, p. 110. Eden later would regret that he did not call for an election to test his standing among his countrymen. Interview with Eden. For an excellent study on the domestic pressures in Britain see Leon D. Epstein, *British Politics in the Suez Crisis* (Urbana, Ill., 1964). Sir John Slessor, Marshal of the Royal Air

Force, was probably the first and only Englishman to see Eisenhower after Eden's ultimatum of October 30. He was summoned to the White House at 2:30 P.M. the next day. Slessor described the meeting in a letter to the London *Times*, June 16, 1964: "The impression he [Eisenhower] left on me was certainly not one of terrible anger or of having lost his head, but more like one of amazed stupefaction at the rashness of our unilateral use of force, involving at least the risk of general war, without consultation with our major ally—especially a few days before the Presidential election which naturally was very much on his mind." Slessor's letter was prompted by the publicity accorded in Britain to Herman Finer's *Dulles over Suez* (Chicago, 1964), which was critical of both Dulles and Eisenhower.

CHAPTER EIGHTEEN

1. "The Amazing Mr. Dulles," New York *Times*, Feb. 25, 1958.

2. Letter of Dec. 4, 1958, Dulles MSS. Also Walter H. Judd to Eisenhower, Jan. 4, 1958, *ibid.* Also W. H. Hale, "Man from Arkansas Goes after Mr. Dulles," *Reporter*, Apr. 18, 1957; "Case against Mr. Dulles," *Nation*, Dec. 14, 1957; "Why Help the Reds Ditch Secretary Dulles?," *Saturday Evening Post*, Feb. 1, 1958; "Dulles Is Wrong," *New Republic*, Oct. 6, 1958; Reinhold Niebuhr, "Moral World of Foster Dulles," *New Republic*, Dec. 1, 1958.

3. Italy tried to shift NATO's purposes from military to economic. See Norman Kogan, *The Politics of Italian Foreign Policy* (New York, 1963), p. 136. Also "The NATO Conference in Paris," broadcast report by Eisenhower and Dulles, Dec. 23, 1957; and John Foster Dulles, "Our Case Will Prevail," *Life*, Dec. 23, 1957.

4. Dulles' draft speech to NATO meeting, Paris, Dec.

8-15, 1956, Dulles MSS. "Remarks" to Council on Foreign Relations, June 7, 1957, *ibid.*

5. "Remarks of the Secretary," opening session, Western European chiefs of mission meeting, Paris, May 9, 1958, Dulles MSS. See also "The Role of Negotiation," address to National Press Club, Washington, Jan. 16, 1958, Dept. of State press releases 18, 19; Dulles to Kingsley Martin, editor of the *New Statesman*, Feb. 6, 1958 (published in *New Statesman*, Feb. 8), Dulles MSS.

6. Draft of a letter to Paul Hoffman, Jan. 21, 1952, Dulles MSS.

7. Also draft outline, talk at Quantico, June 14, 1957, Dulles MSS; "Disarmament and Peace," address to the nation, July 22, 1957, Dept. of State press release 430; "Disarmament: The Intensified Effort, 1955-1958," July, 1958, Dept. of State publication 6676; and Saville R. Davis, "Recent Policy Making in the United States Government," *Daedalus*, vol. 89 (Fall, 1960), 951-966.

8. Interview with Milton Eisenhower. The President's brother welcomed assignments to Latin America, and was appreciative of Dulles' encouragement. According to Milton Eisenhower, Dulles kept abreast of developments in Latin America.

9. *Waging Peace*, p. 515.

10. John Robinson Beal, *John Foster Dulles*, pp. 230-236.

11. *Mandate for Change*, pp. 425-426.

12. *Waging Peace*, p. 519.

13. *Ibid.*, pp. 521, 523-524.

14. Also "Points of Conversation with General De Gaulle, June 30, 1958"; "Paris for talks with De Gaulle, July 3-6, 1958"; "Ideas Used in Talk with De Gaulle, July 3-6, 1958"; Dulles to Adenauer, July 7, 1958, Dulles MSS.

15. Andrew H. Berding, *Dulles on Diplomacy*, p. 42.

16. *Ibid.*, p. 43. Also Adenauer to Dulles, Apr. 30, 1959, Dulles MSS.

17. Letter of Feb. 9, 1959, Dulles MSS.

18. Letter of Apr. 15, 1959, *Waging Peace*, p. 358. Interview with Allen Dulles. The Secretary had elaborated on the meaning of "mission" in "Principles in Foreign Policy," Dept. of State press release 203, Apr. 11, 1955.

19. House of Commons *Debates*, vol. 600, Feb. 19, 1959, copy in Dulles MSS. Also "A broadcast appreciation by the Rt. Hon. Selwyn Lloyd," British Secretary of State for Foreign Affairs, May 28, 1959, copy in Dulles MSS.

20. D.E.B. [?] to Dulles, Apr. 2, 1959, Dulles MSS.

21. Issue of Apr. 30, 1959.

22. "Letter from Washington," Apr. 25, 1959. See also "Dulles Illness Shakes Western Security," *Christian Century*, Feb. 25, 1959; "The Last Journey of John Foster Dulles," *U.S. News and World Report*, June 8, 1959; "World Owes More than Some Realize to Mr. Dulles," *Saturday Evening Post*, June 27, 1959; G. Bernard Noble, "U.S. Foreign Policy: The Dulles Era," Dept. of State *News Letter*, May, 1963.

23. "John Foster Dulles: A Profile in Courage," *American Weekly*, June 14, 1959.

BIBLIOGRAPHICAL ESSAY

I. *Biographical*

For an individual who has passed so recently into the dark corridors of history, John Foster Dulles has had a considerable attention from biographers. The reason may be, of course, not merely because he presided over the Department of State during an era of unprecedented problems and complexities but because he was an interesting individual. Dulles was a "driver," as are almost all persons who make their mark in one activity or another. But he had other qualities: he was articulate to the point where he coined almost too many phrases; and he was a moralist in international politics. His was an unusual combination of talents. The first careful book to appear about him, while he was still in office, was by John Robinson Beal, *John Foster Dulles* (New York, 1957), which appeared in a revised edition in the year of its subject's death, 1959. This is a journalistic account, in that it has a certain raciness and breeziness, and moves rather than ruminates, but its author is an intelligent individual and an able journalist, and he obtained some help from the Dulles family, and the result is a book of continuing usefulness. All inquirers into the life and career of the late Secretary must consult this volume, if only as a point of departure. After Dulles' death there followed several works of varying quality. Roscoe Drummond and Gaston Coblentz, *Dulles at the Brink: John Foster Dulles' Command of American Power* (Garden City, N. Y., 1960) is sketchy. Hans Morgenthau, the pessimistic academic observer of American policy, has contributed an essay on Dulles in Norman A. Graebner, *An Uncertain Tradition: American Secretaries of State in the Twentieth Century* (New York, 1961). A volume of importance, judicious and objective, all in all a splendid effort, is Richard Goold-Adams' *The Time of Power: A Reappraisal of John Foster Dulles* (London, 1962). And then there are two books of firsthand knowledge of their subject. Of preeminent importance is the touching volume by the late Secretary's sister, Eleanor Lansing Dulles, *John Foster Dulles: The Last Year* (New York, 1963). Miss Dulles had a long experience in diplomacy, and was able to judge her brother's record not merely from the closeness of family relations but from her own association with the Department of State. See also the admirable book by Andrew H. Berding, *Dulles on Diplomacy* (Princeton, 1965), memories of a Department officer—indeed the literary assistant of Cordell Hull when that earlier Secretary wrote a two-volume memoir—who often traveled with Dulles and had a close official association. Berding recalls Dulles' remarks on various occasions, and has based his book on notes made at the time.

In a sense biographical because of their authorship are Dulles' own two books, *War, Peace and Change* (New York, 1939) and *War or Peace* (New York, 1950).

II. *Memoirs*

For the period of Dulles' earlier career as adviser to Democratic Administrations there is a vast literature. *The Memoirs of Cordell Hull* (New York, 1948) show Dulles' entry into foreign policy in the electoral year 1944. (See also Julius W. Pratt's two volumes on Cordell Hull in the present Series [New York, 1964].) Walter Millis and E. S. Duffield, eds., *The Forrestal Diaries* (New York, 1951) is a unique volume of hastily declassified materials, a major source for anyone wishing to understand the war and immediate postwar years of American military and foreign policy. Forrestal dealt primarily in military affairs, but there were so many connections with foreign policy—never before had those two often separate strands of American government been so closely tied—that the published diaries, a composite of diary jottings and letters interlarded with editorial comment, are indispensable reading. Arthur H. Vandenberg, Jr., and Joe Alex Morris, eds., *The Private Papers of Senator Vandenberg* (Boston, 1952) contain many diary notes, plus quotation from letters, concerning the career of the late Senator, and while more fancifully literary than the Forrestal diaries are of nearly equal interest, because Vandenberg during the latter years of his long senatorial career was so close to the center of American policy, domestic and foreign. In surveying Dulles' career prior to the Secretaryship one must not overlook the able memoir by the President of much of that time, Harry S. Truman's *Year of Decisions* (New York, 1955) and *Years of Trial and Hope* (1956); the Truman books obviously were written by their author of record, and for this reason command attention. They also are frank and open about the years of the presidency. So many memoirs are bland, so careful with reputations of the author and his contemporaries, predecessors, and successors, that the student cannot get much nourishment out of them; but President Truman is a straight shooter, and if sometimes he misses the target it is not for want of trying. See also the essays by Dean G. Acheson, *A Democrat Looks at His Party* (New York, 1955) and *Power and Diplomacy* (Cambridge, Mass., 1958). Mr. Acheson is one of the most talented individuals ever to reach high office in this country; among his many qualities is a lucid literary style, and combined with his own magnificent perception of individuals and issues the result is always worth reading, even if in the case of the above-mentioned books he has not yet brought forward his literary heavy artillery. He now has finished the first volume of his memoirs, dealing with his early life, and all students of diplomacy look forward to the volume dealing with his Secretaryship and the later, Dulles, years.

Sir Anthony Eden in retirement has been producing memoirs, and published first his volume dealing with the Suez crisis, under title of *Full Circle* (Boston, 1960). The book sometimes circles around some ultradiplomatic problems, such as the question of British collusion with the Israelis at the time of Suez, but in general it is a magnificent memoir, and like the books of Acheson and Truman it is the product of its author and not a collaborative ghost. Eden is his own advocate, and holds that his course against Nasser was the correct one, and that it would have stood the test of time and events, had not the United States under leadership of Secretary Dulles failed to support him. Dulles did try to delay action against Nasser; there can be no doubt of that. Eden castigates the Secretary for intellectual dishonesty. One must admit that the former Prime Minister has produced an argument of considerable proportions in which many points lie on the British side.

After leaving office in 1961, President Eisenhower set to work on his memoirs which appeared a few years later. There was some advance skirmishing by other authors. One book was a survey of the Administration's first term by Robert J. Donovan, *Eisenhower: The Inside Story* (New York, 1956), which used papers of the President to relate cabinet meetings and other intimate gatherings, with considerable treatment of foreign policy. Eisenhower's assistant at the White House, Sherman Adams, brought out a book in advance of the President, *Firsthand Report: The Story of the Eisenhower Administration* (New York, 1961). Students of the Eisenhower presidency must consult this latter volume, the second chapter of which deals with foreign policy and John Foster Dulles. There are some arguable contentions here, such as the author's assertion that President Eisenhower upset Dulles by appointing General Walter Bedell Smith as Under Secretary of State. A. Merriman Smith, the well-known White House correspondent, produced *A President's Odyssey* (New York, 1961), detailing the trips to Europe, Asia, the Middle East, Africa, and South America in 1959-1960. Then came the President's memoirs, *The White House Years: Mandate for Change, 1953-1956* (Garden City, N. Y., 1963) and *Waging Peace* (1965). Doubtless because of the difference in personality, perhaps also because events of the Eisenhower presidency are closer to the present day, Mr. Eisenhower chose not to be as hard-hitting as did former President Truman. The Eisenhower books avoid criticism of associates. One might say, though, that this care with reputations has marked other parts of Mr. Eisenhower's career. For example, during the immediate postwar years, especially under attack by such individuals with monumental reputations as Field Marshal Montgomery, Eisenhower refused to enter the command arguments of the war. Criticism of associates has not been his way. Whatever the precautions or preferences, the memoirs of the presidency are certain on one thing: the enormous respect that "Ike" came to hold for "Foster" Dulles. It was not a veneration born out of the tragedy of the Secretary's death while at the height of his powers, but a respect for the thought of Dulles which in many ways followed Eisenhower's own lines of thinking. The President also liked the Secretary—a liking which developed from early days of the presidency when the two men were virtual strangers into the later years when they saw each other very frequently and talked intimately about affairs of state. Secretary Dulles let down his austerities when dealing especially with the Eisenhower of the second term.

For Latin American policy, a subject which did not attract Dulles, see Milton Eisenhower, *The Wine Is Bitter: The United States and Latin America* (Garden City, N. Y., 1963).

Not long after the Administration departed from Washington there appeared a half memoir, half polemic, by a former presidential speechwriter, and a formidable journalist, Emmet John Hughes, *The Ordeal of Power: A Political Memoir of the Eisenhower Years* (New York, 1963). The continuing crises abroad had given many Americans the feeling that Dulles either had engaged in a balancing act as Secretary or simply had failed to ensure peace. It was an ideal time in 1963 to bring out a critical book on the regime of the 1950s, and Hughes' volume with its extraordinary literary qualities proved popular. Hughes had no use for the late Secretary—although, to be sure, one must question how much "inside" information this writer possessed. See also Hughes' *America the Vincible* (Garden City, N. Y., 1962).

Memoirs by diplomatic participants of the Dulles years have been slow in coming. Thus far there is only David Ben-Gurion, *Israel: Years of Challenge* (New York, 1963), an autobiography containing many points other than the author's part in the war of 1956. Robert D. Murphy, *Diplomat among Warriors* (Garden City, N. Y., 1964) may be overrated, as it displays not merely the writer's long and highly important diplomatic career but relates disagreements over policy during the postwar years which sometimes (as in the case of Murphy's advocacy of an armed convoy to Berlin in 1948) seem to have been dangerously in error. Murphy had an ambivalent view of Dulles, praising and criticizing him. The book's sources are difficult to ascertain, as they appear to be papers or a diary, but Murphy may have written almost entirely from memory and open sources. Chancellor Konrad Adenauer has produced the first volume of *Memoirs: 1945-53* (Chicago, 1965), a disappointing book. One awaits the volume for the Dulles years. President de Gaulle has not brought his memoirs through his new time of power.

III. *Monographs*

The special works on American foreign relations during the 1950s are legion, and it is impossible to set out citations and commentary on anywhere near all of them. Books about policy, so close to events, sometimes almost on top of events, are often present-minded and tendentious. Nonetheless there is much merit in many of these volumes. Never has the interest of Americans in foreign affairs been so strong, and this curiosity has itself inspired a literature of more than ordinary value. Moreover, the huge reporting, both in newspapers and periodicals, has brought a tremendous amount of recent diplomatic negotiation into the public domain. The pryings and questionings of newspapermen and journalists have exceeded in ingenuity—and sometimes in gall—anything in the history of journalism. One has only to recall the stodgy figure of Premier Nikita Khrushchev, patiently making his way through a field of Iowa corn, surrounded and almost engulfed by a horde of journalists who at every stop on this bucolic adventure pushed forward and shouted some such admonition as "Hey, Khrushchev, hold up that ear of corn!" It is strange but true that as the history of American foreign policy has approached very recent times, and presumably the diplomatic documents revealing that policy are more and more difficult to obtain, far more diplomacy has been in the public domain than ever before.

The first special resort of the student of the Dulles years should be to two excellent summaries of international relations published annually in the English-speaking world: *The United States in World Affairs*, published under varying editorship by the Council on Foreign Relations in New York; and the more comprehensive *Survey* published by the Royal Institute of International Affairs in London.

As for introductory accounts in the 1950s, volumes of merit are Chester Bowles' interesting essays, *American Politics in a Revolutionary World* (Cambridge, Mass., 1956); Stephen D. Kertesz, ed., *American Diplomacy in a New Era* (Notre Dame, Ind., 1961), a symposium by academic specialists on events since 1945; Zbigniew K. Brzezinski, *The Soviet Bloc: Unity and Conflict* (Cambridge, 1960), scholarly, informative; Frederick C. Barghoorn, *The Soviet Cultural Offensive: The Role of Cultural Diplomacy in Soviet Foreign Policy* (Princeton, 1960), an excellent analysis.

One then turns to topics in the foreign policy of the era.

Nothing in this regard is more interesting than the connection
during the 1950s of power and diplomacy. The United States
had managed to balance its military forces, if uneasily, between so-called conventional and strategic—that is, atomic—
forces, and it was Secretary Dulles' difficult task to keep
a large literature on the problem of national security, much
of it of high value. See the careful volume edited by William
W. Kaufmann, *Military Policy and National Security* (Prince-
diplomacy and power together in his negotiations. There is
ton, 1956); Henry A. Kissinger's sometimes incautious but,
because it caught the national attention through a feature
story in *Life* magazine, much-remarked-upon *Nuclear Weapons and Foreign Policy* (New York, 1957); Robert E. Osgood,
Limited War: The Challenge to American Strategy (Chicago,
1957); Bernard Brodie, *Strategy in the Missile Age* (Princeton, 1959), a collection of essays by the eminent political
scientist and member of the Rand Corporation; Arnold Wol-
fers, ed., *Alliance Policy in the Cold War* (Baltimore, 1959);
Klaus E. Knorr, ed., *NATO and American Security* (Princeton, 1959); Gordon B. Turner and Richard D. Challener, eds.,
National Security in the Nuclear Age (New York, 1960);
Warner R. Schilling *et al.*, *Strategy, Politics and Defense Budgets* (New York, 1962), especially the chapter by Glenn H.
Snyder, "The 'New Look' of 1953."

The problem of Europe—that perennial topic—appears in
Henry C. Wallich's *Mainsprings of the German Revival* (New
Haven, 1955), analysis of the "German miracle" of economic
reorganization. The American occupation in Germany, 1945-
55, has its accounting in the touchingly written, carefully re-
searched volume by Eugene Davidson, *The Death and Life
of Germany* (New York, 1959). Disengagement, an interesting debate over policy of the latter 1950s, had an eloquent
statement in George F. Kennan's Reith Lectures over the
BBC, published as *Russia, the Atom and the West* (New
York, 1958). See also the admirable summary by Michael
Howard, *Disengagement in Europe* (Harmondsworth, Eng.,

1958), a Penguin Special; and Eugene Hinterhoff, *Disengagement* (London, 1959). The late Edgar S. Furniss, Jr., discussed *France, Troubled Ally: De Gaulle's Heritage and Prospects* (New York, 1960), stressing dependence of French foreign policy upon domestic bases, and the continuity of policy from the Fourth to the Fifth Republics. Gerald Freund's *Germany between Two Worlds* (New York, 1961) is an excellent book. See also the essays in David S. Collier and Kurt Glaser, eds., *Western Integration and the Future of Eastern Europe* (Chicago, 1964).

Relations with the Far East often concerned Dulles, as the USSR in its policy seemed to move out of Europe into Asia. Fortunately, before he became Secretary he had managed to bring Japanese problems onto a better basis—independence. See the general treatment of relations in Edwin O. Reischauer, *The United States and Japan* (Cambridge, 1961), and also Bernard C. Cohen, *The Political Process and Foreign Policy: The Making of the Japanese Peace Settlement* (Princeton, 1957) and Frederick S. Dunn, *Peace-Making and the Settlement with Japan* (Princeton, 1963). On relations with Indochina, or Vietnam, see E. J. Hammer, *he Struggle for Indochina* (Stanford, 1954), a timely book; C. M. Roberts, "The Day We Didn't Go to War," *Reporter*, Sept. 14, 1954, an apparently inside account; and more recent volumes such as Bernard B. Fall, *The Two Vietnams* (New York, 1963), Robert Scheer, *How the United States Got Involved in Vietnam* (Santa Barbara, 1965), and Robert Shaplen, *The Lost Revolution* (New York, 1965). For other parts of Asia, John King Fairbank's *The United States and China* (Cambridge, 1962), Oliver E. Clubb, Jr., *The United States and the Sino-Soviet Bloc in Southeast Asia* (Washington, 1962), and C. Hartley Grattan, *The United States and the Southwest Pacific* (Cambridge, 1961).

As for the Suez crisis, the best place to begin is general literature on American-British relations—which constituted for Americans the most worrisome part of the Suez fiasco.

See Leon D. Epstein, *Britain—Uneasy Ally* (Chicago, 1954), Lionel M. Gelber, *America in Britain's Place: The Leadership of the West and Anglo-American Unity* (New York, 1961), and Herbert Nicholas, *Britain and the U.S.A.* (Baltimore, 1963). For the crisis there is Guy Wint and Peter Calvocoressi, *Middle East Crisis* (Harmondsworth, Eng., 1957), a Penguin Special. Merry and Serge Bromberger, *Secrets of Suez* (London, 1957) is an expose by French journalists, allegedly describing the French-Israeli planning before the invasion. Michael Adams, *Suez and After: Year of Crisis* (Boston, 1958), contains the dispatches, carefully put together, of a first-rate newspaperman. Randolph S. Churchill, *The Rise and Fall of Sir Anthony Eden* (New York, 1959) analyzes the collapse of the Prime Minister's policy. On the subject of Gamal Abdel Nasser see Wilton Wynn, *Nasser of Egypt: The Search for Dignity* (Cambridge, 1959), a sympathetic study, and Robert St. John, *The Boss: The Story of Gamal Abdel Nasser* (New York, 1960), the rise to leadership. An important part of the Middle East appears in George Lenczowski, *Oil and State in the Middle East* (Ithaca, 1960). For American policy in the area, analysis of present and future problems, see John C. Campbell, *Defense of the Middle East: Problems of American Policy* (New York, 1960). Also Samuel Halperin, *The Political World of American Zionism* (Detroit, 1961); John Marlowe, *Arab Nationalism and British Imperialism: A Study in Power Politics* (New York, 1961); Leon D. Epstein, *British Politics in the Suez Crisis* (Urbana, Ill., 1963); E. L. M. Burns, *Between Arab and Israeli* (New York, 1963), by the chief of staff of the UN Truce Supervision Organization in 1954-56; Nadav Safran, *The United States and Israel* (Cambridge, 1963). Bernard Lewis, *The Middle East and the West* (Bloomington, Ind., 1964) contains lectures by a British expert. Recently the Suez literature has expanded, what with three books published within months of each other. Herman Finer, *Dulles over Suez: The Theory and Practice of His Diplomacy* (Chicago, 1964), a massive indictment, caused a furor when it appeared in Britain, as it purported to be based on interviews with leading statesmen. Terence Robertson, *Crisis: The Inside Story of the Suez Conspiracy* (New York, 1965) conveyed Canada's part—in particular that of Lester B. Pearson—in resolving the crisis; like the Finer book, it relied on interviews and commentary from participants. A. J. Barker, *Suez: The Seven Day War* (New York, 1965), by a British officer, set out the military side of events, tactfully pointing to deficiencies among "the politicians" rather than military men. For the conclusion of the crisis, the 1958 troubles over Lebanon, Jordan, and Iraq, see Waldemar J. Gallman, *Iraq under General Nuri* (Baltimore, 1964), by a former American ambassador; and Leila T. Meo, *Lebanon: Improbable Nation* (Bloomington, 1965), by a young and talented political scientist of Lebanese-Arab extraction.

IV. *Periodicals*

For newspapers one must rely on the New York *Times* and *Herald Tribune*, the London *Times*, and their European counterparts. As for periodicals, it is best to be skeptical of news magazines such as *Time, Newsweek,* and *US News and World Report.* They are, however, good sources of contemporary thought. The British for a long time have had numerous periodicals commenting weekly or fortnightly on events at home and abroad, and in recent years the United States has developed similar magazines, such as the *Reporter*. The logical abilities of commentators, or their literary skills, sometimes cover gaps in knowledge.

V. *Printed Sources*

Apart from government publications, such as hearings of Congressional committees, or Command Papers brought out in London, or the printed records of debates in Congress or Parliament, there are two major private sources of documents for the era of Dulles' Secretaryship. *Documents on American Foreign Relations*, published annually by the Council on Foreign Relations, accompanies the annual volume of *The United States in World Affairs. Documents on International Affairs*, published annually by the Royal Institute, accompanies the *Survey*. A special collection is Donald C. Watt, ed., *Documents on the Suez Crisis, 26 July to 6 November 1956* (New York, 1957), compiled for the Royal Institute.

The Department of State has published a series of volumes, *American Foreign Policy*, which begins with 1950-55 (2 vols.), with annual volumes thereafter, and it deserves extended commentary. Its purpose is to bring together documents for the public and scholars until such time as regular volumes appear in the Department's magisterial series, *Foreign Relations of the United States*. The interim series is a worthy venture. How unfortunate, though, that the senior officialdom of the Department has failed to provide staff and budget for the Historical Office to produce volumes of *Foreign Relations* with sufficient regularity. Some years ago the hope was to publish volumes fifteen years after events. The gap moved to twenty years. At the present writing (1966) it is twenty-two years. The series is falling behind a year with every year, until the gap soon will be thirty years. Why not abolish some of the Department's public information activities, the Niagara-like flow of pamphlets and brochures and extracts of speeches which for the most part reach scholarly and other wastebaskets, and advance *Foreign Relations* to the fifteen-year line?

VI. *Manuscript and Other Sources*

The John Foster Dulles MSS are deposited at Princeton University, a large collection which includes Dulles' published writings—books (drafts and proofs), articles, addresses, statements, press releases, testimonies—as well as diaries, journals, notes, memoranda, interviews, motion pictures, newspaper clippings, conference dossiers, and correspondence. These papers are supplemented by the Janet Avery Dulles (Mrs. John Foster Dulles) MSS. An important part of the Dulles collection, consisting of telegrams, memoranda of conversations, minutes of meetings, and other material, carries a United States Government security classification and will not be open until the original files in the Department of State become generally accessible. (The Department files are following a thirty-year rule, with an additional but limited access through subjects published in *Foreign Relations*, that is at the moment—1966—into the year 1944.) It is estimated that by the year 1968 there also will be 10,000 to 12,000 pages of transcribed tape-recorded interviews in the Dulles collection. Transcripts are in four categories: "open"—scholars may read them upon presentation of credentials; "permission required to quote and cite"—open to scholars who pledge to observe requirements; "written permission required to read"—after obtaining permission scholars must adhere to any restrictions on the transcripts; "closed." The author, a member of the committee of the Dulles Oral History Project, did not consult these interviews.

The Allen W. Dulles MSS are in possession of Mr. Dulles, in Washington, D.C.

The Dean Acheson MSS are in possession of Mr. Acheson.

Former Secretary Acheson kindly allowed access to the "Acheson seminar" material at Princeton. After leaving office in 1953, Mr. Acheson journeyed frequently to Princeton to meet with a group of scholars and other individuals who asked him questions about his public work. These seminar sessions were taped and are available to researchers in the Princeton Library, subject to approval by Mr. Acheson. The seminar material is quite interesting. To be sure, there is possibility of error because of faulty memory—but one must hasten to add that Mr. Acheson has a keen memory, and a great sense of history, and his oral commentary is far more important than that usually recorded by oral history projects.

The Harry S. Truman MSS, in the library at Independence, are a vast storehouse of records of Mr. Truman's Administration, and with a few exceptions the papers are open to researchers. Dr. Philip C. Brooks and his able staff are most hospitable.

The Franklin D. Roosevelt MSS at Hyde Park have some material of interest for Dulles' career in the early 1940s.

The Arthur Bliss Lane MSS at the Yale University Library show Republican Party maneuvers for the ethnic vote in the presidential election of 1952, from the viewpoint of a distinguished former diplomat and Ambassador to Poland in the immediate postwar years.

In the Acknowledgments I have expressed my thanks to various individuals for interviews, for which I am very grateful.

INDEX